CASHING IN ON
EDUCATION

CASHING IN ON EDUCATION

Women, Childcare, and Prosperity in
Latin America and the Caribbean

Mercedes Mateo Díaz and Lourdes Rodriguez-Chamussy

WORLD BANK GROUP

IDB
Inter-American
Development Bank

Latin American Development Forum Series

This series was created in 2003 to promote debate, disseminate information and analysis, and convey the excitement and complexity of the most topical issues in economic and social development in Latin America and the Caribbean. It is sponsored by the Inter-American Development Bank, the United Nations Economic Commission for Latin America and the Caribbean, and the World Bank, and represents the highest quality in each institution's research and activity output. Titles in the series have been selected for their relevance to the academic community, policy makers, researchers, and interested readers, and have been subjected to rigorous anonymous peer review prior to publication.

Advisory Committee Members

Alicia Bárcena Ibarra, Executive Secretary, Economic Commission for Latin America and the Caribbean, United Nations

Inés Bustillo, Director, Washington Office, Economic Commission for Latin America and the Caribbean, United Nations

Augusto de la Torre, Chief Economist, Latin America and the Caribbean Region, World Bank

Daniel Lederman, Deputy Chief Economist, Latin America and the Caribbean Region, World Bank

Santiago Levy, Vice President for Sectors and Knowledge, Inter-American Development Bank

Roberto Rigobon, Professor of Applied Economics, MIT Sloan School of Management

José Juan Ruiz, Chief Economist and Manager of the Research Department, Inter-American Development Bank

Ernesto Talvi, Director, Brookings Global-CERES Economic and Social Policy in Latin America Initiative

Andrés Velasco, Cieplan, Chile

Titles in the Latin American Development Forum Series

Keeping the Promise of Social Security in Latin America (2004) by Indermit S. Gill, Truman G. Packard, and Juan Yermo

Lessons from NAFTA: For Latin America and the Caribbean (2004) by Daniel Lederman, William F. Maloney, and Luis Servén

The Limits of Stabilization: Infrastructure, Public Deficits, and Growth in Latin America (2003) by William Easterly and Luis Servén, editors

Globalization and Development: A Latin American and Caribbean Perspective (2003) by José Antonio Ocampo and Juan Martin, editors

Is Geography Destiny? Lessons from Latin America (2003) by John Luke Gallup, Alejandro Gaviria, and Eduardo Lora

Contents

Boxes

Figures

Tables

Foreword

In the first decade of this century, Latin America went through a period of sustained growth accompanied by a reduction in income inequality. Since then, however, in the wake of slower world growth and weaker commodity prices, regional growth has slowed down considerably. Other than a large and sustained rebound in commodity prices, regional growth will depend more on internal factors: faster capital accumulation, increased labor force participation, and higher productivity. Moreover, further reductions in inequality may be harder to achieve, as the wage premium has already fallen significantly, and there is little fiscal space for further social spending.

Fostering inclusive growth in the region in this more complex environment is a substantive challenge indeed, and it highlights the importance of identifying specific areas where policy makers can act to improve efficiency and equity simultaneously. This book is about one of them, namely, the potential for increasing growth and social inclusion through higher female labor force participation. The book explores the effectiveness of childcare provision as a policy tool to lift constraints women face to contribute more actively to the income generation in their households.

The literature has documented the increase in education for the working-age population in Latin America and the closing of gender gaps in terms of school attendance and educational attainment. Nonetheless, the resources invested in improving education for women have not had as high social returns as possible because of their low participation rate. About half of the women who could participate in the labor market in the region fail to do so. This book starts by stating that society and policy makers have substantive reasons to care about this outcome, and it estimates the economic costs of having such low levels of participation. The book analyzes the constraints to more active participation in the labor market that women face, and it explores the impact of childcare as an effective tool to open economic opportunities for Latin American women. By reviewing the factors associated with take-up of existing programs, and by looking at the characteristics of the wide range of childcare programs in the region—often incoherent and lacking an integrated perspective—the authors present a convincing argument in favor of using childcare as a tool to foster participation.

Improved daycare services may facilitate higher female labor force participation, but if they are of low quality they can potentially work against an equally important policy goal: ensuring that toddlers and infants get appropriate attention and care to stimulate their early development. The analysis in this book acknowledges this issue and argues for quality daycare as the way out of this potential conflict. The process of enhancing female labor force participation and stimulating growth thus needs to be accompanied by investing more resources—both budgetary and political—in improving childcare services over time.

This book will become an important reference for anyone interested in how the region can increase growth in a way that is consistent with equity and social advancement. It adds to the efforts that the Inter-American Development Bank has been making to provide careful analysis and empirical evidence to support informed discussions with policy makers and other actors interested in making the Latin American region a better place for all.

Santiago Levy
Vice President for Sectors and Knowledge
Inter-American Development Bank

Acknowledgments

To our own little consumers of early childhood education and care:
Alex, Alan, Adriana,
Emilia, Santiago

This book is the product of both direct experience and research. Our own life projects have made us living subjects of many of the issues described in these pages. It is through those experiences that we connected for this research and policy project.

This project would not have been possible without the support of many people. We thank Santiago Levy, the Vice President for Sectors and Knowledge at the Inter-American Development Bank (IDB), for his intellectual leadership and inspiring ideas, and Andy Morrison, Chief of the Gender and Diversity Division, who believed that this project could lead somewhere and provided financial support through IDB's Gender and Diversity Fund.

We are extremely thankful to Juanita Caycedo Duque, our liaison with program directors, teams, and counterparts in countries, who was crucial in helping us gather the institutional data. We thank her for her wonderful sense of humor, for being an active team player, and for making this journey a great, albeit sometimes tedious, one. We extend a very special thank you to Andrea Atencio, who assembled and processed the household survey data. We thank Maria Olga Peña and Rosa Katherine Rodríguez for their research assistance.

We are very grateful to the peer reviewers of the manuscript, whose comments enriched its content and quality. Raquel Fernández provided insights, vision, and sharpness. Analia Jaimovich, Luis-Felipe López-Calva, Hugo Ñopo, Claudia Piras, Emiliana Vegas, Aimee Verdisco, and members of the IDB Studies and Publication Committee provided important comments and inputs. Paul Lavrakas was extremely helpful in improving the module for household surveys. We are also indebted to the anonymous peer reviewers who provided extremely valuable comments.

Program directors and counterparts in 21 countries patiently and clearly answered our questions throughout the preparation of this book; it could not have been produced without the information they provided. We very gratefully acknowledge them in the appendix.

Finally, we thank Rita Funaro, the editor-in-chief in the Research Department at the IDB, for her support and recommendations; Jewel McFadden (acquisitions editor) and Janice Tuten (publications project manager) in the World Bank's Publishing and Knowledge Department for superb guidance throughout the publication process; and Barbara Karni for doing an excellent job copyediting this book.

About the Authors

Mercedes Mateo Díaz is a lead education specialist at the Inter-American Development Bank. She was a postdoctoral research fellow of the Belgian Scientific Research Foundation (FNRS) in 2004 and an honorary researcher at FNRS until 2007. In 2004 she was a Marie Curie Fellow at the Robert Schumann Center at the European University Institute. An expert on institutional reform and social policy, she is the author of *Representing Women? Female Legislators in West European Parliaments* (2005) and a coeditor of *Democracies in Development: Politics and Reform in Latin America* (2006). She holds a PhD in political science and international relations from the University of Louvain in Belgium.

Lourdes Rodriguez-Chamussy is an economist in the Poverty and Equity Global Practice at the World Bank, where she specializes in applied microeconomic research on labor, development, and gender. She previously worked as a research fellow in the Vice Presidency for Sectors and Knowledge at the Inter-American Development Bank. She has published articles on poverty measurement and was the co-editor of *Human Development Report* on Mexico, published by the United Nations Development Programme. She holds a PhD in agricultural and resource economics from the University of California, Berkeley.

Abbreviations

CCT	conditional cash transfer
ECCE	early childhood care and education
ECD	early childhood development
ELDS	early learning and development standards
EU	European Union
FLFP	female labor force participation
GDP	gross domestic product
LAC	Latin America and the Caribbean
MLFP	male labor force participation
NGO	nongovernmental organization
OECD	Organisation for Economic Co-operation and Development
SEDLAC	Socio-Economic Database for Latin America and the Caribbean

Overview

Countries in Latin America and the Caribbean (LAC) have invested substantial resources in girls' education in recent decades. As a result, the gender gap has disappeared for enrollment in primary school and narrowed significantly for enrollment in secondary school. Improvements in school attainment have been even more impressive, with more girls than boys now completing school in many countries in the region (Ñopo 2012). These achievements are impressive. But to fully realize the gains of these investments, governments need to get more of these female graduates into the labor force.

Almost half of all women of working age in LAC are out of the labor market, including 46 million women 25 and older with some education. At more than 30 percentage points, the participation gap between men and women is one of the largest in the world (ILOSTAT 2015).

Developing and leveraging the professional skills of women is crucial for economic performance. Estimates of the cost of low female labor force participation (FLFP) are high, ranging from 3.4 percent of GDP in Mexico to 17 percent of GDP in Honduras. These losses are much smaller in other countries, for example 9 percent in Japan and 5 percent on average for the Organisation for Economic Co-operation and Development (OECD) countries. (IMF 2013). Raising the levels of FLFP to male levels would increase GDP by an estimated 19 percent in Argentina and 15 percent in Brazil (Aguirre and others 2012; see chapter 1).

The gender gap in labor market participation is present across the lifecycle, but it widens during a woman's childbearing years; most of the population out of the labor market are women between the ages of 24 and 45. One of the main factors behind the gender gap in economic opportunity and participation is childcare demands on women's time (ILO 2013; IMF 2013; Ñopo 2012; World Bank 2012).

This book argues that more and better childcare is an important way to increase FLFP. The main hypothesis is that the success of childcare policies depends on use and that use depends on how programs design quality and convenience features. First-rate educational programs will be useless if children are not enrolled or do not attend; program expansions will be wasted if mothers cannot enroll their children because they are unable to reach the center, if the program is too expensive, or if their work schedules are not compatible with the childcare center's hours.

1

Previous studies have documented that a large share of the potential workforce does not participate in the labor market (McKinsey Global Institute 2015; Ñopo 2012; Paes de Barros and others 2011; Pagés and Piras 2010; Piras 2004; World Bank 2012). They also provide clues about how to increase participation. An extensive body of evidence, particularly from developed countries, shows that the presence of subsidized nonparental childcare is correlated with FLFP (Del Boca 2015; Mateo Díaz and Rodriguez-Chamussy 2013). Almost all random assignment and quasi-experimental studies show consistent positive effects on either the intensive or extensive margins of FLFP. What is missing in the literature is identification and analysis of the factors that affect the take-up of programs and demand for childcare services and other care arrangements.

Systematized sources of information on childcare in the region usually focus on development outcomes for children rather than the effect on FLFP (see Araujo, López Bóo, and Puyana 2013; Berlinski and Schady 2015; Evans, Myers, and Ilfeld 2000; Grun 2008; Vargas-Barón 2009; Vegas and Santibañez 2010). The results, which usually include a range of interventions affecting children's development (conditional cash transfers, health programs, childcare programs, and parenting education), are not necessarily representative of childcare in the region.

This book addresses these gaps. Part I shows why increasing FLFP is important and childcare is the right policy for achieving it. Chapter 1 provides evidence that increased FLFP contributes to growth, poverty reduction, and fiscal sustainability. Lower labor force participation in paid work, particularly among the poorest women, implies both productivity losses and higher probabilities of intergenerational transmission of poverty and inequality. Female labor income accounted for an estimated 28 percent of the sharp decline in inequality experienced in the region between 2000 and 2010; had female labor income not changed during this decade, extreme poverty would have been 30 percent higher in 2010 (World Bank 2012). For each generation of girls that completes primary, secondary, or tertiary education, an estimated $400 billion of the region's investments in education will not be capitalized through the labor market (see figure 1A.1 in the annex to chapter 1)—a sum equivalent to the projected value of LAC's trade with China by 2017 (J. P. Morgan 2013).

Chapter 2 shows that childcare is positively and consistently related to increases in FLFP, that exceptions to this rule are often related to the quality of childcare, and that programs will not work if service features are not properly tailored. Childcare alone is not sufficient to get women into the labor market, however. Interventions must mesh with other policies intended to improve women's outcomes in the labor market, such as education, maternity leave, flexible arrangements at work, and intermediation programs (programs that connect employers and people looking for jobs).

Part II describes FLFP and the use and provision of childcare services in LAC. Chapter 3 overviews current labor market outcomes, describing women's labor force participation, unemployment, informality, earnings, and occupational segregation. Chapter 4 explores the use of childcare. It shows that a mother's decisions to participate in the labor market and to enroll her child in childcare are often made simultaneously and that use of childcare is segmented, with higher attendance among higher-income, better-educated families. If early education programs are to help level the playing field and close learning gaps, countries need to get more disadvantaged children into early education programs.

Chapter 5 overviews the public and private supply of childcare programs in LAC, based on data gathered from specialists and directors of publicly supported childcare programs in 21 countries.[1] It identifies a gap between supply and demand and shows that segmentation in the use of childcare programs affects the incidence of public spending. The chapter describes how different systems structure transitions and service hours (parental leave, publicly subsidized childcare programs, and compulsory education) and identifies the problems families encounter when trying to reconcile family and work schedules.

Part III examines how policy makers can improve services and increase the number of formal, center-based care arrangements for young children. Chapter 6 presents international benchmarks. It compares FLFP and childcare in LAC with other regions, reviewing how some countries outside the region set standards for childcare coverage, organize programs and resources, and design their program features. The exercise shows that many successful economies have higher levels of both FLFP and childcare use and reveals how some countries have solved the problem of segmentation.

Chapter 7 proposes a method for identifying who is not using childcare services and strategies for encouraging them to do so. Based on the experience of Chile, it concludes that successful expansion of childcare requires good administrative data (on stocks, enrollment rates, and attendance rates); good survey data on why parents use or do not use formal childcare; adaptation of program features to the needs of the most vulnerable households and working mothers; and complementary policies that reach households that are more difficult to mobilize for cultural reasons.

Chapter 8 presents a basic package of services. It notes that programs can simultaneously increase FLFP and improve child development outcomes and that policy makers need to consider the trade-offs between the two.

Chapter 9 summarizes key challenges and frames a set of policy recommendations to increase FLFP through childcare provision. It calls for better data with which to assess demand for childcare and presents a sample module that could be added to household or other nationwide surveys.

This book brings new elements to the public policy debate about alternatives that could help remove barriers to FLFP, promote early childhood development, and help reduce inequalities and level the playing field for generations to come. LAC countries currently face favorable demographic conditions for moving forward. They should start cashing in on the benefits of the ambitious educational reforms and social programs of recent decades to achieve faster and more sustainable growth.

Note

1. The information gathered (including legislation on childcare, early childhood development services, early education, public financing of early education and care services, children's rights, family education and support, and maternity and parental leave from work) is available at http://www.iadb.org/en/research-and-data /female-labor-force/list-laws,8525.html.

References

Aguirre, D., L. Hoteit, C. Rupp, and K. Sabbagh. 2012. *Empowering the Third Billion: Women and the World of Work in 2012.* New York: Booz and Company.

Araujo, M. C., F. López Bóo, and J. M. Puyana. 2013. *Overview of Early Childhood Development Services in Latin America and the Caribbean.* Washington, DC: Inter-American Development Bank.

Berlinski, S., and N. Schady, eds. 2015. *The Early Years: Child Well-Being and the Role of Public Policy.* Washington, DC: Inter-American Development Bank.

Del Boca, D. 2015. "Child Care Arrangements and Labor Supply." Working Paper 569, Inter-American Development Bank, Washington, DC.

Evans, J. L., R. G. Myers, and E. M. Ilfeld. 2000. *Early Childhood Counts: A Programming Guide on Early Childhood Care for Development.* Washington, DC: World Bank Institute.

Grun, R. 2008. "Financing Early Childhood Development: A Look at International Evidence and its Lessons." Note for the Department of Education of Khanty-Mansiysk, Russian Federation. World Bank, Washington, DC.

ILO (International Labour Organisation). 2013. *The Informal Economy and Decent Work: A Policy Resource Guide Supporting Transitions to Formality.* Geneva: ILO.

ILOSTAT (database). International Labour Organisation, Geneva. http://www.ilo .org/ilostat/.

IMF (International Monetary Fund). 2013. *Women, Work, and the Economy: Macroeconomic Gains from Gender Equity.* Washington, DC: IMF.

J.P. Morgan. 2013. *Corridors of Power: China's Latin American Linkage.* New York: J.P. Morgan.

Mateo Díaz, M., and L. Rodriguez-Chamussy. 2013. "Childcare and Women's Labor Participation: Evidence for Latin America and the Caribbean." Technical

Note 586, Inter-American Development Bank, Washington, DC. Available at https://publications.iadb.org/handle/11319/6493.

McKinsey Global Institute. 2015. *The Power of Parity: How Advancing Women's Equality Can Add $12 Trillion to Global Growth.* San Francisco.

Ñopo, H. 2012. *New Century, Old Disparities: Gender and Ethnic Earnings Gaps in Latin America and the Caribbean.* Washington, DC: Inter-American Development Bank.

Paes de Barros, R., P. Olinto, T. Lunde, and M. Carvalho. 2011. "The Impact of Free Childcare on Women's Labor Force Participation: Evidence from Low-Income Neighborhoods of Rio de Janeiro." Paper presented at 2011 World Bank Economists' Forum, Washington, DC.

Pagés, C., and C. Piras. 2010. *The Gender Dividend: Capitalizing in Women's Work.* Washington, DC: Inter-American Development Bank. Available at https://publications.iadb.org/handle/11319/450?locale-attribute=en.

Piras, C., ed. 2004. *Women at Work: Challenges for Latin America.* Washington, DC: Inter-American Development Bank.

Vargas-Barón, E. 2009. *Going to Scale: Early Childhood Development in Latin America.* Rise Institute, Washington, DC.

Vegas, E., and L. Santibañez. 2010. *The Promise of Early Childhood Development in Latin America and the Caribbean.* Washington, DC: World Bank.

PART I

Why Is Increasing Female Labor Supply Important and Childcare the Right Policy to Help Achieve It?

CHAPTER 1

Economic Gains from Increasing Female Labor Force Participation

Promoting the economic participation of women and reducing gender inequalities in the labor market are goals in themselves, because all individuals deserve the same opportunities to be economically active. Beyond fairness, however, countries are paying a high price for low female labor force participation (FLFP).

Countries in Latin America and the Caribbean (LAC) should be concerned about FLFP for three main economic reasons. First, evidence points to massive gains in per capita gross domestic product (GDP) from the incorporation of women into the labor market. Second, female labor income is critical for reducing poverty and inequality. Third, narrowing gender gaps in labor outcomes would increase the fiscal sustainability of social protection systems.

Given their current demographic situations, most LAC countries have a unique opportunity to cash in on the tremendous investments made in education over recent decades. To do so, they need to capitalize on the full potential of their workforces (see annex 1A, which provides estimates of the magnitude of the investment in education that is not being capitalized in the labor market).

This chapter presents estimates of per capita GDP gains from incorporating into the labor force women who completed primary, secondary, and tertiary education and are currently out of the labor market; reviews the evidence on the effect of FLFP on poverty reduction; and discusses the impact on long-term fiscal sustainability of FLFP, calculating the number of additional years of demographic bonus LAC countries could enjoy from increasing it.

Growth and Productivity Gains from Female Labor Force Participation

Evidence points to significant GDP per capita gains as gender gaps in the labor market shrink, given that suboptimal use of talent has consequences for aggregate productivity (Hsieh and others 2013). A report by the McKinsey Global Institute (2015) shows that women's contribution to GDP in LAC (33 percent) is below the world average (37 percent). The share of output produced by women is lower only in the Middle East/North Africa and South Asia. According to their estimates, $28 trillion could be added to global 2025 GDP if the participation of women in the economy were identical to men's. If all countries matched the best-performing country in their region rather than achieved parity, $12 trillion could be added in 2025. The McKinsey report estimates that achieving parity in LAC would add 34 percent to the region's 2025 GDP, and raising all countries to the level of the best performer in the region would add 14 percent.

Aguirre and others (2012) estimate the impact on GDP of increasing FLFP to country-specific male levels. Results for the only two LAC countries in their study indicate that doing so would increase GDP by 19 percent in Argentina and 15 percent in Brazil.[1]

Cuberes and Teignier (2016) estimate that existing labor market gender gaps in entrepreneurship and participation in the workforce lead to average income losses of 15.7 percent in the short run and 17.2 percent in the long run for LAC.

Our estimates are partial equilibrium calculations of gains from the incorporation into the labor market only of women who completed some level of education, assuming that current returns to each education level remain unchanged. Potential productivity gains from incorporating women who complete primary, secondary, or tertiary education but then do not enter the labor market range from 3.5 percent of GDP in Mexico to 10.4 percent in Costa Rica and 16.8 percent in Honduras (table 1.1).

Estimated increases in GDP in LAC from raising FLFP are about 7 percent on average. Estimated economic gains are lowest in Mexico (3.5 percent) and Guatemala (4.0 percent), where current labor returns to women are very low. Breaking the vicious circle of low productivity and low participation could bring about significantly larger economic gains. In countries like these, economic gains would be greater if interventions to improve productivity were introduced (chapter 2 discusses complementary policies that affect FLFP).

Effect on Poverty and Inequality Reduction

Growth in female labor income in LAC between 2000 and 2010 accounted for 28 percent of the reduction in inequality and 30 percent of the reduction in extreme poverty (World Bank 2012). Increased female labor income thus pulled about 5 million of the region's people out of extreme poverty.

TABLE 1.1 Estimated productivity loss from women staying out of labor market in selected countries in Latin America and the Caribbean

Country	Percentage of current GDP
Honduras	16.8
Costa Rica	10.4
Peru	9.0
Argentina	7.0
Chile	6.8
Paraguay	6.7
Ecuador	6.5
El Salvador	6.3
Panama	5.8
Colombia	5.7
Uruguay	5.5
Brazil	4.7
Guatemala	4.6
Dominican Republic	4.0
Belize	3.9
Mexico	3.5

Sources: Data from UIS UNESCO for Educational Attainment by gender; ILOSTAT for labor force participation rate by gender and education; SEDLAC for average monthly wage in nominal local currency units by gender; and World Development Indicators for GDP.
Note: Increased labor force participation is by women who completed some level of education only.

Increases in female economic participation and earnings can reduce current and future poverty by raising levels of consumption and savings. There is also evidence of differential consumption and saving propensities of men and women that affect household members. Higher FLFP is associated with lower infant mortality rates and higher life expectancy, for example, and it has positive effects on children's development and well-being.[2] Higher FLFP thus has positive impacts on the earnings capability of the next generation, which may reduce the intergenerational transmission of poverty (Morrison, Raju, and Sinha 2007). Doing so is especially important for the most vulnerable households, among whom a larger proportion of households have at least one child younger than 5 (see annex 1B).

A lower rate of economic activity for women than men is not the only gender inequality linked to poverty. Higher rates of female employment in the informal sector and unemployment, a higher probability of working in low-productivity industries, and lower remuneration are important factors in the relationship between labor and poverty.

Costa and Silva (2008) simulate counterfactual scenarios in which gender inequalities are reduced and estimate their impact on poverty levels in Argentina, Brazil, Chile, the Dominican Republic, El Salvador, Mexico, Paraguay, and Uruguay. They estimate that the potential reduction in the incidence of poverty from increasing FLFP ranges from 15 percent in Uruguay to 34 percent in Chile. Their findings suggest that reduction in all three types of gender inequality in the labor market would significantly reduce poverty but that promoting women's (and particularly mothers') participation has the greatest potential for poverty reduction.

Effect on Fiscal Sustainability

Long-term fiscal sustainability depends on the participation in the labor market and employment of the population considered to be in an economically active age bracket. Demographics therefore play an important role in the planning and priorities of each country.

Many LAC countries are benefiting from favorable demographic conditions. The number of dependents per economically active person will reach historic lows in many countries during the next decade, before increasing again for the rest of the century. This demographic dividend provides a critical window of opportunity in which to grow, save, and strengthen public finances by bringing as many of these potential workers into the labor force as possible. Greater FLFP and improved labor market outcomes can increase governments' capacities to consolidate social security systems and potentially reduce dependency on social assistance programs.[3]

By maintaining the current structure of labor participation, countries can only partially cash the demographic dividend, because only a little more than two-thirds of the population 15–64 are actively contributing to the economy. We estimate that a sustained increase in the region's FLFP at the average annual rate of increase observed over the past 20 years (1.03 percent) would delay by 25 years the moment when the economic dependency ratio will bottom out and start rising again.[4] These calculations assume an increase in the FLFP rate from 57 percent in 2012 to 62 percent (the level in the Organisation for Economic Co-operation and Development [OECD]) in 2020 and to 80 percent (male levels) in 2045 (scenario 2 in figure 1.1). The assumption of a 1.03 percent rate increase is not unrealistic; some LAC countries have already achieved such an increase. Colombia, for example, increased its FLFP at an average annual rate of 2.4 percent over the past 20 years (World Development Indicators 2015).

LAC countries have the opportunity to take advantage of their demographic dividends, whether the dependency ratio is still falling or the population is aging.

FIGURE 1.1 Projected number of dependents and inactive people per 100 economically active people in Latin America and the Caribbean, 2015–50

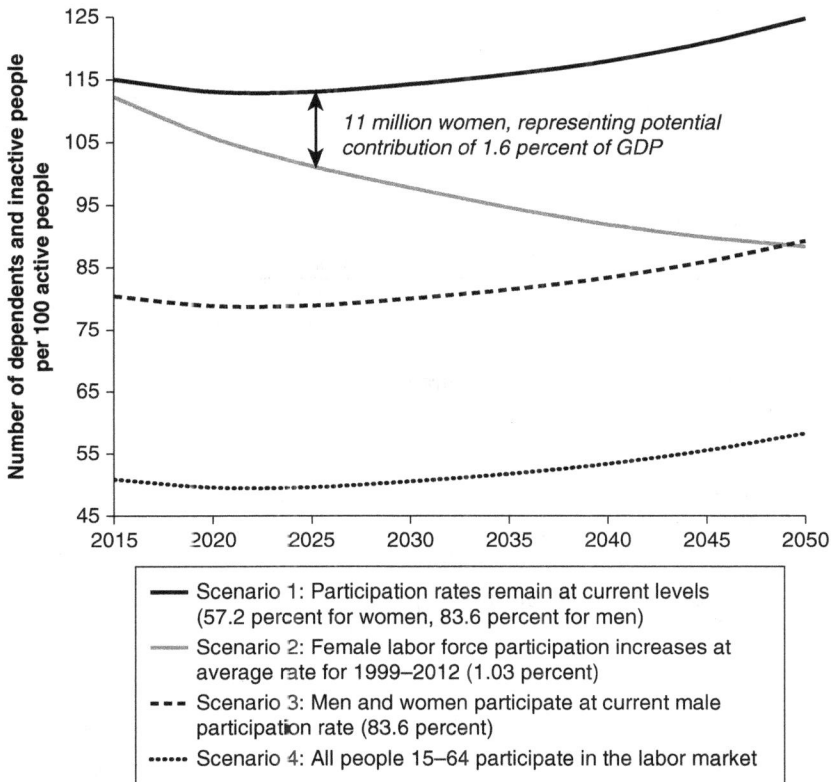

Source: UN 2014.

Figure 1.2 shows the rates of FLFP against the remaining number of years before the projected dependency rate reaches its minimum level for each country (see annex 1D for a detailed description of projected demographic trends by country for the next 25 years). Countries can be divided into three groups according to their demographic situation and the challenges they face in terms of gender gaps in the labor market.

The first group comprises countries in which incorporation of women into the labor market should be a priority. It includes Chile and Costa Rica, which have important time constraints to make the most of their demographic bonus and which have FLFP that is below the region's average. Other countries in this group include Guyana and Mexico, where reaching the minimum level of the dependency ratio is less imminent but where FLFP rates are still significantly

FIGURE 1.2 Dependency rate thresholds and female labor force participation levels in selected countries in Latin America and the Caribbean, circa 2012

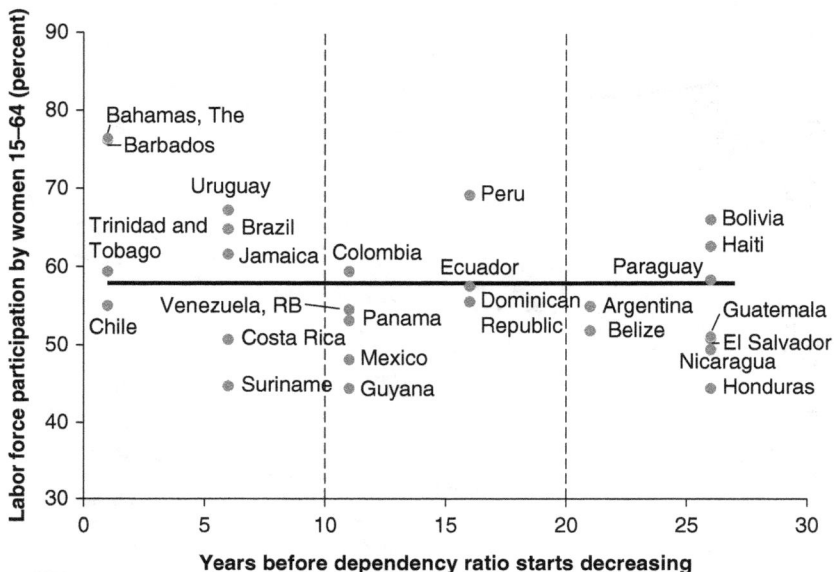

Sources: World Development Indicators 2014; UN 2014.
Note: Horizontal line shows average for Latin America and the Caribbean.

below the region's average. Mexico also has a large gender gap in the intensive margin of participation (hours worked) and high levels of informality (see annex 1E for a description of the evolution of FLFP rates by country over the past two decades).

The second group comprises countries that are pressed for time to benefit from the demographic bonus but where a relatively high proportion of women already participate in the labor market. This group includes Brazil, Peru, and Uruguay. Productivity gains in these countries are fundamental to preparing for population aging.

The third group comprises mainly countries with large cohorts of young people. These countries have an opportunity to reduce vulnerability and strengthen solid social security systems, because the ratio of dependents to the active population will not start declining for more than 20 years. Among countries in this group, Bolivia and Paraguay are above the regional average in terms of FLFP, whereas El Salvador, Guatemala, Honduras, and Nicaragua have among the lowest FLFP in the region. They could significantly increase savings and strengthen social security by increasing the number of women in the labor force and strengthening their attachment to the labor market over the long run.

To gain a sense of the opportunities and urgencies faced by each country, it is important to look not only at the level of FLFP but also at the pace at which FLFP has been changing. Estimates of the number of years it will take LAC countries to reach the average FLFP in the OECD (62 percent) provide a sense of urgency for countries that are incorporating women into the labor market slowly and whose active population will eventually start shrinking. For example, even though Argentina and Paraguay have relatively large shares of young people, they have experienced very low—even negative growth—of FLFP. Therefore, they face a steep slope to grab the opportunities provided by the demographic dividend (figure 1.3).

FIGURE 1.3 Difference between number of years left to capitalize on the demographic dividend and number of years to reach OECD average

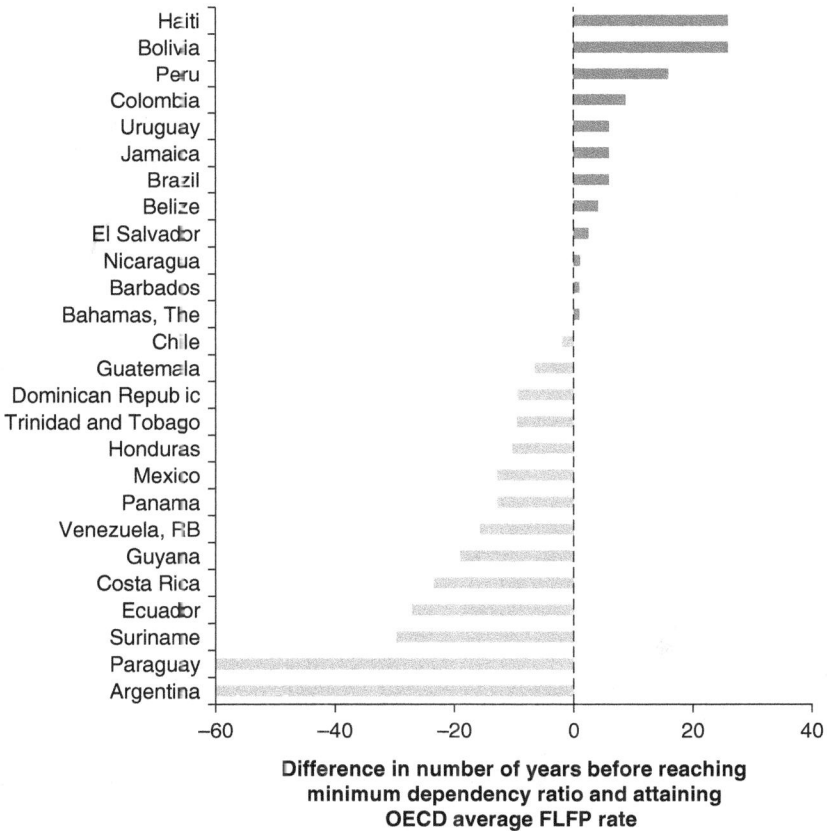

Sources: World Development Indicators 2014; UN 2014.
Note: FLFP = female labor force participation; OECD = Organisation for Economic Co-operation and Development.

Annex 1A: Investments in Education in Latin America and the Caribbean

Making sure more girls attend school has been a priority in LAC in recent decades. Governments have invested in differential conditional cash transfers, in some cases providing 40 percent more for girls than for boys of school age. Several countries have implemented programs that aim to reduce the rates of pregnant girls who leave school prematurely.

The gender education gap has closed significantly and even reversed in secondary school in many LAC countries. Together with lower fertility rates and a growing acceptance of women in the workplace, more schooling for girls has expanded the supply of women workers.

Translating these gains in human capital into productivity, earnings, and other benefits for children and families requires more effective engagement of women in paid work. Malhotra, Pande, and Grown (2003) note that these benefits often materialize only when real economic options exist. Education allows women to extricate themselves from violent situations, for example, only if it empowers them economically.

Where data were available, we produced rough estimates of government investments in education for both genders by educational attainment. We started with the proportions of men and women who had completed each level of education (primary, lower-secondary, upper-secondary, and tertiary). Based on population data, we calculated the number of people in each category and multiplied it by the annual costs per student in order to estimate investments in girls and boys. Educational expenses for students who had not completed each level were not included. Higher costs for men or women reflect higher levels of educational attainment for that group.

Female educational attainment is higher at all levels except lower-secondary, where there are no significant gender differences. In 13 of 20 countries studied, educational attainment, and therefore related expenses, is higher for women than for men. Labor participation rates, however, are higher for men in all countries, with Guatemala, Honduras, and Mexico showing the largest differences (35–40 percentage points).

For girls the highest return to education in terms of labor participation is completion of tertiary education. For the region as a whole, FLFP increases significantly at every level of education: About 40 percent of women with completed primary and lower-secondary education, 55 percent of women with completed upper-secondary education, and 71 percent of women with completed tertiary education are active in the labor market. These differences are not evident for men, among whom labor participation is about 80 percent in all cases (slightly lower for lower-secondary).

Figure 1A.1 shows the percentage of investment in education for people who completed each level of education that is not "capitalized" in terms of labor outcomes. It suggests that LAC is optimizing about 60 percent of its educational investments in women and more than 80 percent of its investments in men. The largest gaps between educational investment and labor opportunities for women are in Argentina, Costa Rica, Chile, and República Bolivariana de Venezuela. These rough estimates suggest that, for a single generation of girls that completed different levels of education, some $400 billion of the region's investments will not be capitalized through the labor market.

FIGURE 1A.1 Investment in education that is not "capitalized" through labor force participation in selected countries in Latin America and the Caribbean, circa 2012

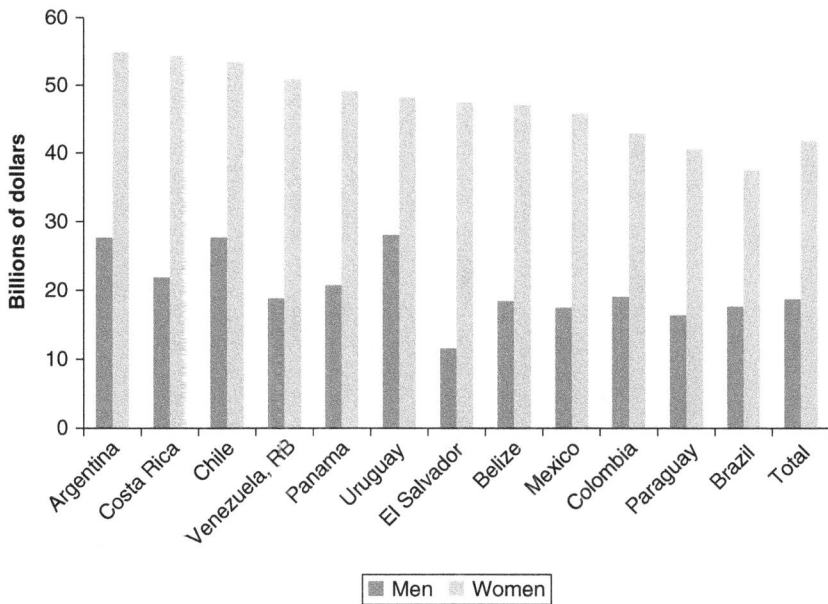

Sources: UIS 2014 for educational attainment by gender and government expenditure by student; ILOSTAT 2014 for labor force participation; World Development Indicators 2014 for labor force participation rate.

TABLE 1A.1 Estimated expenditure on education of girls and boys in selected countries in Latin America and the Caribbean, by level of completed education, circa 2012

(millions of 2005 dollars)

Country	Primary		Lower secondary		Upper secondary		Tertiary		Total	
	Boys	Girls	Boys	Girls	Boys	Girls	Boys	Girls	Boys	Girls
Argentina	39,370	42,452	14,538	12,160	26,227	29,228	9,822	13,817	89,956	97,657
Barbados	165	153	546	572	87	89	20	26	818	839
Belize	44	47	87	88	59	62	16	15	206	213
Bolivia	316	239	469	337	521	425	1,684	1,590	2,991	2,591
Brazil	191,930	198,110	71,540	71,434	102,146	113,803	77,913	105,498	443,528	488,845
Chile	6,860	8,415	8,983	8,980	14,950	15,165	8,303	8,649	39,096	41,208
Colombia	29,644	31,476	5,769	6,588	8,701	9,382	15,903	18,369	60,017	65,815
Costa Rica	2,920	2,868	668	597	834	877	2,885	2,918	7,307	7,260
Dominican Republic	862	806	889	752	744	878	—	—	2,495	2,436
Ecuador	3,310	2,998	677	762	1,926	1,948	—	—	5,913	5,707
El Salvador	465	539	223	218	230	262	260	294	1,179	1,314
Guatemala	1,506	1,508	139	140	113	141	—	—	1,758	1,789
Honduras	—	—	—	—	626	833	305	285	931	1,118

(continued on next page)

18

TABLE 1A.1 Estimated expenditure on education of girls and boys in selected countries in Latin America and the Caribbean, by level of completed education, circa 2012 *(continued)*

Country	Primary		Lower secondary		Upper secondary		Tertiary		Total	
	Boys	Girls	Boys	Girls	Boys	Girls	Boys	Girls	Boys	Girls
Mexico	46,045	58,581	28,608	30,962	30,965	37,408	80,216	71,492	185,834	198,444
Panama	779	670	56	47	1,427	1,391	1,311	1,739	3,572	3,847
Paraguay	1,105	1,084	239	166	795	669	394	507	2,533	2,426
Peru	4,886	4,730	409	413	3,006	2,362	3,627	3,568	11,927	11,074
Trinidad and Tobago	2,380	2,289	114	135	—	—	—	—	2,494	2,424
Uruguay	2,035	2,088	862	872	504	676	647	1,126	4,047	4,762
Venezuela, RB	26,029	23,207	4,403	3,949	10,459	11,473	8,710	12,335	49,600	50,963
Average	18,982	20,119	7,327	7,325	10,754	11,951	13,251	15,139	45,810	49,537
Total	360,650	382,261	139,219	139,172	204,317	227,071	212,015	242,229	916,202	990,733

Source: UIS 2014.

Note: Data for Bolivia, Costa Rica, the Dominican Republic, El Salvador, Guatemala, Honduras, Mexico, Peru, and Uruguay are for 2012. Data for other years are as follows: Argentina (2003), Barbados (2000), Belize (2010), Brazil (2011), Chile (2010), Colombia (2011), Ecuador (2010), Panama (2010), Paraguay (2008), Trinidad and Tobago (2009), and Republica Bolivariana de Venezuela (2009).
— = Not available.

TABLE 1A.2 Labor force participation rates of men and women in selected countries in Latin America and the Caribbean, by level of completed education, circa 2012

Country	Primary		Lower secondary		Upper secondary		Tertiary		Total	
	Men	Women	Men	Women	Men	Women	Men	Women	Men	Women
Argentina	68.0	35.9	52.9	24.6	86.7	55.8	80.3	69.3	81.7	54.9
Barbados	—	—	—	—	—	—	—	—	84.8	76.5
Belize	87.1	46	80.1	45	77.3	61.4	90.8	85.3	84.7	51.8
Bolivia	—	—	—	—	—	—	—	—	82.3	66
Brazil	77.6	50.6	78.1	53.8	89.1	72	89.5	80.5	85.4	64.8
Chile	54.6	24.7	77.8	44.6	73.5	49.2	79.1	65.8	79.3	55
Colombia	80.5	45.3	52	35.4	85.2	62.5	90.0	82.6	82.3	59.4
Costa Rica	78.0	24.9	68.5	39.6	77.7	39.4	80.6	69.4	83.9	50.7
Dominican Republic	77.8	37.2	78.1	48.2	76.7	51.8	83.9	75.1	82.8	55.5
Ecuador	86.0	46.5	65.0	37.5	73.2	43.6	78.6	66.4	85.4	57.5
El Salvador	91.8	51.6	92.2	64.0	94.5	78.7	73.9	22.3	82.2	50.9
Guatemala	89.4	39.4	72.5	39.5	75.4	51.4	82.2	75.9	90.1	51.1
Honduras	—	—	—	—	—	—	—	—	84.6	44.4
Mexico	75.9	37.1	78.9	42.9	80.0	51.7	88.8	74.4	83.3	48.1

(continued on next page)

TABLE 1A.2 Labor force participation rates of men and women in selected countries in Latin America and the Caribbean, by level of completed education, circa 2012 *(continued)*

Country	Primary		Lower secondary		Upper secondary		Tertiary		Total	
	Men	Women	Men	Women	Men	Women	Men	Women	Men	Women
Panama	83.2	27.7	73.2	35.2	82.2	37.7	74.0	70.8	86.2	53.1
Paraguay	85.6	53.8	75.8	49.2	81.2	57.2	88.1	78.2	87.9	58.3
Peru	—	—	—	—	—	—	85.7	74	86.7	69.1
Trinidad and Tobago	—	—	—	—	—	—	—	—	82.2	59.4
Uruguay	66.4	35.2	69.3	47.5	87.7	70.7	80.9	74.6	85.7	67.2
Venezuela, RB	84.2	41	77.3	43.5	79.4	48.1	76.5	67.3	82.6	54.5
Average	79.0	39.8	73.0	43.4	81.0	55.4	83.0	70.7	84.2	57.4

Sources: ILOSTAT 2014 for labor force participation by education level; World Development Indicators for labor force participation rate.

Note: Total labor force participation is for population 15–64. Calculation of total expenditure on education assumes six years of primary, three years of lower-secondary, three years of upper-secondary, and four years of tertiary education. Estimates do not include post-secondary nontertiary education. Data for Bolivia, Costa Rica, the Dominican Republic, El Salvador, Guatemala, Honduras, Mexico, Peru, and Uruguay are for 2012. Data for other years are as follows: Argentina (2003), Barbados (2000), Belize (2010), Brazil (2011), Chile (2010), Colombia (2011), Ecuador (2010), Panama (2010), Paraguay (2008), Trinidad and Tobago (2009), and República Bolivariana de Venezuela (2009).

— = Not available.

Annex 1B: Income Distribution of Households with at Least One Child Younger than 5

FIGURE 1B.1 Households in selected countries in Latin America and the Caribbean with at least one child younger than 5, by income level, circa 2014

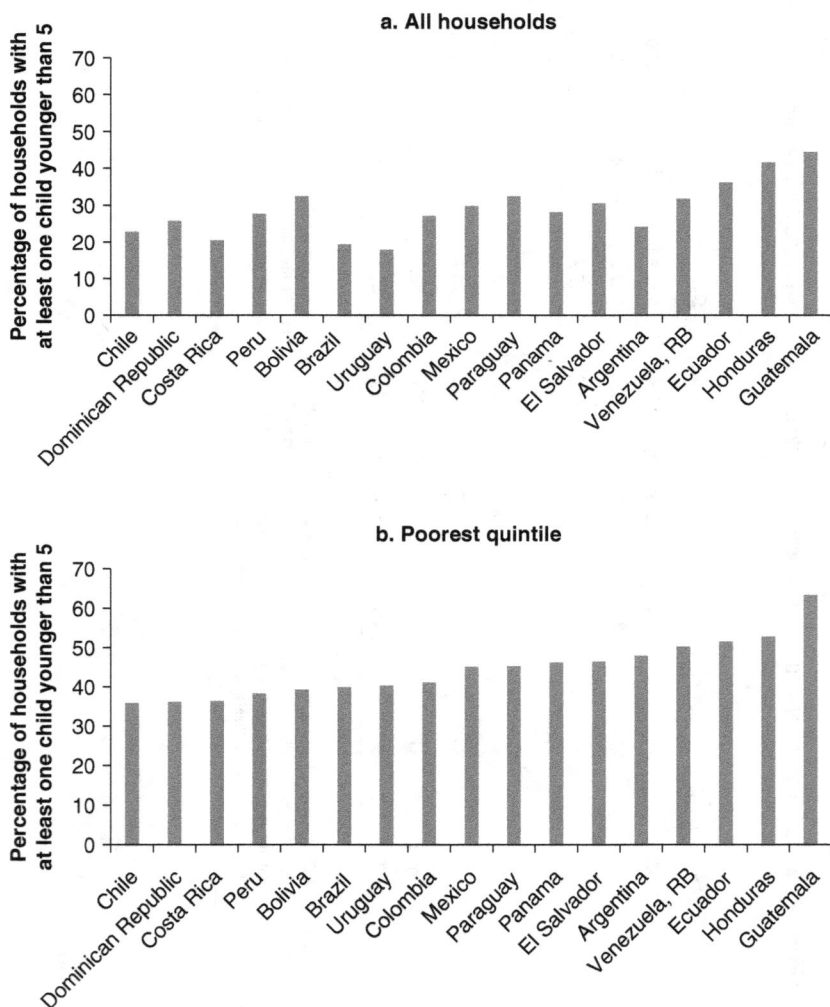

a. All households

b. Poorest quintile

(continued on next page)

FIGURE 1B.1 Households in selected countries in Latin America and the Caribbean with at least one child younger than 5, by income level, circa 2014 *(continued)*

c. Richest quintile

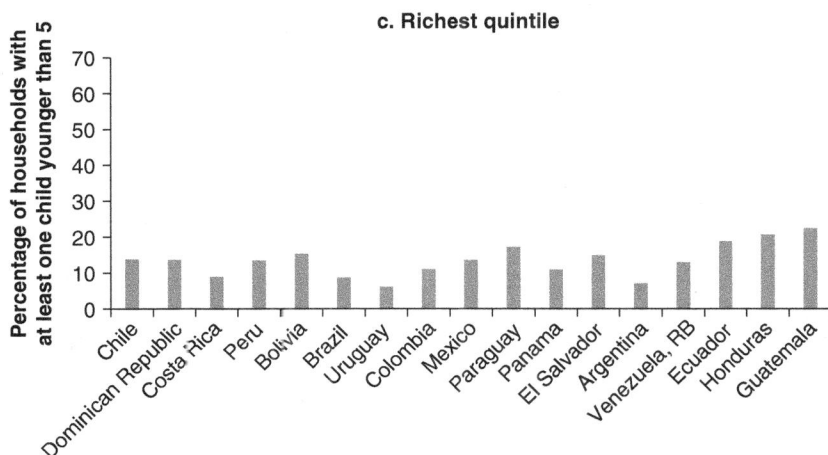

Source: Sociometro-BID (DB 2015), available at http://www.iadb.org/en/research-and-data//sociometro-bid,6981.html.

Annex 1C: Share of Population in Selected Countries Receiving Social Assistance or Noncontributory Pensions

TABLE 1C.1 Share of population in selected countries in Latin America and the Caribbean that receives social assistance through conditional cash transfer programs

Country	Program	Year	Thousands of beneficiaries		Percentage of population	Cost of program (percentage of GDP)
			Households	Individuals		
Argentina	Asignación Universal por Hijo	2013	1,905	8,383	20.2	0.47
Bolivia	Bono Juancito Pinto	2013	1,135	5,786	52.4	0.19
Brazil	Bolsa Família	2013	14,086	57,753	28.7	0.44
Chile	Chile Solidario	2011	264	1,109	6.4	0.13
Colombia	Familias en Acción	2013	2,682	11,263	23.9	0.23
Costa Rica	Avancemos	2013	132	641	13.6	0.19
Dominican Republic	Progresando con Solidaridad	2013	683	2,324	22.3	0.46

(continued on next page)

TABLE 1C.1 Share of population in selected countries in Latin America and the Caribbean that receives social assistance through conditional cash transfer programs *(continued)*

Country	Program	Year	Thousands of beneficiaries		Percentage of population	Cost of program (percentage of GDP)
			Households	Individuals		
Ecuador	Bono de Desarrollo Humano	2012	1,203	5,031	32.4	0.64
El Salvador	Comunidades Solidarias Rurales	2013	96	620	9.8	0.39
Guatemala	Mi Bono Seguro	2012	758	4,168	27.6	0.20
Honduras	Programa de Asignación Familiar	2013	246	1,228	15.2	0.84
Mexico	Oportunidades	2013	6,600	32,340	27.3	0.41
Panama	Red de Oportunidades	2013	73	353	9.5	0.14
Paraguay	Tekoporã	2013	76	395	5.8	0.09
Peru	Juntos	2013	718	3,819	12.3	0.14
Uruguay	Asignaciones Familiares (Plan Equidad)	2013	184	791	23.3	0.40
Latin America and the Caribbean (population-weighted average)			30,841	136,004	25.1	0.38

Source: Data from the Inter-American Development Bank, available at http://www.iadb.org/en/research-and-data //social-transfers,7531.html.

TABLE 1C.2 Share of population in selected countries in Latin America and the Caribbean that receives noncontributory pensions

Country	Name	Year	Minimum age for receiving benefits	Thousands of beneficiaries	Percentage of people older than minimum age for receiving benefits covered	Size of transfer Monthly payment (dollars)	Cost of program (percentage of GDP)
Argentina	Programa de Pensiones No Contributivas (Vejez)	2013	70	26	0.8	373	0.02
Bolivia	Renta Universal de Vejez "Renta Dignidad"	2013	60	871	100	81	1.24
Brazil	Benefício de Prestação Continuada	2013	65	1,863	12.4	378	0.31
Brazil	Previdência Rural	2012	60	5,821	27.2	363	0.99
Chile	Pensión Básica Solidaria de Vejez	2013	65	584	33.4	207	0.42
Colombia	Programa de Protección Social al Adulto Mayor	2013	57	1,250	21.4	47	0.12
Costa Rica	Régimen No Contributivo de Pensiones por Monto Básico	2013	65	93	27.3	205	0.34
Ecuador	Pensión para Adultos Mayores	2013	65	569	56.9	88	0.36
El Salvador	Nuestros Mayores Derechos	2013	60	28	4.6	95	0.07
Guatemala	Programa de Aporte Económico o del Adulto Mayor	2013	65	103	14.5	99	0.12
Mexico	Pensión para Adultos Mayores	2013	65	5,600	72.5	56	0.22
Panama	Asistencia Económica para Adultos Mayores de 70 y más	2013	70	88	47.7	204	0.31

(continued on next page)

TABLE 1C.2 Share of population in selected countries in Latin America and the Caribbean that receives noncontributory pensions *(continued)*

Country	Name	Year	Minimum age for receiving benefits	Thousands of beneficiaries	Percentage of people older than minimum age for receiving benefits covered	Size of transfer	
						Monthly payment (dollars)	Cost of program (percentage of GDP)
Paraguay	Pensión Alimentaria para Adultos Mayores en Pobreza	2013	65	94	25.2	175	0.36
Peru	Programa Nacional de Asistencia Solidaria "Pensión 65"	2013	65	306	15.7	77	0.08
Uruguay	Pensión No Contributiva por Vejez e Invalidez	2013	70	86	24.8	368	0.62
Venezuela, RB	Gran Misión Amor Mayor	2013	60	522	18.1	427	0.48
Latin America and the Caribbean (population-weighted average)				17,384	31.9	236	0.47

Source: Data from the Inter-American Development Bank, available at http://www.iadb.org/en/research-and-data//social-transfers,7531.html.

Annex 1D: Total Dependency Ratio in Selected Countries

The total dependency ratio is the ratio of the number of people considered economically dependent (people younger than 14 and older than 65) to every 100 people ages 15–64. It is usually used to measure the pressure on the productive population given the demographic structure in a country.

Estimates of the year in which each country will reach the lowest total dependency ratio before it starts rising are based on the *World Population Prospects: The 2012 Revision* (UNDP 2013). These series are projected for five-year intervals, assuming a medium fertility rate. Figure 1D.1 shows the trends for selected countries in LAC from 2015 to 2040.

FIGURE 1D.1 Projected total dependency ratio in selected countries in Latin America and the Caribbean, 2015–40

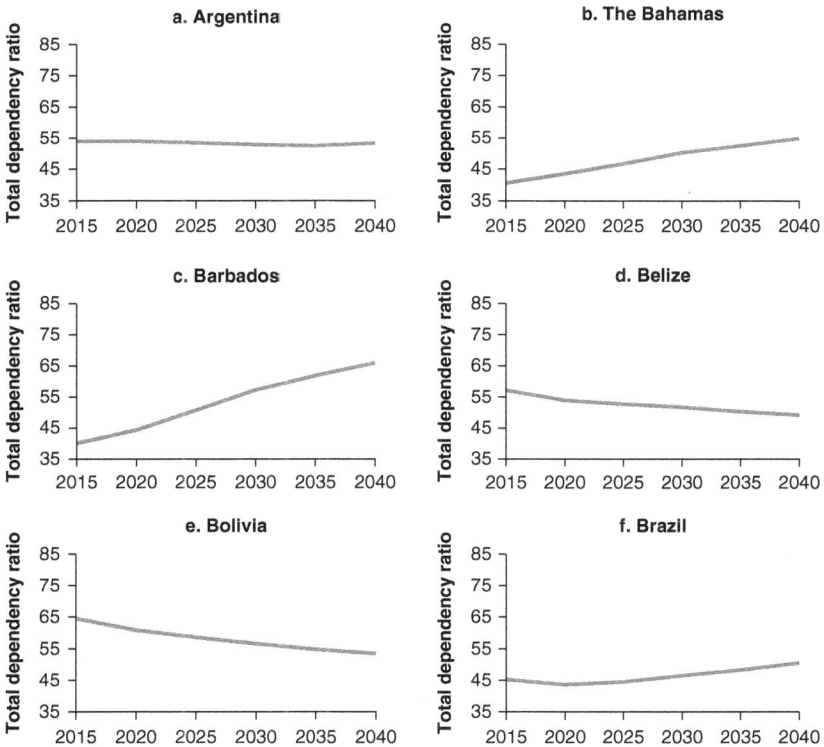

(continued on next page)

FIGURE 1D.1 Projected total dependency ratio in selected countries in Latin America and the Caribbean, 2015–40 *(continued)*

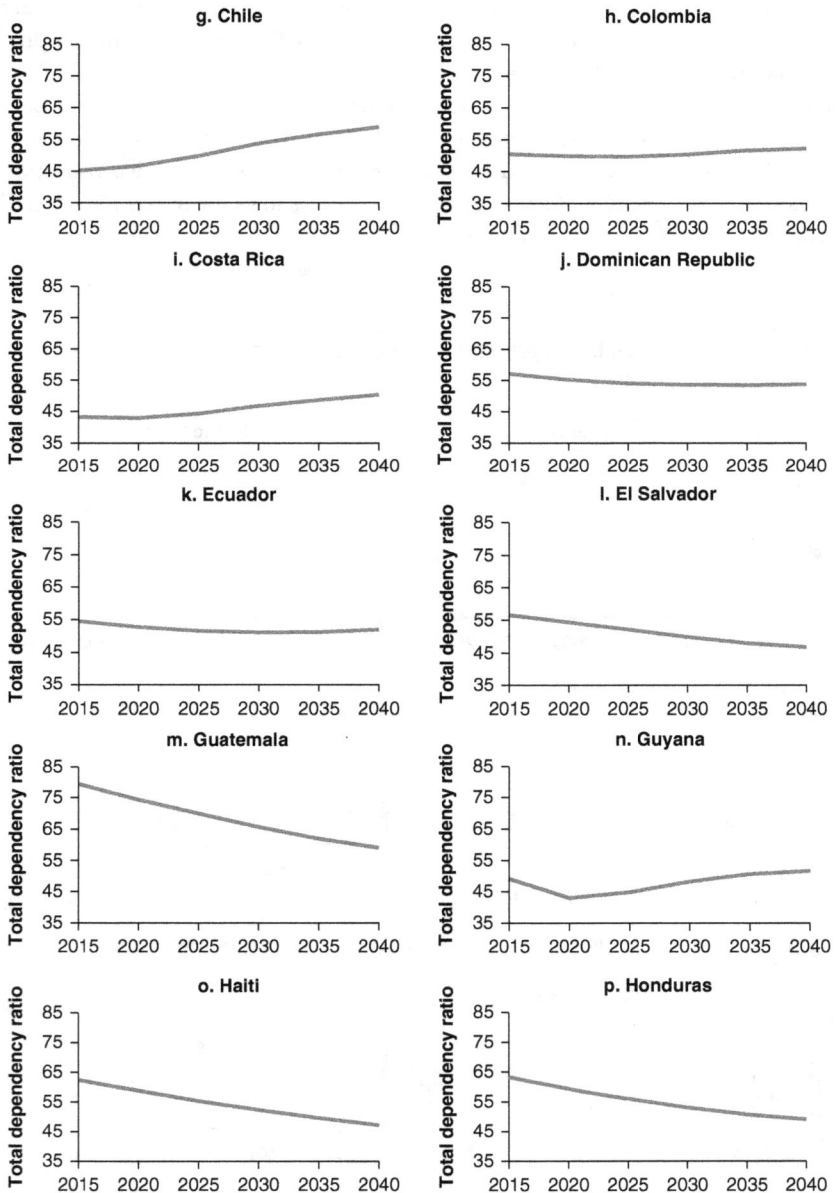

g. Chile

h. Colombia

i. Costa Rica

j. Dominican Republic

k. Ecuador

l. El Salvador

m. Guatemala

n. Guyana

o. Haiti

p. Honduras

(continued on next page)

FIGURE 1D.1 Projected total dependency ratio in selected countries in Latin America and the Caribbean, 2015–40 *(continued)*

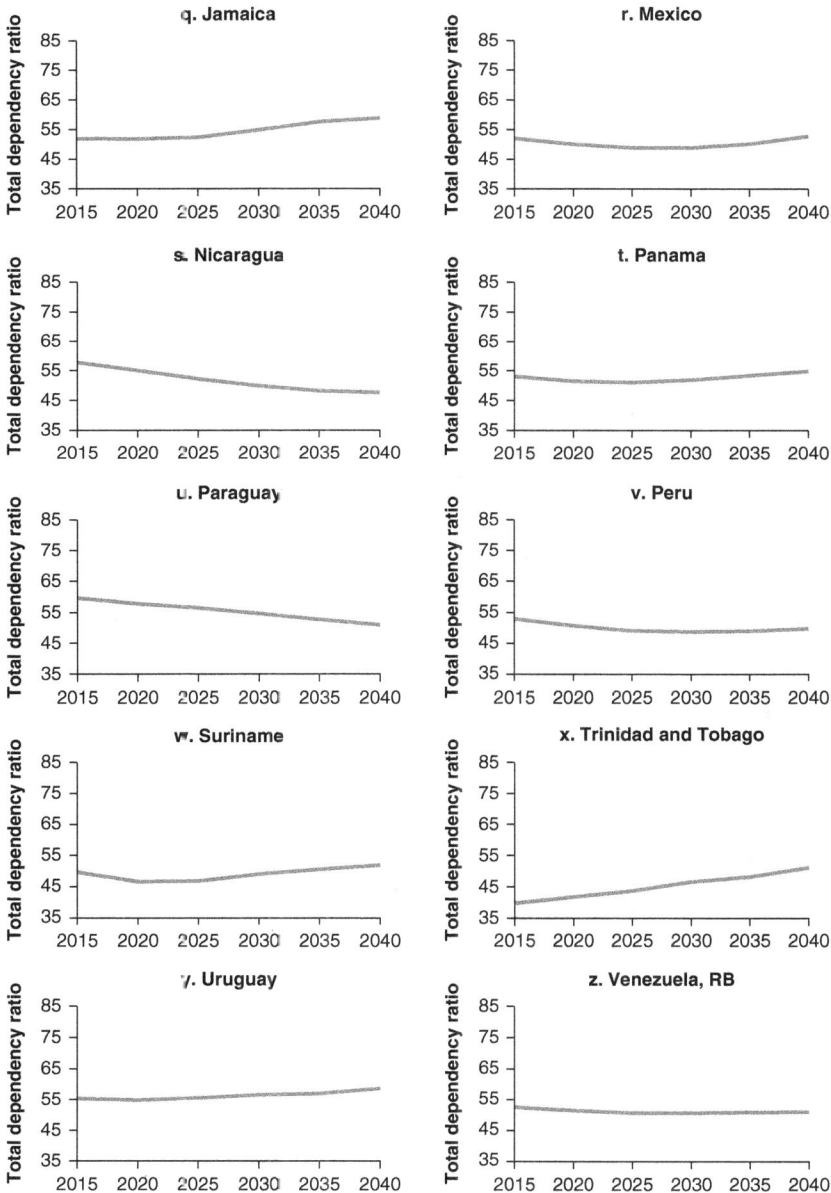

q. Jamaica

r. Mexico

s. Nicaragua

t. Panama

u. Paraguay

v. Peru

w. Suriname

x. Trinidad and Tobago

y. Uruguay

z. Venezuela, RB

Source: UNDP 2013.
Note: Dependency ratio is the number of dependents per 100 working-age people.

Annex 1E: Female Labor Force Participation in Latin America and the Caribbean

FIGURE 1E.1 Women 15–64 in the labor force in Latin America and the Caribbean, 1990–2012

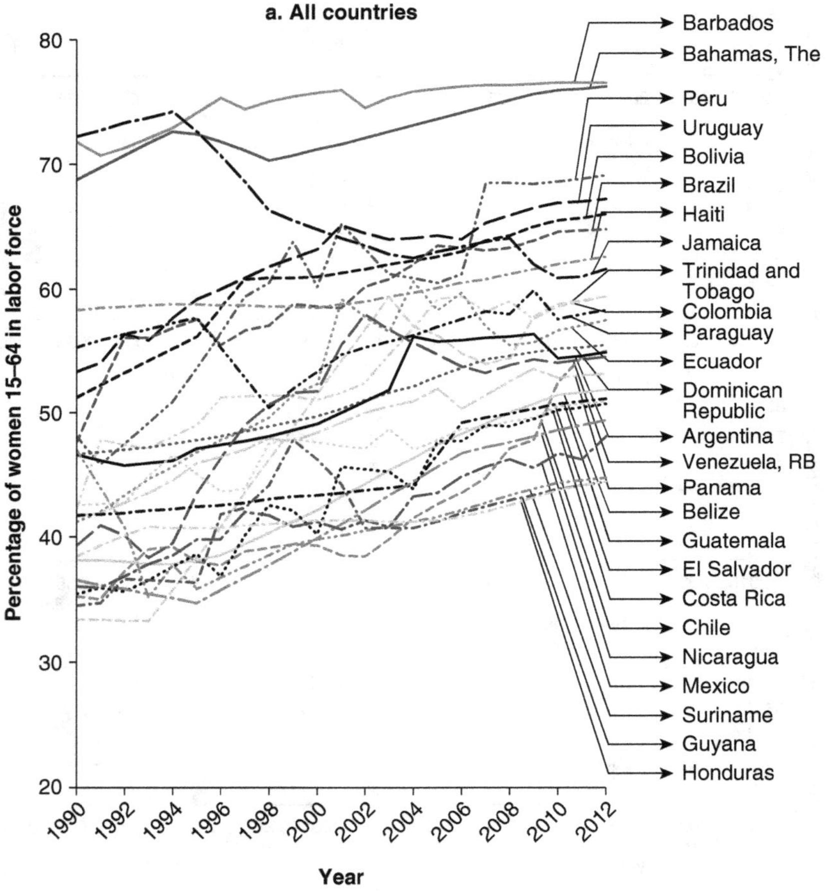

a. All countries
Percentage of women 15–64 in labor force
80
70
60
50
40
30
20
1990
1992
1994
1996
1998
2000
2002
2004
2006
2008
2010
2012
Year
Barbados
Bahamas, The
Peru
Uruguay
Bolivia
Brazil
Haiti
Jamaica
Trinidad and Tobago
Colombia
Paraguay
Ecuador
Dominican Republic
Argentina
Venezuela, RB
Panama
Belize
Guatemala
El Salvador
Costa Rica
Chile
Nicaragua
Mexico
Suriname
Guyana
Honduras

(continued on next page)

FIGURE 1E.1 Women 15–64 in the labor force in Latin America and the Caribbean, 1990–2012 *(continued)*

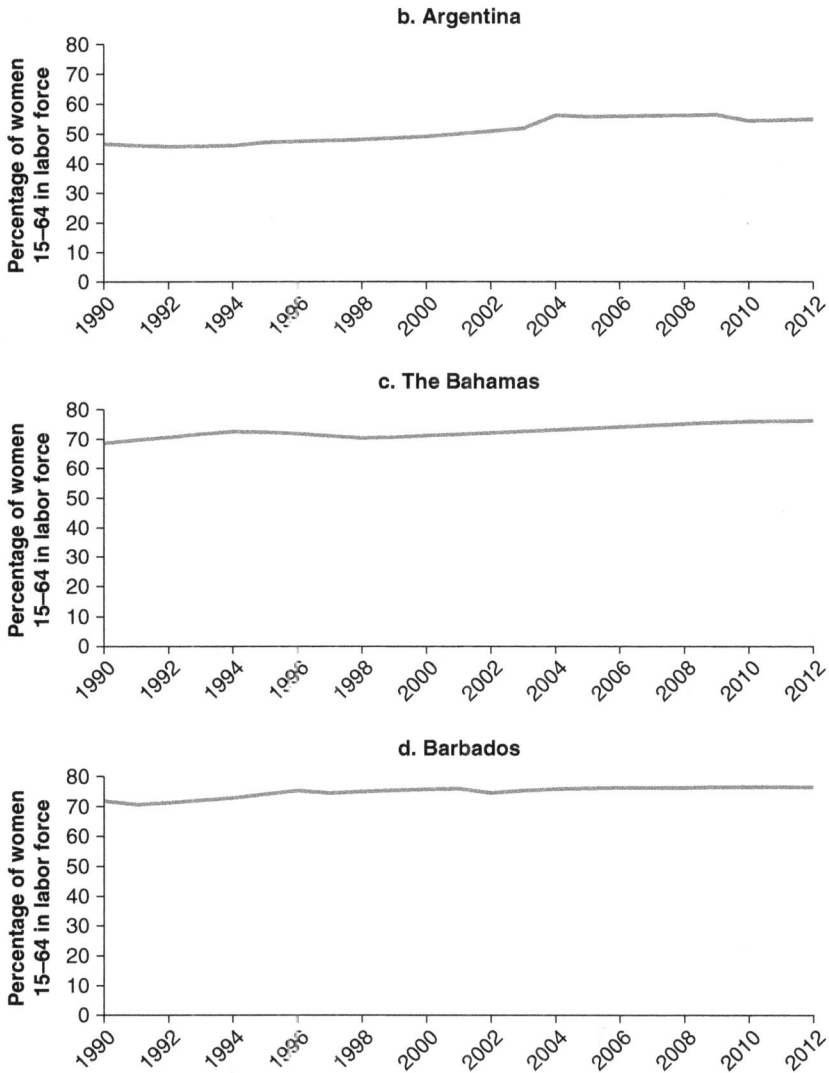

b. Argentina

c. The Bahamas

d. Barbados

(continued on next page)

FIGURE 1E.1 Women 15–64 in the labor force in Latin America and the Caribbean, 1990–2012 *(continued)*

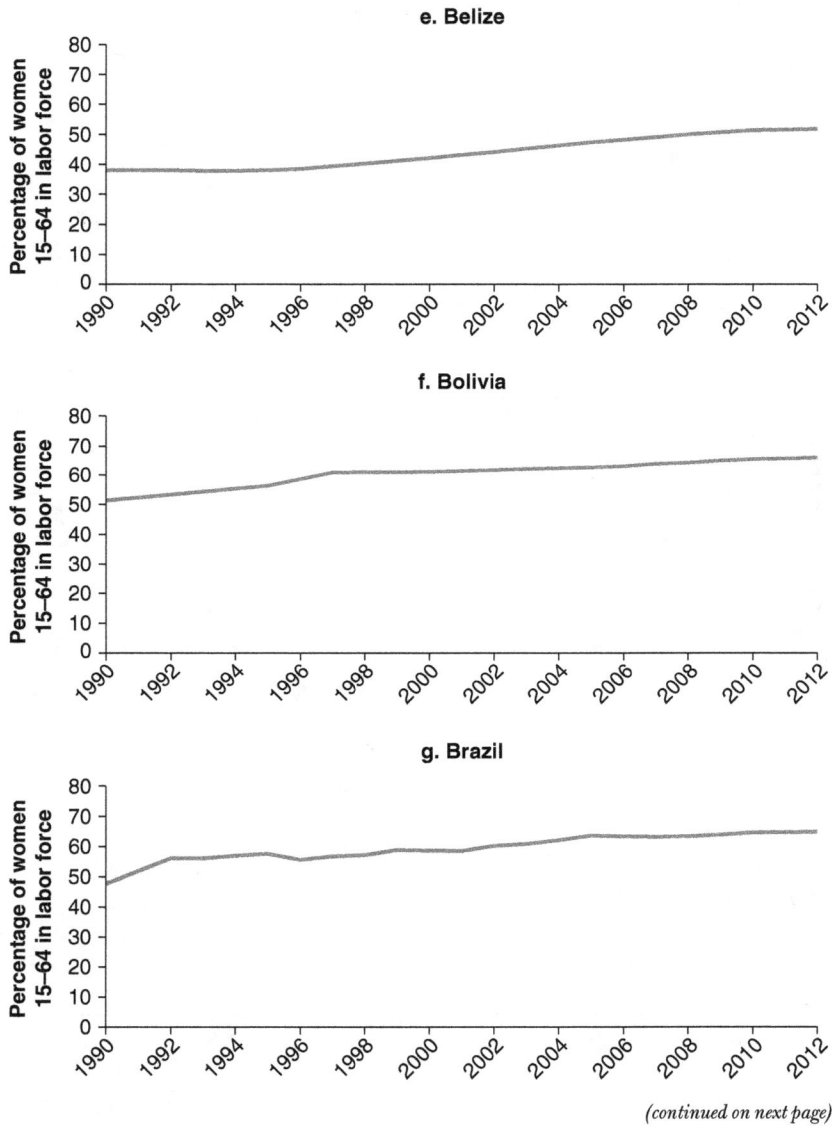

e. Belize

f. Bolivia

g. Brazil

(continued on next page)

FIGURE 1E.1 Women 15–64 in the labor force in Latin America and the Caribbean, 1990–2012 *(continued)*

h. Chile

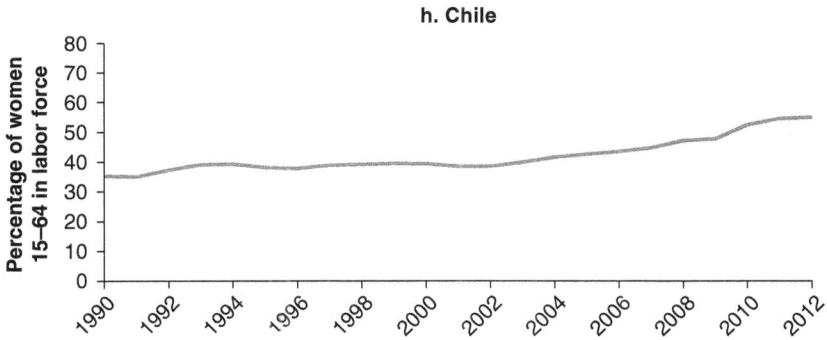

i. Colombia

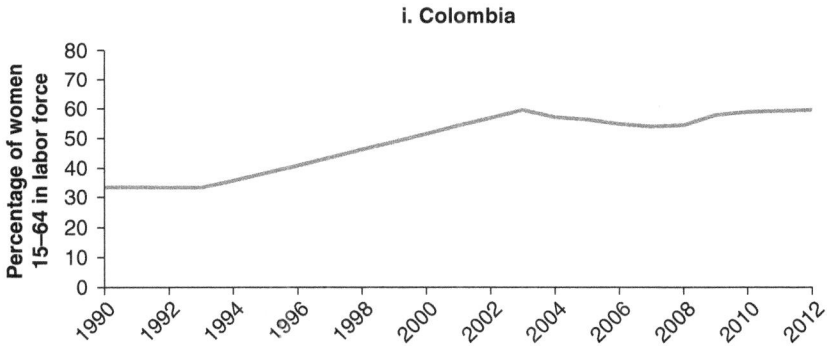

j. Costa Rica

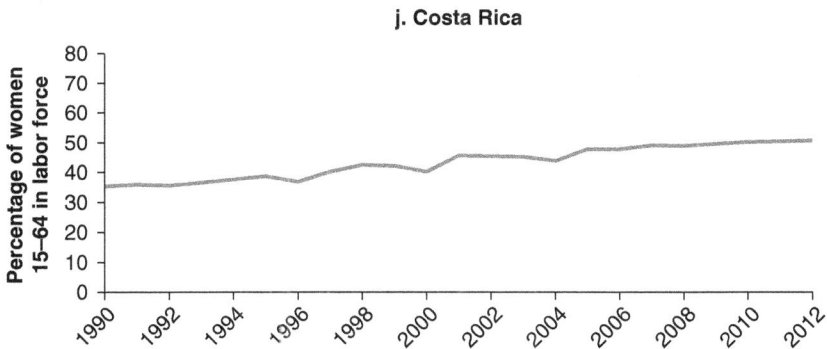

(continued on next page)

FIGURE 1E.1 Women 15–64 in the labor force in Latin America and the Caribbean, 1990–2012 *(continued)*

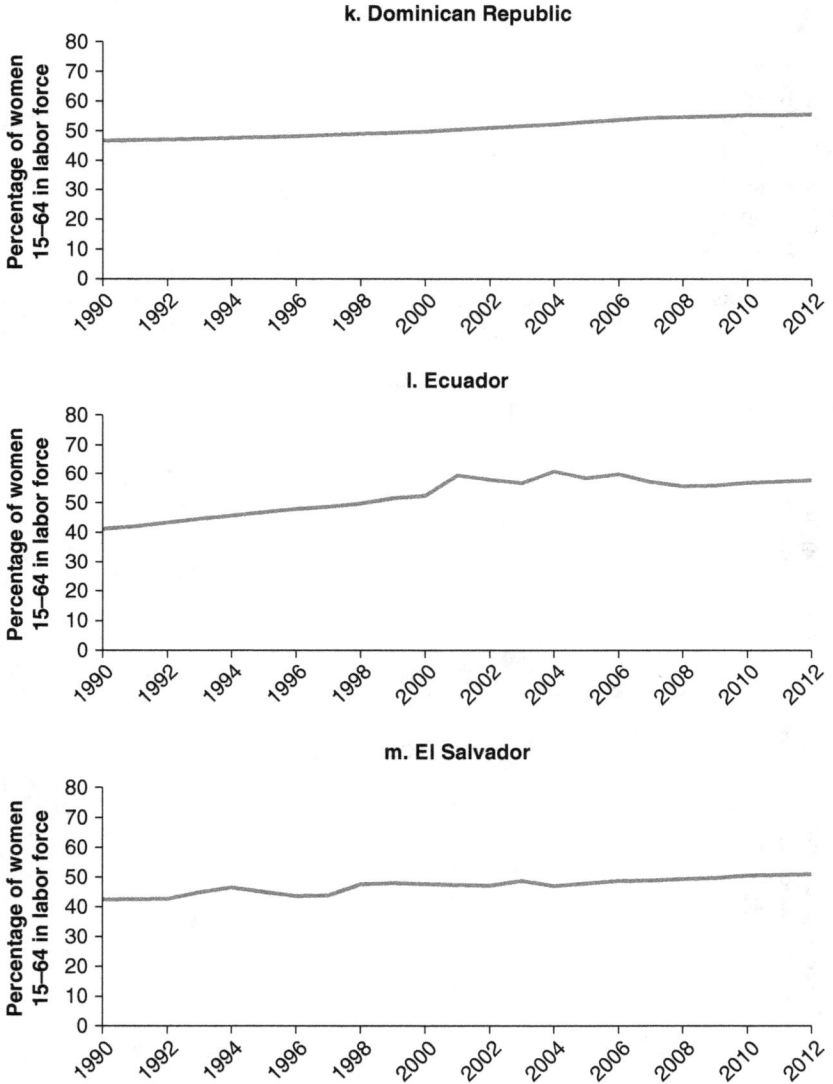

k. Dominican Republic

l. Ecuador

m. El Salvador

(continued on next page)

FIGURE 1E.1 Women 15–64 in the labor force in Latin America and the Caribbean, 1990–2012 *(continued)*

n. Guatemala

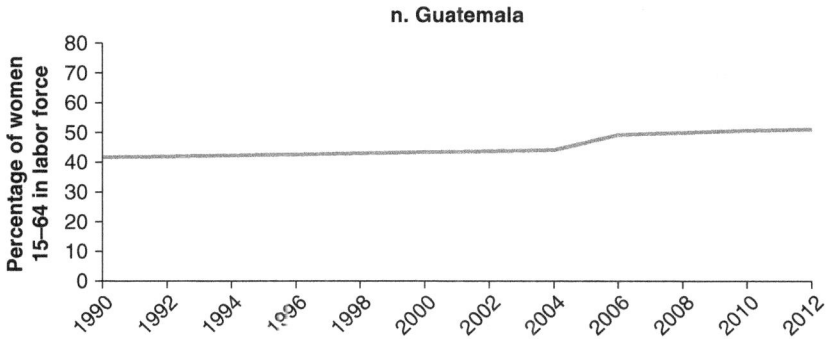

o. Guyana

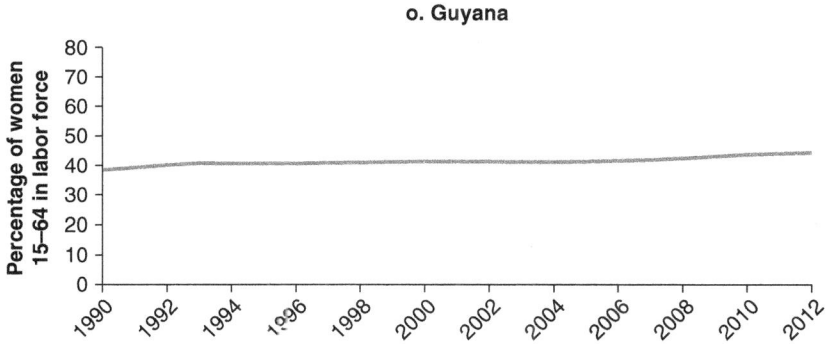

p. Haiti

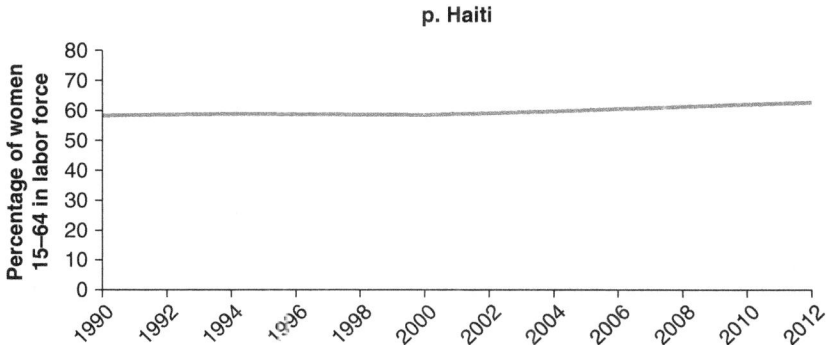

(continued on next page)

FIGURE 1E.1 Women 15–64 in the labor force in Latin America and the Caribbean, 1990–2012 *(continued)*

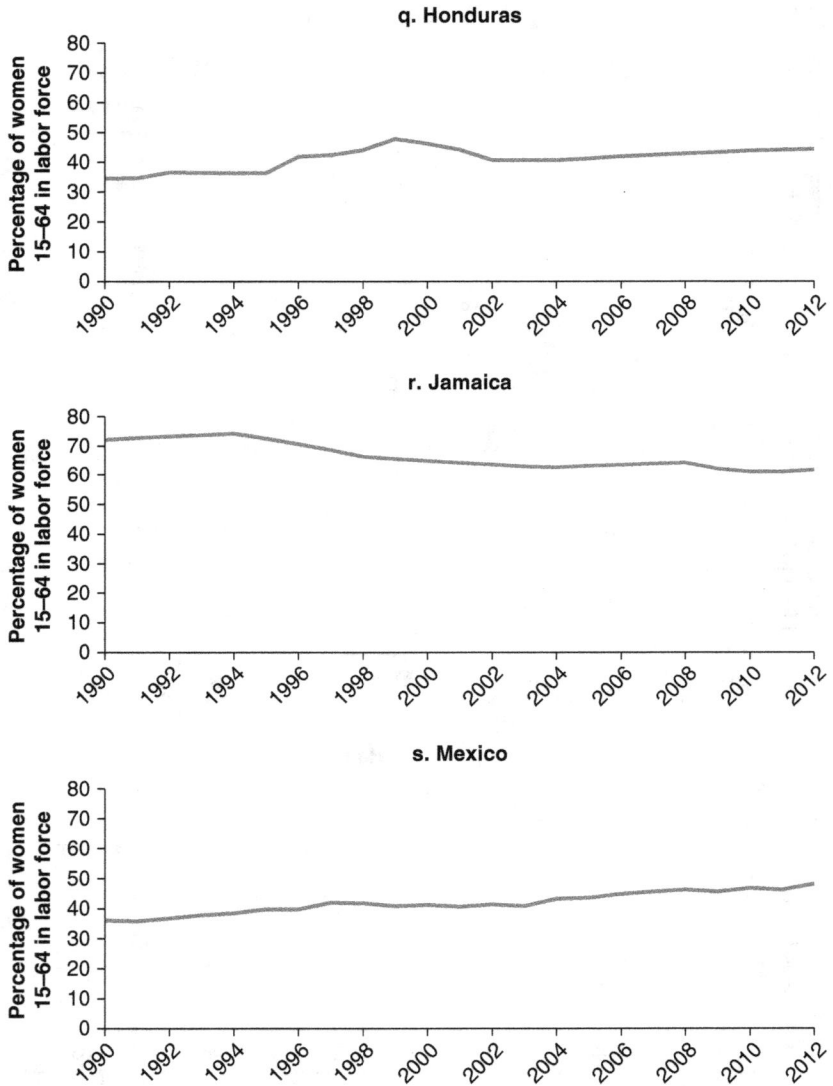

q. Honduras

r. Jamaica

s. Mexico

(continued on next page)

FIGURE 1E.1 Women 15–64 in the labor force in Latin America and the Caribbean, 1990–2012 *(continued)*

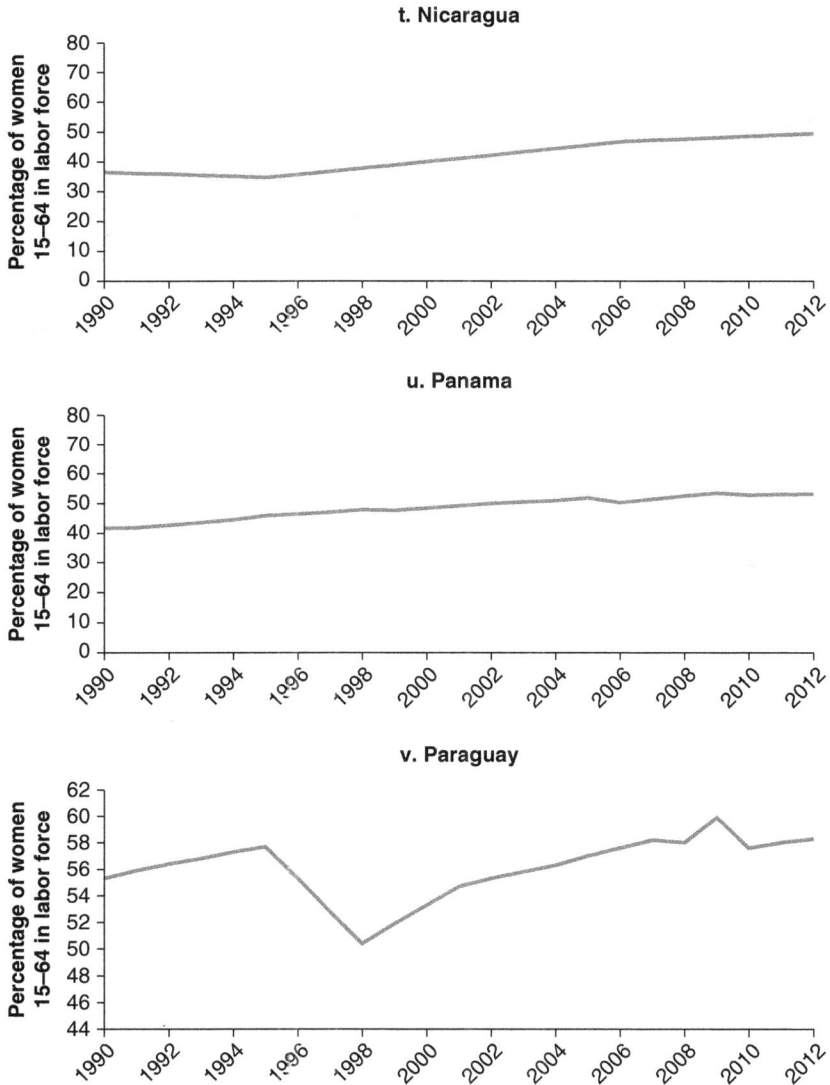

t. Nicaragua

u. Panama

v. Paraguay

(continued on next page)

FIGURE 1E.1 Women 15–64 in the labor force in Latin America and the Caribbean, 1990–2012 *(continued)*

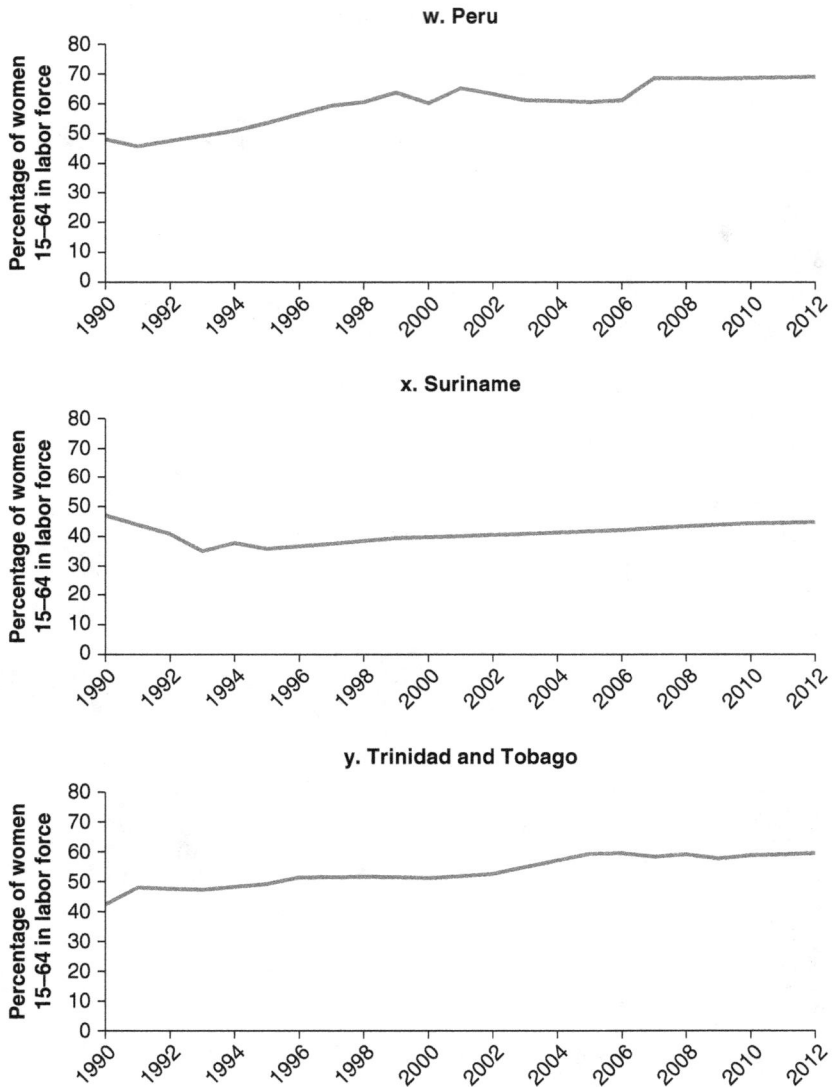

w. Peru

x. Suriname

y. Trinidad and Tobago

(continued on next page)

FIGURE 1E.1 Women 15–64 in the labor force in Latin America and the Caribbean, 1990–2012 *(continued)*

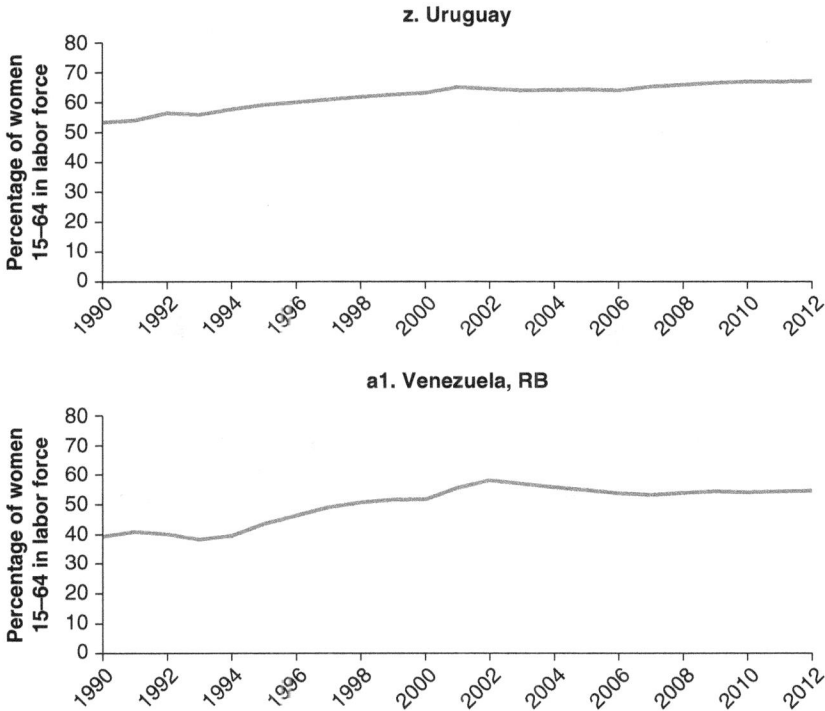

z. Uruguay

a1. Venezuela, RB

Source: World Development Indicators 2014.

Notes

1. Estimates for the increase in GDP in other countries are as follows: China: 8 percent; Denmark: 4 percent; Egypt: 56 percent; France: 7 percent; Germany: 7 percent; India: 45 percent; Italy: 19 percent; Japan: 15 percent; South Africa: 17 percent; Spain: 10 percent; Sweden: 3 percent; Tanzania: 3 percent; United Arab Emirates: 19 percent; United Kingdom: 8 percent; and United States: 8 percent (Aguirre and others 2012).

2. For studies on the effects of FLFP, see Behrman and Deolalikar (1988); Behrman, Duryea, and Székely (1999); Blumberg (2006); Dollar and Gatti (1999); Fernandez and Perova (2013). King and Hill (1993); Klasen and Lamanna (2009); Krogh and others (2009); McGinn, Ruiz Castro, and Long Lingo. (2015); Ñopo (2012); Psacharopoulos (1994); Psacharopouls and Tzannatos (1992); Schultz (1993); World Bank (2011, 2012).

3. About 29 million households in LAC receive some kind of government transfer through conditional cash transfer (CCT) programs, which reach about 25 percent of the total population (about 131 million people). Another 13 million people—including more than a quarter of the region's elderly population—receive noncontributory pensions (see annex 1C). These transfers represent about 0.7 percent of regional GDP (0.37 percent for CCTs and 0.33 percent for noncontributory pensions).

4. For details on demographic trends and dependency ratios, see annex 1D. Estimates assume that medium fertility rates stay unchanged; we recognize that fertility rates likely will decline as more women join the labor force.

References

Aguirre, D., L. Hoteit, C. Rupp, and K. Sabbagh. 2012. *Empowering the Third Billion: Women and the World of Work in 2012*. Booz and Company, New York.

Behrman, J., and A. Deolalikar. 1988. "Health and Nutrition." In *Handbook of Development Economics*, edited by H. Chenery and T. N. Srinivasan. Amsterdam: North-Holland.

Behrman, J., S. Duryea, and M. Székely. 1999. "Schooling Investments and Macroeconomic Conditions: A Micro-Macro Investigation for Latin America and the Caribbean." Research Department Working Paper 407, Inter-American Development Bank, Washington, DC.

Blumberg, R. 2006. "How Mother's Economic Activities and Empowerment Affect Early Childhood Care and Education (ECCE) for Boys and Girls: A Theory-Guided Exploration across History, Cultures and Societies." Background paper prepared for the *Education for All Global Monitoring Report 2007*.

Costa, J., and E. Silva. 2008. "The Burden of Gender Inequalities for Society." In *Poverty in Focus*. Brasilia: International Poverty Centre.

Cuberes, D., and M. Teignier. 2016. "Aggregate Costs of Gender Gaps in the Labor Market: A Quantitative Estimate." *Journal of Human Capital* 10 (1): 1–32.

Dollar, D., and R. Gatti. 1999. "Gender Inequality, Income, and Growth: Are Good Times Good for Women?" Gender and Development Working Paper 1, World Bank, Washington, DC.

Fernandez, R., and E. Perova. 2013. "Eradicating Extreme Poverty and Sharing Prosperity: A Gendered Perspective." World Bank, Poverty and Equity Global Practice, Washington, DC.

Hsieh, C.-T., E. Hurst, C. I. Jones, and P. J. Klenow. 2013. "The Allocation of Talent and U.S. Economic Growth." Stanford University, Palo Alto, CA, and the National Bureau for Economic Research (NBER), Cambridge, MA.

ILOSTAT (database). International Labour Organisation, Geneva. http://www.ilo.org/ilostat/.

King, E. M., and M. A. Hill, eds. 1993. *Women's Education in Developing Countries*. Washington, DC: World Bank.

Klasen, S., and F. Lamanna. 2009. "The Impact of Gender Inequality in Education and Employment on Economic Growth: New Evidence for a Panel of Countries." *Feminist Economics* 15 (3): 91–132.

Krogh, E., T. N. Hansen, S. Wendt, and M. Elkjaer. 2009. "Promoting Employment for Women as a Strategy for Poverty Reduction." Organisation for Economic Co-operation and Development (OECD), Paris.

Malhotra, A., R. Pande, and C. Grown. 2003. "Impact of Investments in Female Education on Gender Equality." International Center for Research on Women, Washington, DC.

McGinn, K. L., M. Ruiz Castro, and E. Long Lingo. 2015. "Mums the Word! Cross-National Effects of Maternal Employment on Gender Inequalities at Work and at Home." Harvard Business School Working Paper 15-094, Cambridge, MA.

McKinsey Global Institute. 2015. *The Power of Parity: How Advancing Women's Equality Can Add $12 Trillion to Global Growth*. McKinsey and Company, San Francisco.

Morrison, A., D. Raju, and N. Sinha. 2007. "Gender Equality, Poverty and Economic Growth." Policy Research Working Paper 4349, World Bank, Washington, DC.

Ñopo, H. 2012. *New Century, Old Disparities: Gender and Ethnic Earnings Gaps in Latin America and the Caribbean*. Washington, DC: Inter-American Development Bank.

Psacharopoulos, G. 1994. "Returns to Investment in Education: A Global Update." *World Development* 22 (9): 1325–43.

Psacharopoulos, G., and Z. Tzannatos. 1992. "Latin American Women's Earnings and Participation in the Labor Force." Policy Research Working Paper 856, World Bank, Washington, DC.

Schultz, T. P. 1993. "Economics of Women's Schooling." In *The Politics of Women's Education*, edited by J. K. Conway and S. C. Bourque. Ann Arbor, MI: University of Michigan Press.

Socio-Economic Database for Latin America and the Caribbean (SEDLAC). CEDLAS and World Bank. http://sedlac.econo.unlp.edu.ar/eng/.

UIS (UNESCO Institute for Statistics) (database). Montreal. http://www.uis.unesco.org/Pages/default.aspx.

UN (United Nations). 2014. *Probabilistic Population Projections based on the World Population Prospects: The 2012 Revision*. New York: UN.

UNDP (United Nations Development Programme). 2013. *World Population Prospects: The 2012 Revision*. New York: UNDP.

World Bank. 2011. "Una (R)evolución de género en marcha. Ampliación de las oportunidades económicas para las mujeres en América Central: Revisión de la última década." Washington, DC. http://documents.worldbank.org/curated/en/901171468012925649/pdf/691260ESW0P1140CA0Estudio0de0Genero.pdf.

———. 2012. *The Effect of Women's Economic Power in Latin America and the Caribbean*. Washington, DC: World Bank.

World Development Indicators (database). World Bank, Washington, DC. http://data.worldbank.org/data-catalog/world-development-indicators.

CHAPTER 2

Childcare Policies: Key for Female Labor Participation

Evidence from both developed and developing countries reveals that access to childcare is associated with higher female labor force participation (FLFP). This chapter reviews this research and shows that, even if different policies are needed to overcome the constraints women face to access jobs, childcare seems to be the policy that has the most consistent positive effects on women's engagement in the labor force (Busso and Romero Fonseca 2015). Given the simultaneous nature of women's decisions to work and to use childcare, ensuring the appropriate support for meeting childcare needs is a necessary condition for the success of every other policy intended to improve women's outcomes in the labor market.

In addition to the importance of childcare for working mothers, compelling evidence demonstrates that early childhood education has an impact on children's cognitive and socioemotional development as well as long-term outcomes. Good-quality childcare can thus be a key instrument for increasing productivity and growth.

Increasing access to childcare improves the stock of human capital (by helping working families) and the flow of human capital (by fostering early childhood development). This strong intergenerational feature of childcare policies is particularly important for vulnerable households. Enabling parents to work (or study) and young children to benefit from early education has the potential to close gaps in school achievement, employment, and earnings between the poor and nonpoor.

This chapter reviews the evidence on the impact of childcare on FLFP and child outcomes. The first section analyzes the effects on female labor supply. It examines the conditions under which childcare policies achieve their intended effects, identifying mismatches between the services provided and the services working women need. The second section assesses the effects of childcare on child outcomes. The last section analyzes the cost-effectiveness of childcare.

Effects of Childcare on Female Labor Supply

Most of the evidence shows that reductions in the costs of childcare and increases in its availability boost FLFP.

International Evidence of Positive Effects

Effect of formal childcare

Much the literature focuses on the relationship between the cost of childcare and FLFP, testing the hypothesis that the more affordable the service, the more it is used and the higher the probability that women participate in the labor market. Anderson and Levine (2000) and Blau and Currie (2006) provide detailed reviews of estimates of the elasticity of female labor supply with respect to the cost of childcare in the United States. Most of their findings suggest that as the price of childcare falls, FLFP increases. There is, however, wide variation in the magnitude of the estimates.

Gustafsson and Stafford (1992) find that in Sweden, high-quality public childcare encourages labor market participation of women with preschoolers. Lokshin (2000) and Fong and Lokshin (2000) model mothers' participation in the labor force, working hours, and household demand for childcare in Romania (Fong and Lokshin) and the Russian Federation (Lokshin). They find that the decision to take a job and use childcare is sensitive to the price of the service. Hallman and others (2005) find that reductions in formal childcare prices in Guatemala do not predict mothers' labor force participation but have a large positive effect on work hours. Wrohlich (2008) shows that an increase in the availability of childcare has larger effects on maternal labor supply than reducing childcare costs. Baker, Gruber, and Milligan (2008) study the expansion of subsidized provision of childcare for children 0–4 in Quebec, where they find a positive effect on maternal labor supply for married (and cohabiting) mothers. Consistent with this evidence, Bick (2015) finds that increasing the supply of subsidized childcare for younger children (0–2) increases the maternal FLFP rate and that a large proportion of part-time working mothers would work full time if they had greater access to subsidized childcare. Simonsen (2010) uses local variation across municipalities in the availability and price of high-quality publicly subsidized daycare in Denmark. She shows that guaranteed access to childcare has a significant and positive effect on the employment of mothers of children younger than 1 and that the price effect is significantly negative. Gathmann and Sass (2012) find that an increase in the price of childcare may result in reductions in use and a decline in FLFP. Del Boca (2015) summarizes results based on international studies that show increases in FLFP ranging from 5.2 percentage points for subsidies covering half of childcare costs in the United States to 25.4 percentage points for subsidies covering the total cost of childcare in the United Kingdom.

Effect of informal childcare

The use of informal childcare arrangements also shows positive effects on maternal labor supply. Using U.S. longitudinal data, Posadas and Vidal-Fernández (2012) find that childcare by grandparents increases maternal labor force participation by 15 percentage points on average, with most of the effect driven by families from socioeconomically disadvantaged backgrounds. Arpino, Pronzato, and Tavares (2010) find similar results in Italy. Both Compton and Pollak (2011) (for the United States) and Compton (2011) (for Canada) show that proximity to mothers or mothers-in-law has a substantial positive effect on the labor supply of married women with young children. Using data from 10 European countries, Dimova and Wolff (2011) show that regular childcare by grandparents has a small positive effect on maternal labor force participation but no effect on the type of employment (full-time or part-time). Using the same countries, Zamarro (2009) finds a significant effect of availability of regular childcare arrangements on FLFP only in Greece and the Netherlands.

Effect of public school enrollment

Gelbach (2002) finds that free public school enrollment of 5-year-olds in the United States increases labor supply among mothers whose youngest child is 5 by 6–24 percent, depending on the specification. Cascio (2009) finds that maternal labor supply increased with the introduction of kindergartens into U.S. public schools but only for single mothers of 5-year-olds with no younger children. Schlosser (2011) takes advantage of the staggered implementation of free public preschool in Israel to study the effects of a reduction in childcare costs on preschool enrollment and Arab mothers' labor supply. Her results show a sharp increase in maternal labor supply, mainly among more educated mothers.

Evidence from Latin America and the Caribbean of Positive Effects

Experimental or rigorous quasi-experimental evaluations of childcare interventions in LAC show a consistently positive effect of access to affordable childcare on FLFP and mixed evidence on female and household income (table 2.1). Results indicate increases of 2–22 percent in the probability of the mother being employed if given access to subsidized childcare. There are also sizable increases in the number of hours worked. In Argentina, for example, a youngest child attending public preschool was associated with an increase of 7.8 hours of work a week; in Mexico access to subsidized childcare was associated with an increase of 6.0 weekly work hours. Contreras, Puentes, and Bravo (2012) find that daycare location and opening hours that are compatible with working hours are positively correlated with female labor supply in Chile.

TABLE 2.1 Research findings on impact of childcare policies on female labor outcomes in Latin America and the Caribbean

Type of intervention/study/country	Effect
Access to free childcare	
Paes de Barros and others (2011)/ Brazil	• 9–17 percent increase in employment of mothers who were not working before • 16 percent increase in household income
Rosero and Oosterbeek (2011)/ Ecuador	• 22 percentage point increase in probability that mother works • 7-hour a week increase in number of hours worked • Positive but not significant effect on mothers' incomes • Significantly positive effect on income of household head
Access to subsidized childcare	
Ángeles and others (2011)/Mexico	• 18 percent increase in probability of being employed • 6-hour a week increase in number of hours worked • No effect on job stability for mothers • No effect on mothers' or household income • 7-hour a week reduction in time mothers allocated to care
Calderon (2014)/Mexico	• 1.8 percentage point increase in probability of being employed • 4.5 percent increase over average income increase in urban population of eligible women • No effect on household income
Access to public childcare	
Medrano (2009)/Chile	• 2.6–10 percent increase in female labor force participation, but effect disappears after controlling for observable family and individual characteristics • No effect on employment or work hours
Access to low-cost childcare	
Attanasio and Vera-Hernandez (2004)/Colombia	• Increase in probability of employment from 12 percent to 37 percent • 75-hour a month increase in number of hours worked
Access to public preschool	
Berlinski and Galiani (2007)/ Argentina	• 7.5 percent point increase in probability of preprimary school attendance • One additional classroom with full take-up of new places increased likelihood of maternal employment by 7 percentage points
Berlinski, Galiani, and McEwan (2011)/Argentina	• 13 mothers start work for every 100 youngest children in household that start preschool • 19 percentage point increase in likelihood of working more than 20 hours a week • 7.8-hour a week increase in hours worked if youngest offspring attends preschool; no effect if child is not youngest in household

Source: Mateo Díaz and Rodriguez-Chamussy 2013.

The effect size on FLFP in the studies shown in table 2.1 compares with the effect size found in Israel from the reduction of childcare costs (Schlosser 2011) and in France from the provision of free public school enrollment (Goux and Maurin 2010).

Busso and Romero Fonseca (2015) argue that the increase in childcare use in Latin America over recent decades has had short- and long-term effects on increases in female labor supply. It has also likely contributed to the convergence between advantaged and disadvantaged groups.

Other Effects on Female Labor Supply

Most empirical results show a positive and significant relationship between child-care and FLFP. Some studies show otherwise. Medrano (2009) and Encina and Martinez (2009) find no significant effects of childcare on FLFP in Chile, where rates are low.[1] Havnes and Mogstad (2011) find no significant effects on maternal labor supply in Norway, where the expansion to universal public childcare mostly crowded out the use of informal arrangements.

In an extension of the results of Gelbach (2002) on Oklahoma, Fitzpatrick (2010) finds that universal availability of preschool increases preschool enrollment but has no effect on the labor supply of most women. One possible explanation for these results differences, according to Fitzpatrick, is the change in the profile of women at the margin of participating in the labor market. In earlier studies using data spanning 1950–1990, the baseline rates of maternal employment were 17–55 percent; at the time of Fitzpatrick's study (2010), the figure was 77 percent. Women who had already made the decision to participate in the labor market may simply have readjusted their childcare arrangements by substituting them with cheaper formal care at the preschool.

The mediating role of quality and service characteristics

Another potential explanation for the lack of effects of childcare provision on FLFP is low take-up rates. Low take-up may reflect low quality or lack of service characteristics crucial for families. There may also be problems with the incentive design of childcare programs in the context of multiple obstacles for the incorporation of women into paid work (for example, mismatches between the service features of particular interventions and the needs of working mothers).

Many factors affect the decision to enroll a child in a formal daycare program. They include having a job, being able to afford the program, finding a facility with a convenient location and opening times, and trusting the service provided. There is very little rigorous empirical evidence on which factors matter most to families.

Quality is very important, but research results are scarce and inconclusive because of the difficulty of defining and measuring quality (box 2.1).

Many factors affect demand for childcare:

- The presence of alternative caregivers in households reduces demand for formal childcare services (Attanasio and Vera-Hernandez 2004; Connelly DeGraff, and Levison 1996; Deutsch 1998; Hallman and others 2005).

- Children's age increases the probability of enrollment (Bernal and Fernández 2013; Leibowitz, Klerman, and Waite 1992; Schlosser 2011; Urzúa and Veramendi 2011).

- A higher level of mother's education increases the probability of enrollment (Bernal and Fernández 2013; Hallman and others 2005; Urzúa and Veramendi 2011).

- Female-headed households are more likely to be eligible for and to participate in subsidized childcare programs (Herbst 2008).

- Higher price tends to reduce demand, although it is difficult to control for quality and possible that high prices are positively correlated with demand when they imply high quality (Fong and Lokshin 2000; Lokshin 2000).

- Distance to the childcare center is negatively correlated with enrollment (Attanasio and Vera-Hernandez 2004; Urzúa and Veramendi 2011). Distance to the childcare center also has a significant negative effect on attendance (Contreras, Puentes, and Bravo 2012).

- Access to childcare centers that operate during typical working hours increases participation (Contreras, Puentes, and Bravo 2012).

Some of these factors may explain why the provision of free childcare increases enrollment without having an effect on maternal labor supply. They suggest that low quality induces low take-up and reinforces negative perceptions about daycare centers (box 2.2).

BOX 2.1 Features of quality of childcare services as defined by users

Focus group discussions carried out in four cities in Mexico in 2012 reveal some of the features mothers consider indicators of good quality in childcare services:

"The interaction, the trust, the hygiene . . . the satisfaction that your child is happy to be there and comes home every day having learned something new."—Working mother, Ciudad Juaréz

"I cannot complain because [my son] went to a daycare center where he was well taken care of, given the attention he deserves, fed on time, and came home like a new boy, clean, combed—I mean, in good shape."—Nonworking mother, Tepic

Childcare in different institutional settings

Depending on how services are funded, mandated childcare and parental leave could have negative effects on employment or women's wages (Gruber 1994; Prada, Rucci, and Urzúa 2015). To avoid creating a wedge between the labor costs of men and women, policy makers could progressively equalize leave and care benefits for mothers and fathers, replacing maternity and paternity leave with family leave that is identical for both parents (Ñopo 2012).

A mother's decision to use nonparental childcare arrangements is frequently made simultaneously with the decision to work (Blau and Robins 1998; Connelly 1992; Del Boca and Vuri 2007). Especially for mothers of younger children (0–3), the decision to enrol a child in full-time formal care is usually made after the mother has secured a job or the possibility of a job with earnings that more than cover the direct and indirect costs of childcare. Childcare needs for young children and the availability of jobs for women foster one another. Childcare provision without possibilities of new female employment in the short term would likely affect only the number of hours worked by women who already hold jobs.

The existence of universal benefits (for example, public preschool), subsidized childcare, and parental leave schemes affects the choices women make about fertility and employment. In recent decades, developed countries experienced huge decreases in birth rates along with increases in FLFP, although in many countries participation among mothers of children younger than 3 is significantly lower than it is among mothers of older children (OECD 2011). The demographic challenges these countries face have motivated them to adopt policies that encourage both FLFP and fertility. Evidence on the effect of these policies is mixed; the experience of countries such as Germany and the United Kingdom have shown that tackling both problems at the same time is difficult. Haan and Wrohlich (2011) show that childcare subsidies for working mothers in Germany induced sizable employment effects but had positive fertility effects only for two subgroups, highly educated women and women previously without children.

Effects of Childcare on Child Development

The last two decades have seen growing interest from researchers and policy makers in the potential short- and long-term benefits of early intervention programs, the features that characterize effective programs, and the returns to investments in early childhood development. An extensive body of literature shows that children who receive nutrition and stimulation in their early years perform better in school and have higher rates of employment and earnings as adults than children who do not have such opportunities.[2] The results of research on early child development can be summarized as follows:[3]

- There is consensus on the importance of investing in education in the first five years of life: The findings of positive effects on cognitive development, academic success, health, and social behavior are remarkably consistent.

- The evidence that preschool has long-term benefits for economically disadvantaged children is strong, although effects vary in size and persistence by type of program.

- There is less agreement about the most effective and efficient programs and policies, but the most effective interventions—at least for children in vulnerable socioeconomic conditions—seem to combine intensive center-based education and some form of family involvement.

- Better-trained caregivers and lower child-to-staff ratios are associated with improved outcomes from center-based childcare.

- Cost-benefit ratios indicate substantial returns from investing in well-designed early childhood programs.

Early childhood care and education (ECCE) policies are an important mechanism for closing the gaps between low- and high-income groups. Structured childcare permits long-term development, is more effective and costs less than interventions later in life, and levels the playing field by benefiting disadvantaged children in particular (Havnes and Mogstad 2015).

A frequent concern about children's well-being is the potential negative impact of increases in labor market participation of women and the reduction in mothers' time with their children. The research findings are mixed, ranging from negative to neutral to beneficial (see Del Boca 2015 and Ermisch and Francesconi 2005 for summaries of the literature).

Modeling of the decision to use childcare requires a series of assumptions about the relationship between the time parents spend with their children and the time they spend at work. Research on European countries suggests that the inputs mothers use to substitute their time when working are crucial: Substitution of a mother's time with high-quality childcare may compensate for the impact of her absence (Brilli 2014; Del Boca, Flinn, and Wiswall 2014).

The empirical results on the impact on children's cognitive and noncognitive outcomes when a parent's time is substituted with a grandparent's care are especially relevant for Latin American, where grandmothers are often the primary caregiver (see chapter 4). Using data from the United Kingdom, Del Boca, Pronzato, and Piazzalunga (2014) find that children looked after by their grandparents perform as well as children in formal childcare on vocabulary but less well in terms of school readiness. Bernal (2014) suggests that the greatest impact on cognitive development of children attending the subsidized care program in Colombia is on children who would have been looked after by their grandmother.

Evidence from 24 countries shows that daughters of employed mothers are more likely to be employed, hold supervisory positions, earn higher wages, and spend less time on housework and that sons of working mothers tend to spend more time providing unpaid care for family members (McGinn, Long Lingo, and Ruiz Castro 2015).

Cost-Effectiveness of Childcare Policies

Subsidizing childcare tends to increase enrollment, which increases female labor supply and has positive outcomes on child development. These interventions are costly, however. Are these programs cost-effective? Are they a sustainable strategy for realizing better labor outcomes?

Cost-benefit analyses show high economic returns, with some programs yielding rates of return of 7–16 percent (Gertler and others 2014; Heckman and Masterov 2007; OECD 2012). Table 2.2 summarizes key features of three emblematic center-based programs in the United States: the Perry Preschool Experiment, the Chicago Child-Parent and Expansion Program, and the Abecedarian Program. The interventions required large investments of resources, with estimated annual per child costs of $5,000–$15,000. But estimates suggest that the returns to these programs were 8.6, 7.1, and 3.7 times the invested amounts and that the benefits to society as a whole were large relative to the benefits to program participants.

TABLE 2.2 Features and cost-benefit ratios of early childhood interventions for high-risk children in the United States

Feature	Perry Preschool Experiment	Chicago Child-Parent Center and Expansion Program	Abecedarian Project
Parental involvement	Yes	Yes	No
Age of children	3–4 years	3–4 years	First months of life (mean age at entry: 4.4 months)
Program duration (years)	2	2	5
Program intensity	2½ hours a day in classroom plus 90-minute teacher home visit once a week for 30 weeks	3 hours a day for 9 months plus 6-week summer program	Year round, full-day
Child-teacher ratio	5.7: 1	Preschool: 17: 2 Kindergarten: 25: 2	Infants: 3: 1 Toddlers: 6: 1
Class size	13	17	12
Staff qualification	Bachelor's degree plus certificate to teach elementary school, early childhood, or special education	Bachelor's degree plus certification	Bachelor's degree or equivalent
Estimated annual cost per child (in 2004 dollars)	$9,785	$5,237[a]	$15,000
Return per dollar invested	$8.6 (16 percent rate of return: 4 percent for participants, 12 percent for society)	$7.1	$3.7

Sources: Heckman and Masterov 2007; OECD 2012.
Note: a. Estimated based on data from the Chicago Longitudinal Study (http://www.waisman.wisc.edu/cls/).

Among the studies reviewed by Karoly, Kilburn, and Caroll (2005), economic returns were significant for programs that required very large investment (more than $40,000 per child), but they were also positive for programs that cost less than $2,000 per child. The most cost-effective programs are programs that involve parents (Baker-Henningham and López Bóo 2010; Karoly, Kilburn, and Caroll 2005).

Many analyses do not incorporate the benefits of improved labor market outcomes for the mother (and father) and other benefits that may be difficult to monetize (such as reductions in crime and improvement in health). Many cost–benefit estimates therefore represent lower bounds.

From an economic perspective, the soundness of high-quality early childhood interventions is well-established. Further evidence on the comparative effectiveness of different programs and their components would help guide policy decisions. Including the impact of childcare policies on mothers' labor outcomes and household income is important in comparing the cost-effectiveness of programs and provides a strong argument for the sustainability of ECCE policies that is often lacking.

Notes

1. The quasi-experimental study by Medrano (2009) uses variation in the number of childcare centers by municipality resulting from the expansion of the national daycare program to compare female labor supply of eligible mothers in municipalities with different degrees of childcare availability. However, it is very likely that the expansion in the number of daycare centers is endogenous; eligibility is proxied by income quintile, which may be endogenous to labor participation. Encina and Martinez (2009) fail to identify causality.

2. See, for instance, Brilli, Del Boca, and Pronzato (2013); Bernal and Fernandez (2013); EACEA (2009); Engel and others (2011); Heckman and Masterov (2007); Heckman, Stixrud, and Urzúa (2006); Magnuson and Waldfogel (2005); OECD (2012, 2016); and Schady and others (2014). Also see the systematic reviews by Berlinski and Schady (2015) and Leroy, Gadsden, and Guijarro (2011) for Latin America and Zoritch, Roberts, and Oakley (2000) for the United States.

3. See Alderman and Vegas (2011); Baker-Henningham and López Bóo (2010); Conti and Heckman (2012); EACEA (2009); Karoly, Kilburn, and Cannon (2005); Nores and Bennett (2010) and UNICEF (2015) for a review of this evidence.

References

Alderman, H., and E. Vegas. 2011. "The Convergence of Equity and Efficiency in ECD Programs." In *No Small Matter: The Interaction of Poverty, Shocks, and Human Capital Investments in Early Childhood Development*, edited by H. Alderman. Washington, DC: World Bank.

Anderson, P. M., and P. B. Levine. 2000. "Child Care and Mothers' Employment Decisions." In *Finding Jobs: Work and Welfare Reform*, edited by D. Card and R. M. Blank. New York: Russell Sage Foundation.

Ángeles, G., P. Gadsen, S. Galiani, P. Gertler, A. Herrera, P. Kariger, and E. Seira. 2011. *Evaluacion de impacto del programa estancia infantiles para apoyar a madres trabajadoras: Informe final de la evaluación de impacto.* National Institute of Public Health, Moreles, Mexico.

Arpino, B., C. Pronzato, and L. Tavares. 2010. "All in the Family: Informal Childcare and Mothers' Labour Market Participation." ISER Working Paper 2010-24, Institute for Economic and Social Research, Essex, United Kingdom.

Attanasio, O., and M. Vera-Hernandez. 2004. *Medium and Long Run Effects of Nutrition and Child Care: Evaluation of a Community Nursery Programme in Rural Colombia.* Report EWP04/06, Institute for Fiscal Studies, London.

Baker, M., J. Gruber, and K. Milligan. 2008. "Universal Childcare, Maternal Labor Supply and Family Well-Being." *Journal of Political Economy* 116 (4): 709–45.

Baker-Henningham, H., and F. López Bóo. 2010. "Early Childhood Stimulation Interventions in Developing Countries: A Comprehensive Literature Review." Working Paper 213, Inter-American Development Bank, Washington, DC.

Berlinski, S., and S. Galiani. 2007. "The Effect of a Large Expansion of Pre-Primary School Facilities on Preschool Attendance and Maternal Employment." *Labour Economics* 14 (3): 665–80.

Berlinski, S., S. Galiani, and P. J. McEwan. 2011. "Preschool and Maternal Labor Market Outcomes: Evidence from a Regression Discontinuity Design." *Economic Development and Cultural Change* 59 (2): 313–44.

Berlinski, S., and N. Schady, eds. 2015. *The Early Years: Child Well-Being and the Role of Public Policy*. Washington, DC: Inter-American Development Bank.

Bernal, R. 2014. "Diagnóstico y recomendaciones para la atención de calidad a la primera infancia en Colombia." *Cuadernos Fedesarrollo* 51: 82.

Bernal, R., and C. Fernández. 2013. "Subsidized Child Care and Child Development in Colombia: Effects of Hogares Comunitarios de Bienestar as a Function of Timing and Length of Exposure." *Social Science & Medicine* 97: 241–49.

Bick, A. 2015. "The Quantitative Role of Child Care for Female Labor Force Participation and Fertility." MPRA Paper 31713, University Library of Munich.

Blau, D. M., and J. Currie. 2006. "Pre-School, Day Care and After-School Care: Who's Minding the Kids?" *Handbook of the Economics of Education*, Vol. 2, edited by E. A. Hanushek and F. Welch. Amsterdam: North-Holland.

Blau, D. M., and P. K. Robins. 1998. "A Dynamic Analysis of Turnover in Employment and Child Care." *Demography* 35 (1): 83–96.

Brilli, Y. 2014. "Public Investments in Children's Human Capital. Evidence from the Literature on Non-Parental Child Care." *Rivista italiana degli economisti* 1.

Brilli, Y., D. Del Boca, and C. D. Pronzato. 2013. "Does Child Care Availability Play a Role in Maternal Employment and Children's Development? Evidence from Italy." CHILD Working Paper 13, Centre for Household, Income, Labour and Demographic Economics, Turin.

Busso, M., and D. Romero Fonseca. 2015. "Female Labor Force Participation in Latin America: Patterns and Explanations." Working Paper 18, Centro de Estudios Distributivos, Laborales y Sociales, University of la Plata, Argentina.

Calderon, G. 2014. "The Effects of Child Care Provision in Mexico." Working Paper 2014-07, Bank of Mexico.

Cascio, E. U. 2009. "Maternal Labor Supply and the Introduction of Kindergartens into American Public Schools." *Journal of Human Resources* 44 (1): 140–70.

Compton, J. 2011. "The Mom Effect: Family Proximity and the Labour Force Attachment of Women in Canada." Canadian Labour Market and Skills Researcher Network (CLSRN) Working Paper 87 (November).

Compton, J., and R. A. Pollak. 2011. "Family Proximity, Childcare and Women's Labor Force Attachment." NBER Working Paper 17678, National Bureau of Economic Research, Cambridge, MA.

Connelly, R. 1992. "The Effect of Child Care Costs on Married Women's Labor Force Participation." *Review of Economics and Statistics* 74 (1): 83–90.

Connelly, R., D. DeGraff, and D. Levison. 1996. "Women's Employment and Child Care in Brazil." *Economic Development and Cultural Change* 44 (3): 619–56.

Conti, G., and J. J. Heckman. 2012. "The Economics of Child Well-Being." IZA Discussion Paper 6930, Institute for the Study of Labor, Bonn.

Contreras, D., E. Puentes, and D. Bravo. 2012. "Female Labor Supply and Child Care Supply in Chile." Working Paper SDT 370, Department of Economics, University of Chile, Santiago.

Del Boca, D. 2015. "Child Care Arrangements and Labor Supply." Working Paper 569, Inter-American Development Bank, Washington, DC.

Del Boca, D., and D. Vuri. 2007. "The Mismatch between Employment and Child Care in Italy: The Impact of Rationing." *Journal of Population Economics* 20 (4): 805–32.

Del Boca, D., C. Flinn, and M. Wiswall. 2014. "Household Choices and Child Development." *Review of Economic Studies* 81 (1): 137–85.

Del Boca, D., C. Pronzato, and D. Piazzalunga. 2014. "Early Child Care and Child Outcomes: The Role of Grandparents." IZA Discussion Paper 8565, Institute for the Study of Labor, Bonn.

Deutsch, R. 1998. "Does Child Care Pay? Labor Force Participation and Earnings Effects of Access to Child Care in the Favelas of Rio de Janeiro." Working Paper 384, Inter-American Development Bank, Washington, DC.

Dimova, R., and F.-C. Wolff. 2011. "Do Downward Private Transfers Enhance Maternal Labor Supply? Evidence from around Europe." *Journal of Population Economics* 24 (3): 911–33.

EACEA (Education, Audiovisual and Culture Executive Agency). 2009. *Tackling Social and Cultural Inequalities through Early Childhood Education and Care in Europe.* Brussels: EACEA.

Encina, J., and C. Martinez. 2009. "Efecto de una mayor cobertura de salas cuna en la participación laboral femenina: Evidencia de Chile." Working Paper SDT 303, Department of Economics, University of Chile, Santiago.

Engel, P. L., L. Fernald, H. Alderman, J. Behrman, C. O'Gara, A. Yousafzai, M. Cabral de Mello, M. Hidrobo, N. Ulkuer, I. Ertem, and S. Iltus. 2011. "Strategies for Reducing Inequalities and Improving Developmental Outcomes for Young Children in Low-Income and Middle-Income Countries." *The Lancet* 378 (9799): 133–53.

Ermisch, J., and M. Francesconi. 2005. "Parental Employment and Children's Welfare." In *Women at Work: An Economic Perspective*, edited by T. Boeri, D. Del Boca, and C. Pissarides. Oxford: Oxford University Press.

Fitzpatrick, M. D. 2010. "Preschoolers Enrolled and Mothers at Work? The Effects of Universal Pre-Kindergarten." *Journal of Labor Economics* 28 (1): 51–85.

Fong, M., and M. Lokshin. 2000. "Child Care and Women's Labor Force Participation in Romania." Policy Research Working Paper 2400, World Bank, Washington, DC.

Gathmann, C., and B. Sass. 2012. "Taxing Childcare: Effects on Family Labor Supply and Children." IZA Discussion Paper 6440, Institute for the Study of Labor, Bonn.

Gelbach, J. B. 2002. "Public Schooling for Young Children and Maternal Labor Supply." *American Economic Review* 92 (1): 307–22.

Gertler, P., J. Heckman, R. Pinto, A. Zanolini, C. Vermeersch, S. Walker, S. M. Chang, and S. Grantham-McGregor. 2014. "Labor Market Returns to an Early Childhood Stimulation Intervention in Jamaica." *Science* 344 (6187): 998–1001.

Goux, D., and E. Maurin. 2010. "Public School Availability for Two-year Olds and Mothers' Labour Supply." *Labour Economics* 17: 951–62.

Gruber, J. 1994. "State Mandated Benefits and Employer Provided Insurance." *Journal of Public Economics* 55 (3): 433–64.

Gustafsson, S., and F. Stafford. 1992. "Child Care Subsidies and Labor Supply in Sweden." *Journal of Human Resources* 27 (1): 204–30.

Hallman, K., A. R. Quisumbing, M. Ruel, and B. de la Briere. 2005. "Mothers' Work and Child Care: Findings from the Urban Slums of Guatemala City." *Economic Development and Cultural Change* 53 (4): 855–85

Haan, P., and K. Wrohlich. 2011. "Can Child Care Policy Encourage Employment and Fertility? Evidence from a Structural Model." *Labour Economics* 18 (4): 498–512.

Havnes, T., and M. Mogstad. 2011. "Money for Nothing? Universal Childcare and Maternal Employment." *Journal of Public Economics* 95: 1455–65.

———. 2015. "Is Universal Child Care Leveling the Playing Field?" *Journal of Public Economics* 127: 100–14.

Heckman, J. J., and D. V. Masterov 2007. "The Productivity Argument for Investing in Young Children." *Review of Agricultural Economics* 28 (3): 446–93.

Heckman, J. J., J. Stixrud, and S. Urzúa. 2006. "The Effects of Cognitive and Noncognitive Abilities on Labour Market Outcomes and Social Behavior." *Journal of Labour Economics* 24 (3): 411–82.

Herbst, C. M. 2008. "Who Are the Eligible Non-recipients of Child Care Subsidies?" *Children and Youth Services Review* 30: 1037–54.

Karoly, L. A., M. Rebecca Kilburn, and J. S. Cannon. 2005. *Proven Benefits of Early Childhood Interventions*. RAND Corporation, Santa Monica, CA.

Leibowitz, A., J. A. Klerman, and L. J. Waite. 1992. "Employment of New Mothers and Child Care Choice: Differences by Children's Age." *Journal of Human Resources* 27 (1): 112–33.

Leroy, J. L., P. Gadsden, and M. Guijarro. 2011. *The Impact of Daycare Programs on Child Health, Nutrition and Development in Developing Countries: A Systematic Review*. 3ie Inc., Washington, DC.

Lokshin, M. 2000. "Household Childcare Choices and Women's Work Behavior in Russia." *Journal of Human Resources* 39 (4): 1094–115.

Magnuson, K. A., and J. Waldfogel. 2005. "Early Childhood Care and Education: Effects on Ethnic and Racial Gaps in School Readiness." *Future Child* 15 (1): 169–96.

Mateo Díaz, M., and L. Rodriguez-Chamussy. 2013. "Childcare and Women's Labor Participation: Evidence for Latin America and the Caribbean." Technical Note IDB-TN-586, Inter-American Development Bank, Washington, DC.

McGinn, K. L., E. Long Lingo, and M. Ruiz Castro. 2015. "Mums the World! Cross-national Effects of Maternal Employment on Gender Inequalities at Work and at Home." Harvard Business School Working Paper 15-094, Cambridge, MA.

Medrano, P. 2009. "Public Day Care and Female Labor Force Participation: Evidence from Chile." Working Paper SDT 306, Department of Economics, University of Chile, Santiago.

Ñopo, H. 2012. *New Century, Old Disparities: Gender and Ethnic Earnings Gaps in Latin America and the Caribbean*. Washington, DC: Inter-American Development Bank.

Nores, M., and W. S. Bennett. 2010. "Benefits of Early Childhood Interventions across the World: (Under) Investing in the Very Young." *Economics of Education Review* 29 (2): 271–82.

OECD (Organisation for Economic Co-Operation and Development). 2011. "Reducing Barriers to Parental Employment." In *Doing Better for Families.* Paris: OECD Publishing.

———. 2012. *Starting Strong III: A Quality Toolbox for Early Childhood Education and Care.* Paris: OECD Publishing.

———. 2016. *Low-Performing Students: Why They Fall Behind and How to Help Them Succeed.* Paris: OECD Publishing.

Paes de Barros, R., P. Olinto, T. Lunde, and M. Carvalho. 2011. "The Impact of Free Childcare on Women's Labor Force Participation: Evidence from Low-Income Neighborhoods of Rio de Janeiro." Paper presented at the World Bank Economists' Forum, Washington, DC.

Posadas, J., and M. Vidal-Fernández. 2012. "Grandparents' Childcare and Female Labor Force Participation." IZA Discussion Paper 6398, Institute for the Study of Labor, Bonn.

Prada, M. F., G. Rucci, and S. S. Urzúa. 2015. "The Effect of Mandated Child Care on Female Wages in Chile." NBER Working Paper 21080, National Bureau of Economic Research, Cambridge, MA.

Rosero, J., and H. Oosterbeek. 2011. "Trade-offs between Different Early Childhood Interventions: Evidence from Ecuador." Discussion Paper TI 2011-102/3, Tinbergen Institute, Amsterdam.

Schady, N., J. Behrman, M. Caridad Araujo, R. Azuero, R. Bernal, D. Bravo, F. López Bóo, K. Macours, D. Marshall, C. Paxson, and R. Vakis 2014. "Wealth Gradients in Early Childhood Cognitive Development in Five Latin American Countries." PIER Working Paper Archive 14-010, Penn Institute for Economic Research, Department of Economics, University of Pennsylvania, Philadelphia.

Schlosser, A. 2011. "Public Preschool and the Labor Supply of Arab Mothers: Evidence from a Natural Experiment." Working Paper, Eitan Berglas School of Economics, Tel Aviv University, Tel Aviv.

Simonsen, M. 2010. "Availability and Price of High Quality Day Care and Female Employment." *Scandinavian Journal of Economics* 112 (3): 570–94.

UNICEF (United Nations Children's Fund). 2015. "Evidence for ECD Investment." New York. Available at http://www.unicef.org/earlychildhood/index_69851.html.

Urzúa, S., and G. Veramendi. 2011. "The Impact of Out-of-Home Childcare Centers on Early Childhood Development." Working Paper, Inter-American Development Bank, Washington, DC.

Wrohlich, K. 2008. "The Excess Demand for Subsidized Child Care in Germany." *Applied Economics* 40 (10): 1217–28.

Zamarro, Gema. 2009. "Family Labor Participation and Childcare Decisions: The Role of Grannies." RAND Labor and Population Working Papers Series, RAND Corporation, Santa Monica, CA.

Zoritch, B., I. Roberts, and A. Oakley. 2000. "Daycare for Pre-school Children." Cochrane Database of Systematic Reviews 2000, 3, CD000564, London.

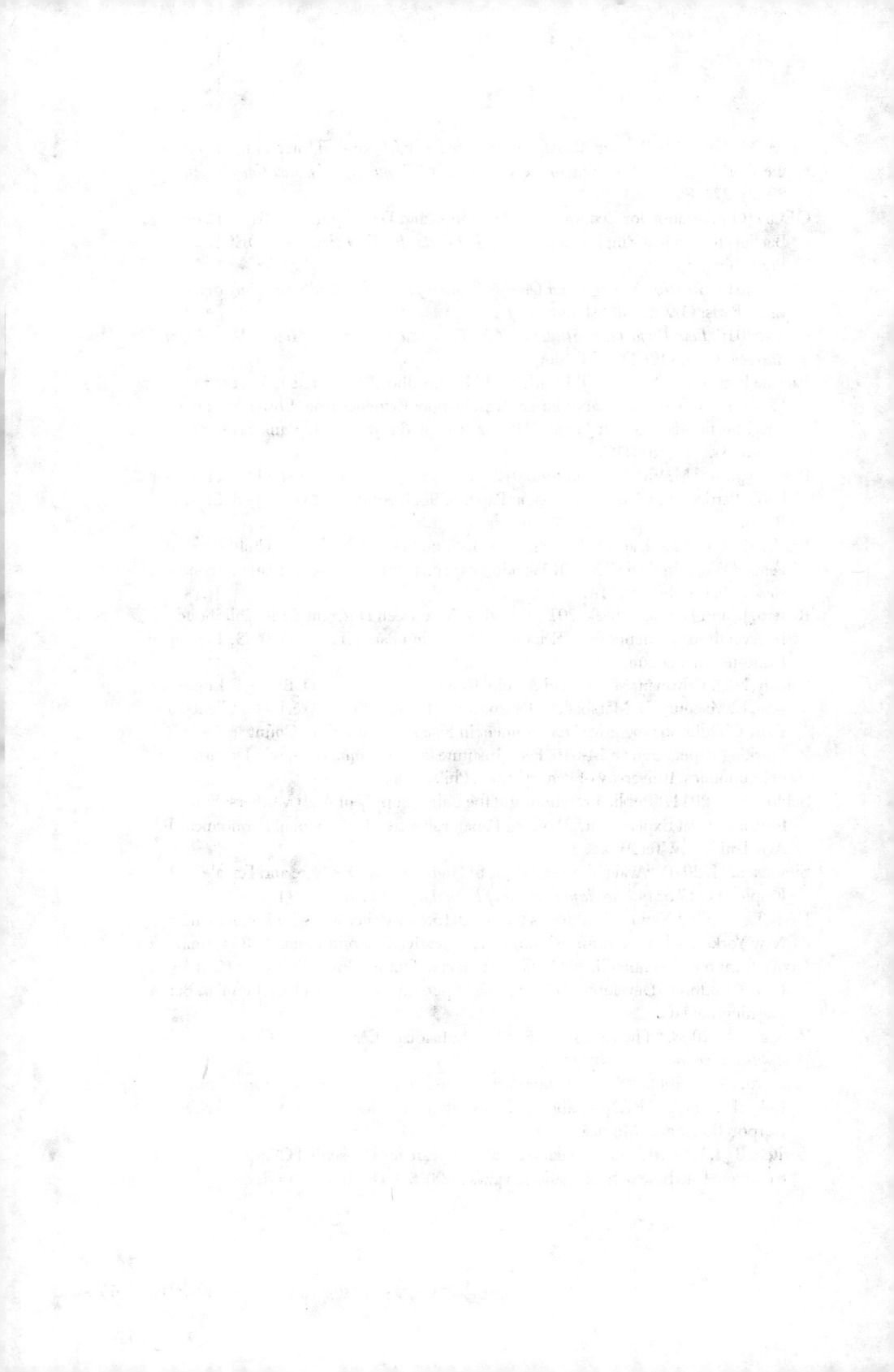

PART II

Where Are We Now?

CHAPTER 3

Female Labor Force Participation and Labor Market Outcomes in Latin America and the Caribbean

Women's participation in the labor market increased 35 percent in Latin America and the Caribbean (LAC) over the past 20 years. These gains notwithstanding, almost half of women 15–64 are still out of the labor force. Although the average rate of female labor force participation (FLFP) is now approaching the average rate in the Organisation for Economic Co-operation and Development (OECD), progress has not been homogeneous, and many countries still have a steep hill to climb. In addition, gender gaps in wages, vulnerability to unemployment, and informality remain salient in most countries.

This chapter describes women's participation and outcomes in the labor market relative to men's across the life cycle. It compares results across countries, shedding light on the dynamics of mothers' and fathers' behavior in the labor market and identifying patterns of women's engagement in paid employment, such as segregation by employment status and sector.

Economic Participation by Women

LAC has made significant progress on gender equality and women's welfare over the past few decades. Most countries experienced significant improvements in women's health and education outcomes. Maternal health improved, and mortality rates dropped by 40 percent on average in the past 20 years (WHO and others 2014). For the region as a whole, the gender gap in primary education enrollment disappeared and significantly narrowed in secondary education, and the gender gap in schooling attainment now favors women (Ñopo 2012). Improvements in other dimensions, such as political empowerment and economic participation, are still pending.

Despite the closing of the education gap between boys and girls in the region, women's participation in the labor force remains much lower than men's. In Brazil and Costa Rica—where gender gaps in access to education are similar to those in the Netherlands and Canada—women's economic participation is significantly lower than men's (figure 3.1). Chile ranks 36th and Mexico 75th out of 145 countries on the educational component dimensions of the Global Gender Gap Index (World Economic Forum 2015) (comparable to the United Kingdom and Hungary). In contrast, they rank 123rd and 126th on economic participation.[1] Colombia and Uruguay have smaller differences in ranking positions in educational attainment and economic participation (Colombia ranks 61st on educational attainment but 37th on economic participation; Uruguay ranks 48th on educational attainment and 91st on economic participation). Only three LAC countries (Barbados, The Bahamas, and Colombia) rank among the top 50 on the Index of Economic Participation and Opportunity (a subindex of the Global Gender Gap Index).

Characteristics of Female Labor Supply

FLFP rates in LAC increased over the past two decades, converging to the average FLFP rates in OECD countries. As of 2013, the last year for which comparable data are available, the average labor force participation rates in LAC were 84 percent for men and 58 percent for women, a gap of 26 percentage points (figure 3.2). This gap is smaller than in South Asia or the Middle East and North Africa, where it reaches 50 percentage points or more, but it is very heterogeneous across countries. At one extreme, FLFP in Guyana, Mexico, and most countries in Central America is 30–40 percentage points lower than male labor force participation (MLFP). At the other extreme, in The Bahamas, Barbados, and Haiti, the gender gap is less than 10 points, comparable to gaps in Sub-Saharan Africa and the European Union. With gaps of 10–20 percentage points, the situation in Bolivia, Jamaica, Peru, and Uruguay is comparable to that in the Europe and Central Asia and in the East Asia and Pacific regions.

Countries such as Bolivia, Brazil, Colombia, and Peru experienced rapid incorporation of women into the labor market; FLFP rates are now similar to top-ranking OECD countries. The trajectory in those countries was similar to that of Ireland and Spain (figure 3.3). In contrast, the FLFP rate is still very low (below 50 percent) in Guyana, Mexico, Suriname, and most countries in Central America (figure 3.4).

As in other regions, labor force participation in LAC varies with education, economic conditions, and age group. However, variation according to socioeconomic

FIGURE 3.1 Ranking of selected countries in Latin America and the Caribbean on the Global Gender Gap Index

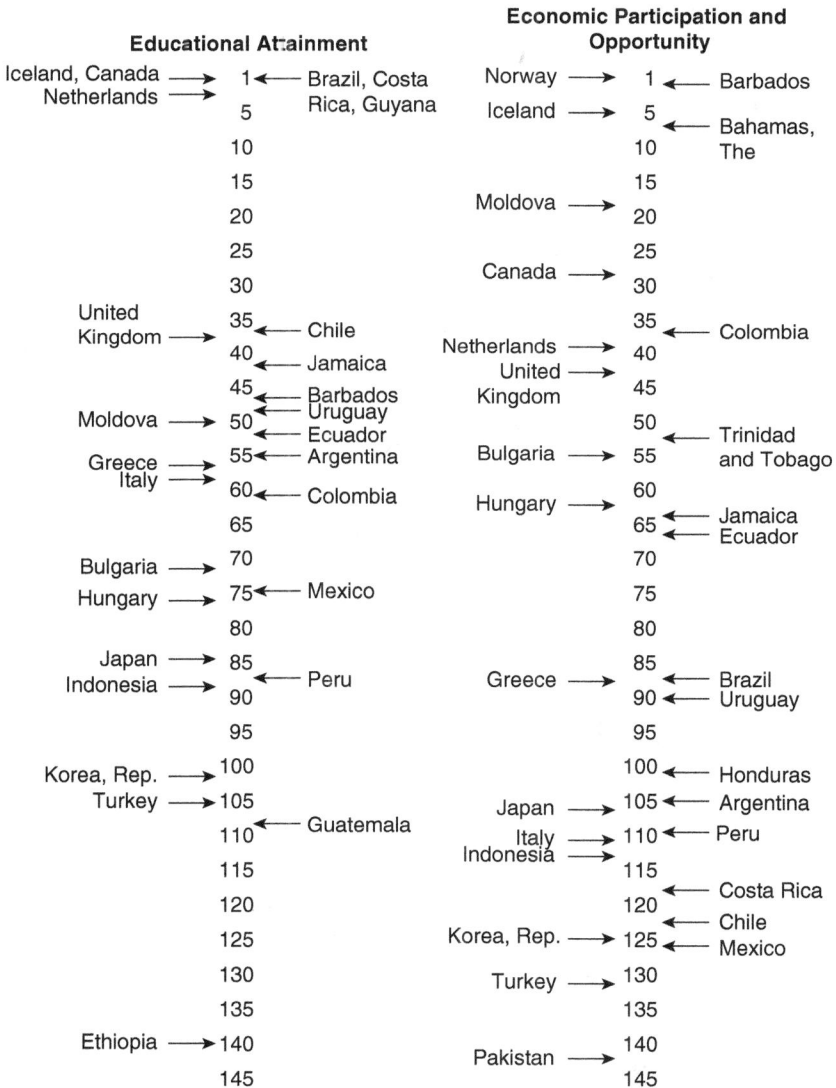

Educational Attainment

Left	Rank	Right
Iceland, Canada →	1	← Brazil, Costa Rica, Guyana
Netherlands →	5	
	10	
	15	
	20	
	25	
	30	
United Kingdom →	35	← Chile
	40	← Jamaica
	45	← Barbados
Moldova →	50	← Uruguay
		← Ecuador
Greece →	55	← Argentina
Italy →	60	← Colombia
	65	
Bulgaria →	70	
Hungary →	75	← Mexico
	80	
Japan →	85	
Indonesia →	90	← Peru
	95	
Korea, Rep. →	100	
Turkey →	105	
	110	← Guatemala
	115	
	120	
	125	
	130	
	135	
Ethiopia →	140	
	145	

Economic Participation and Opportunity

Left	Rank	Right
Norway →	1	← Barbados
Iceland →	5	
	10	← Bahamas, The
	15	
Moldova →	20	
	25	
Canada →	30	
	35	← Colombia
Netherlands →	40	
United Kingdom →	45	
	50	
Bulgaria →	55	← Trinidad and Tobago
	60	
Hungary →	65	← Jamaica
		← Ecuador
	70	
	75	
	80	
Greece →	85	← Brazil
	90	← Uruguay
	95	
	100	← Honduras
Japan →	105	← Argentina
Italy →	110	← Peru
Indonesia →	115	
	120	← Costa Rica
Korea, Rep. →	125	← Chile
		← Mexico
Turkey →	130	
	135	
Pakistan →	140	
	145	

Source: World Economic Forum 2015.

FIGURE 3.2 Gender gap in labor force participation in selected countries and regions, 2013

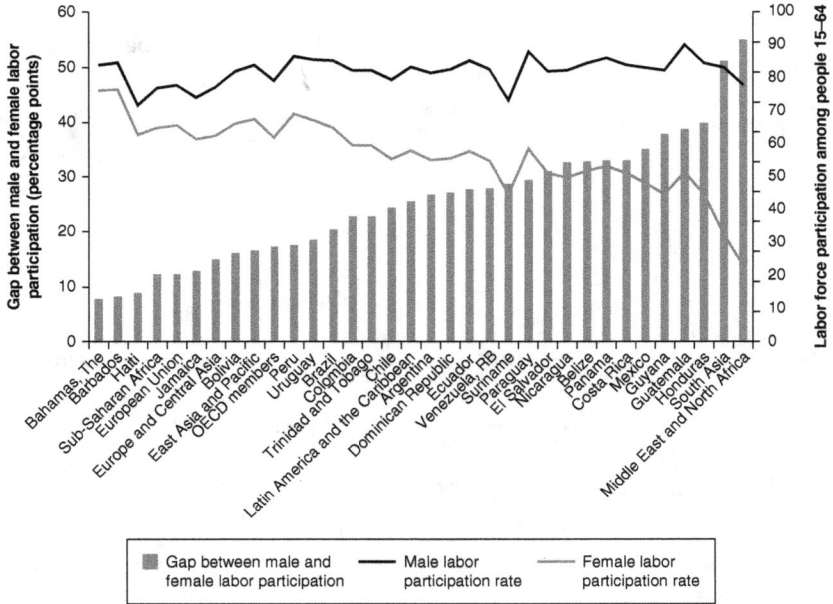

Source: World Development Indicators 2015.
Note: OECD = Organisation for Economic Co-operation and Development.

FIGURE 3.3 Female labor force participation rate in selected countries and country groups, 1990–2013

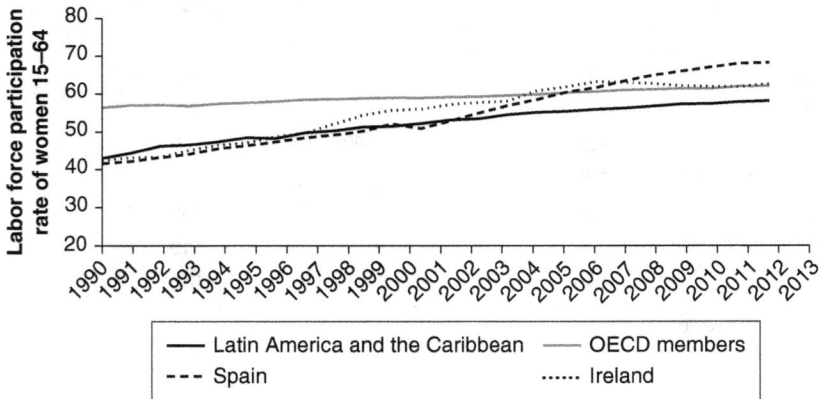

Source: World Development Indicators 2015.
Note: OECD = Organisation for Economic Co-operation and Development.

FIGURE 3.4 Female labor force participation rate in selected countries in Latin America and the Caribbean, 2013

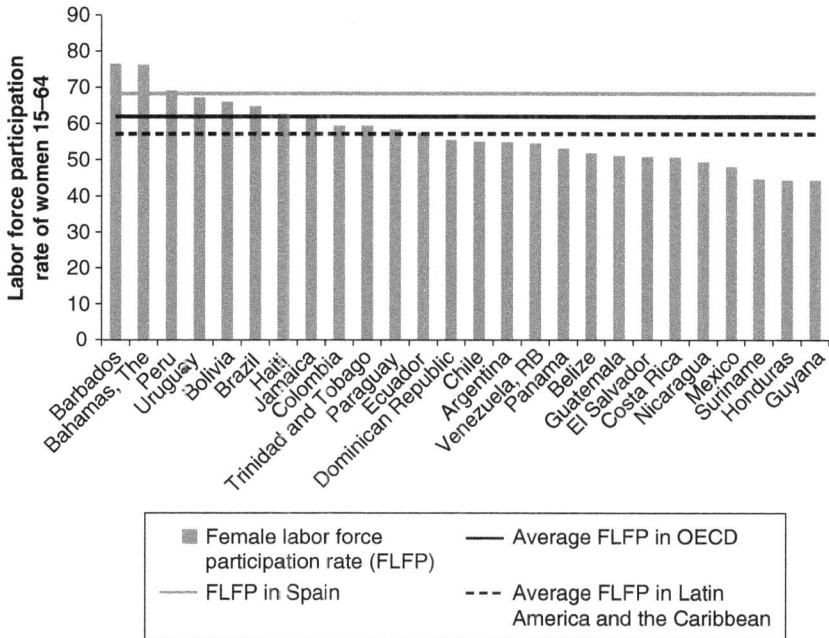

Source: World Development Indicators 2015.
Note: OECD = Organisation for Economic Co-operation and Development.

characteristics differs for women and men. Women in the region with tertiary education are four times more likely to participate in the labor market than women with less than basic education (ILO 2015). In contrast, men with tertiary education are only 20 percent more likely to be active in the labor force than men with less than basic education (figure 3.5).

Higher FLFP among better-educated women is evident outside LAC as well, but the range of differentials is narrower. Figure 3.6 illustrates the cases of Germany, Hungary, the Netherlands, and Norway—countries where the heterogeneity in education attainment gender gaps is similar to that in LAC. FLFP among women with intermediate education levels is much higher in these countries than in LAC; MLFP rates are more similar (figure 3.6).

Labor force participation rates also differ by household income levels, with the gradient much more pronounced among women than men. In most countries in LAC, FLFP is correlated with household income: Women from households in the top quintile of the income distribution are 2.2 times more likely to participate in the labor force than women from households in the bottom quintile (figure 3.7). The exceptions are Bolivia, Panama, and Peru, where households from the bottom and top income quintiles tend to have higher labor force participation rates than households in the middle of the distribution.

The labor force participation rate is less heterogeneous for men than for women. In Bolivia, Ecuador, Guatemala, Honduras, Mexico, Panama, Peru, and Uruguay, there are no significant differences in rates for men by income quintile. For other countries for which data are available, men in households from the top income quintile participate more than men in households at the bottom, but the differences are not as large as they are for women (CEDLAS and World Bank 2014).

FLFP also varies by age group. Worldwide, women tend to perform most unpaid household work and provide most care for family members. These responsibilities greatly constrain the amount of time they can devote to paid work (Anxo and

FIGURE 3.5 Labor force participation rates of men and women in selected countries in Latin America and the Caribbean, by education level, circa 2013

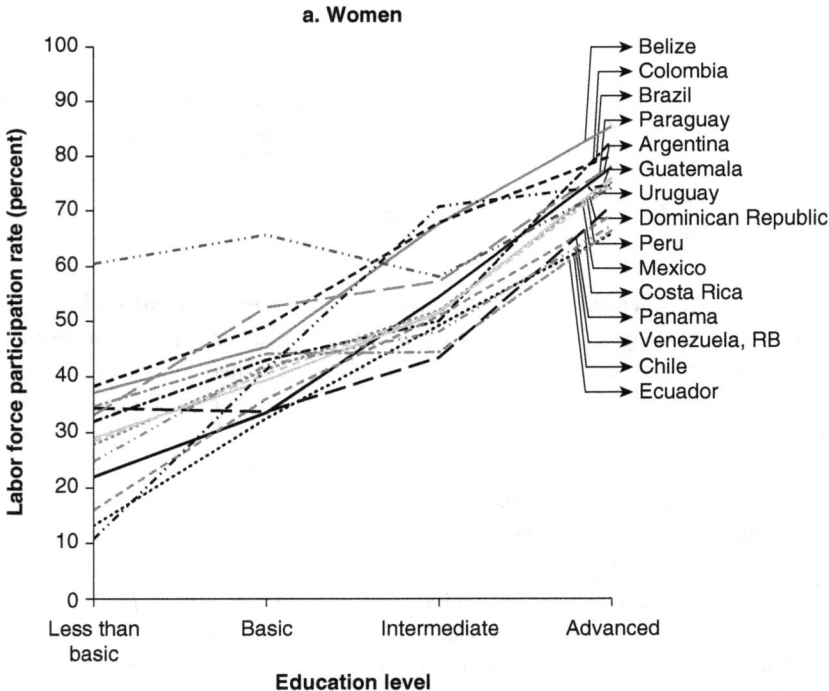

a. Women

Belize
Colombia
Brazil
Paraguay
Argentina
Guatemala
Uruguay
Dominican Republic
Peru
Mexico
Costa Rica
Panama
Venezuela, RB
Chile
Ecuador

(continued on next page)

FIGURE 3.5 Labor force participation rates of men and women in selected countries in Latin America and the Caribbean, by education level, circa 2013 *(continued)*

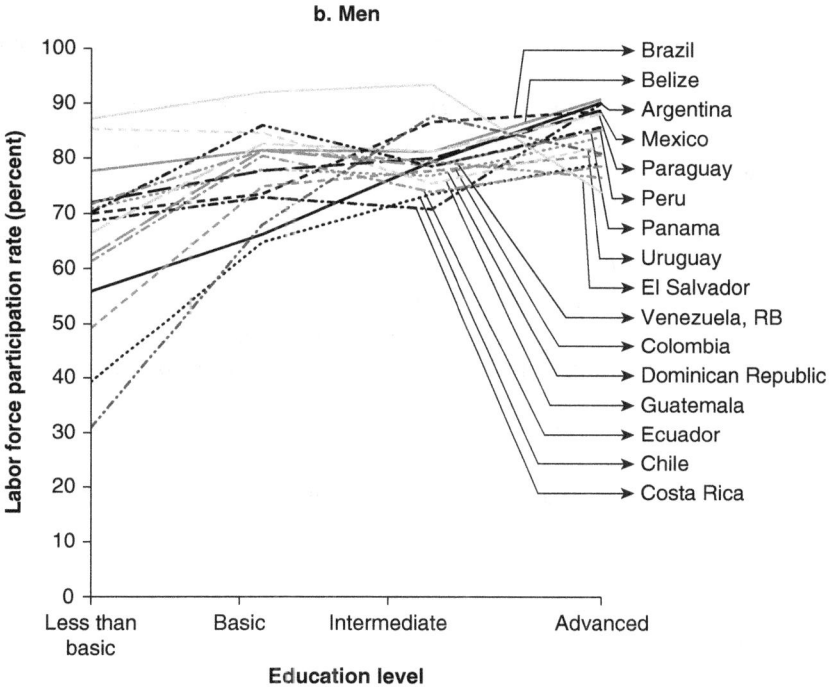

b. Men

Source: ILO 2015.
Note: Education level refers to the highest level completed, classified according to the International Standard Classification of Education.

Boulin 2005; Fagan and Burchell 2002; Lee, McCann, and Messenger 2007). Time constraints, combined with economic structures and institutional arrangements, lead to substantially different patterns of labor supply by men and women (figure 3.8).

For people 25–34, the gap between MLFP and FLPF rates ranges from 21 percentage points in Brazil to 41 percentage points in Guatemala. It widens over the life cycle, reaching in some cases 50 percentage points among people 50 years and older.

Among mothers, unmarried women have higher participation rates than married women, and mothers with school-age children are more likely to participate in the labor force than mothers with younger children (younger than 6). In the United States, for example, there is a persistent gap of 13 percentage points in the participation rates of mothers with older and younger children, although the FLFP rates of women with children has increased over time (U.S. Bureau of Labor Statistics 2014).

Parenthood affects men and women differently. About half of the 85.5 million women who are out of the labor force in LAC are 25–44 (the age range in which women are most likely to have young children). In contrast, parenthood tends to be positively correlated with men's labor force participation rates, wages, and earnings (Choi, Joesch, and Lundberg 2005; Lundberg and Rose 2002).

These differences are present not only in labor force participation rates but also in employment characteristics and conditions: Women tend to work fewer hours, and large proportions of them work part-time and in the informal economy (Lee, McCann, and Messenger 2007). On average women work fewer hours than men in the labor market (although combining work hours in and out of the labor market, they tend to work more than men (Pagés and Piras 2010). The gap varies significantly across countries (figure 3.9). It is widest in Colombia, Guatemala, and Mexico, where women work on average 10 fewer hours a week than men. The gap partly reflects the larger share of part-time workers among women.

FIGURE 3.6 Labor force participation rate in selected countries in Europe, by education level, 2013

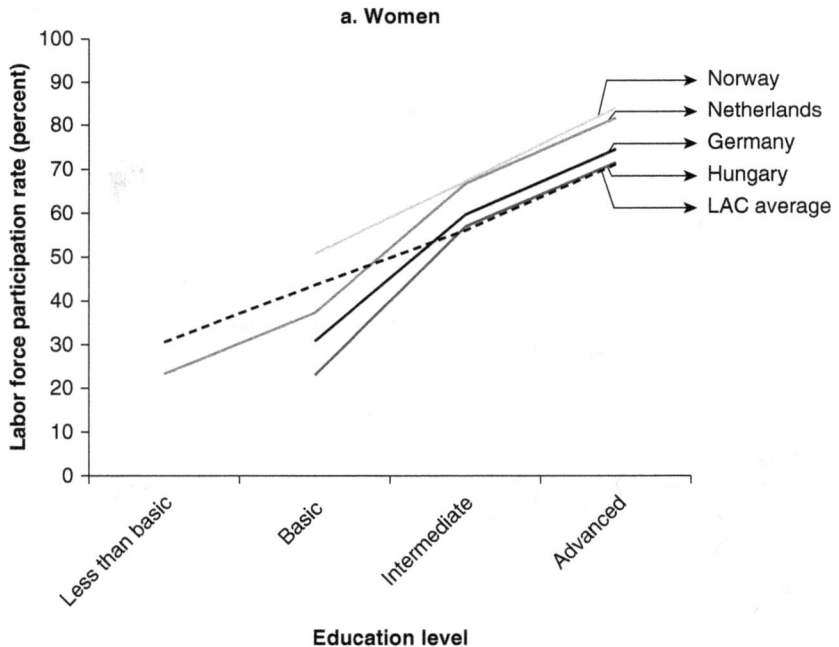

a. Women

Norway
Netherlands
Germany
Hungary
LAC average

Education level

(continued on next page)

FIGURE 3.6 Labor force participation rate in selected countries in Europe, by education level, 2013 *(continued)*

b. Men

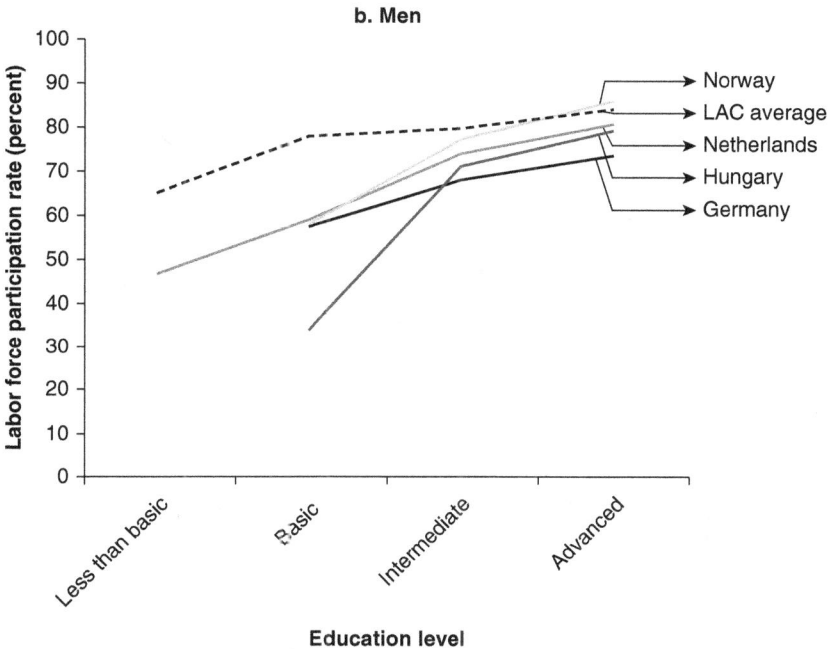

Education level

Source: ILO 2015.
Note: Education level refers to the highest level completed, classified according to the International Standard Classification of Education. LAC = Latin America and the Caribbean.

The Closing of the Gender Gap

FLFP increased over the past two decades in LAC, although not all countries moved at the same pace. Increases tended to be greater during the 1990s than between 2000 and 2010 (figure 3.10). They were larger in countries with lower FLFP at the beginning of this period. In The Bahamas, Barbados, and Jamaica, for example, about 70 percent of working-age women already participated in the labor market in 1990. In these countries, where FLFP was already above average OECD levels there was limited room to grow. Of the 14 LAC countries with FLFP rates of 30–40 percent in the 1990s, Chile, Colombia, and Costa Rica increased FLFP faster than the regional average; Mexico and Trinidad and Tobago increased FLFP by 1–2 percent a year; El Salvador, Guatemala, Guyana, and Panama increased FLFP by below-average rates; and Ecuador and República Bolivariana de Venezuela experienced rapid growth during the 1990s that stagnated during the 2000s.

FIGURE 3.7 Labor force participation rate in selected countries in Latin America and the Caribbean, by household income quintile, circa 2012

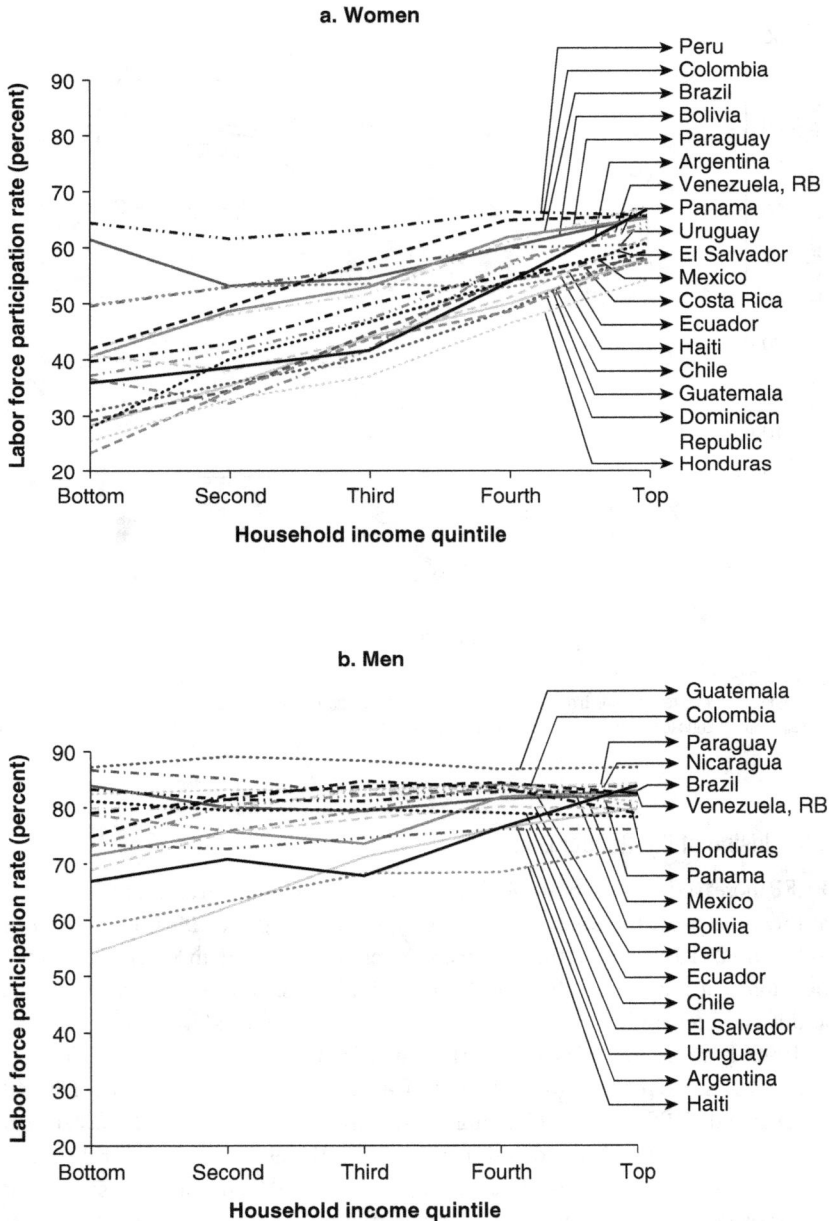

a. Women

Peru
Colombia
Brazil
Bolivia
Paraguay
Argentina
Venezuela, RB
Panama
Uruguay
El Salvador
Mexico
Costa Rica
Ecuador
Haiti
Chile
Guatemala
Dominican
Republic
Honduras

b. Men

Guatemala
Colombia
Paraguay
Nicaragua
Brazil
Venezuela, RB
Honduras
Panama
Mexico
Bolivia
Peru
Ecuador
Chile
El Salvador
Uruguay
Argentina
Haiti

Source: CEDLAS and World Bank 2014.

FIGURE 3.8 Labor force participation rates in selected countries, by gender and age, circa 2013

a. Female labor force participation rate in selected countries in Latin America and the Caribbean

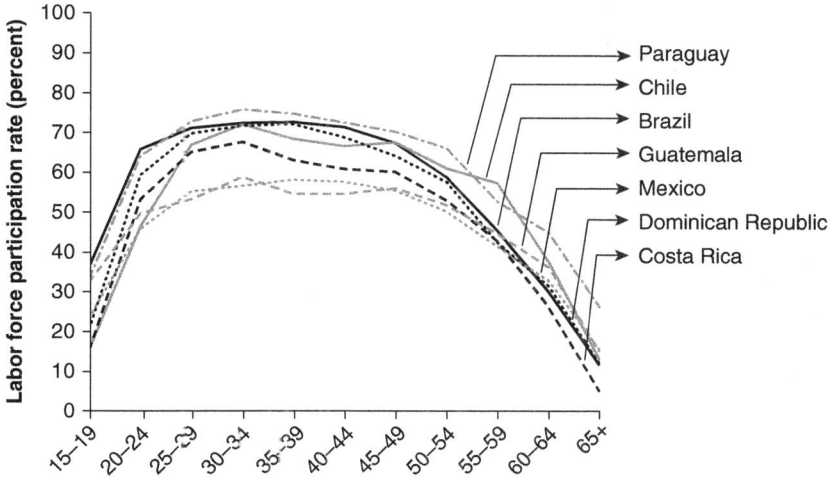

Paraguay
Chile
Brazil
Guatemala
Mexico
Dominican Republic
Costa Rica

b. Female labor force participation rate in selected OECD countries

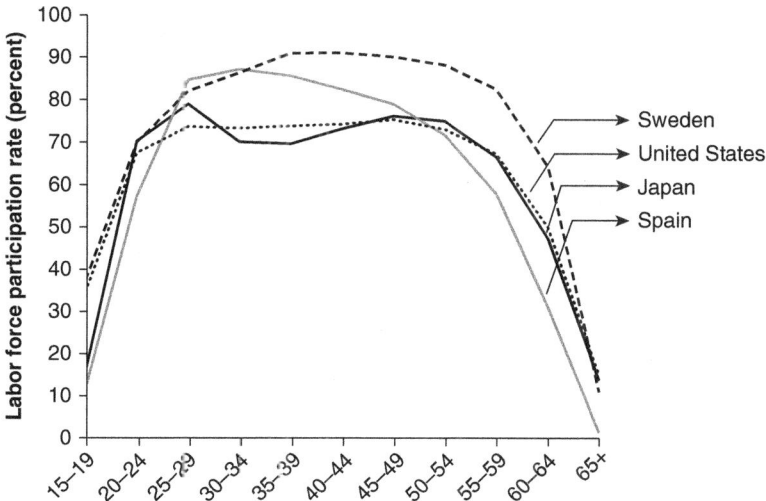

Sweden
United States
Japan
Spain

(continued on next page)

FIGURE 3.8 Labor force participation rates in selected countries, by gender and age, circa 2013 *(continued)*

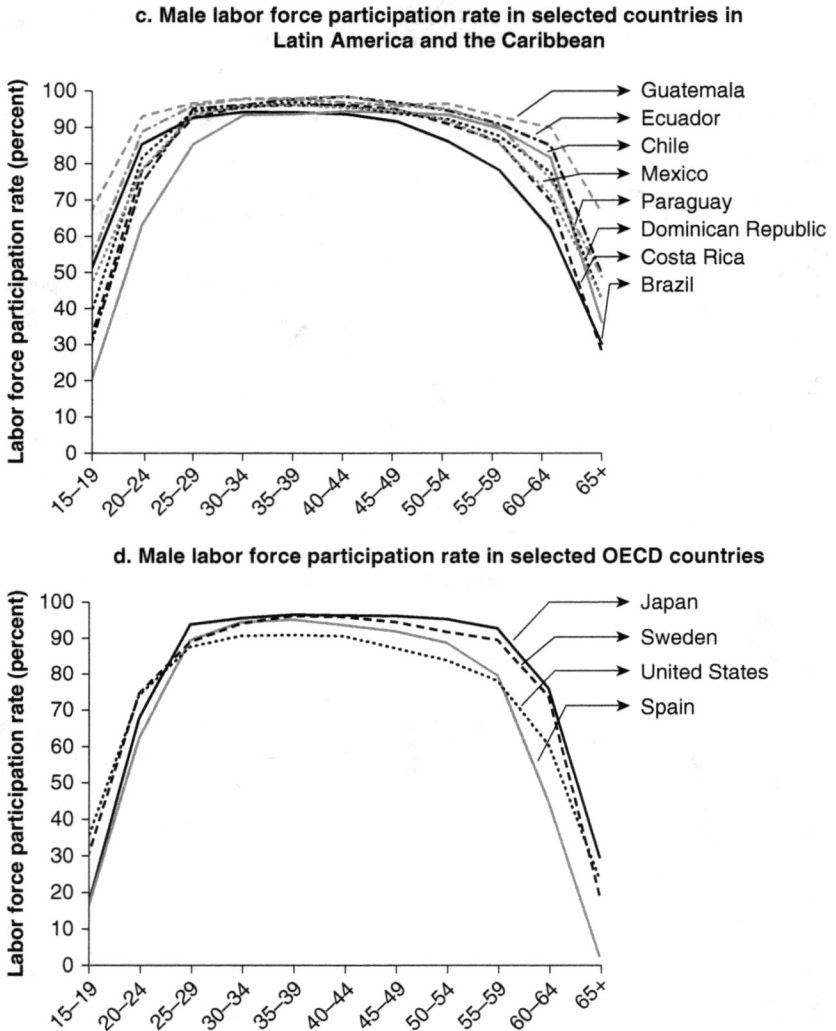

c. Male labor force participation rate in selected countries in Latin America and the Caribbean

Guatemala
Ecuador
Chile
Mexico
Paraguay
Dominican Republic
Costa Rica
Brazil

d. Male labor force participation rate in selected OECD countries

Japan
Sweden
United States
Spain

Source: ILO 2015.
Note: OECD = Organisation for Economic Co-operation and Development.

FIGURE 3.9 Gender gap in hours worked in selected countries in Latin America and the Caribbean, circa 2012

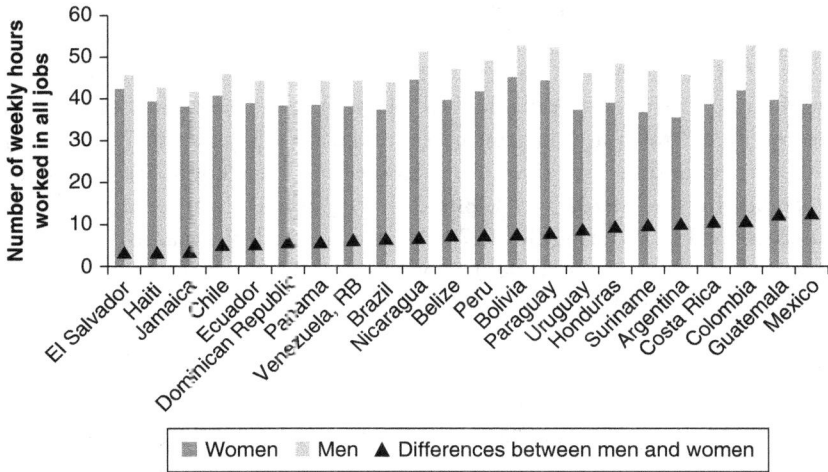

Source: CEDLAS and World Bank 2014.

FIGURE 3.10 Average annual increase in female labor force participation rate in selected countries in Latin America and the Caribbean, 1990–2010

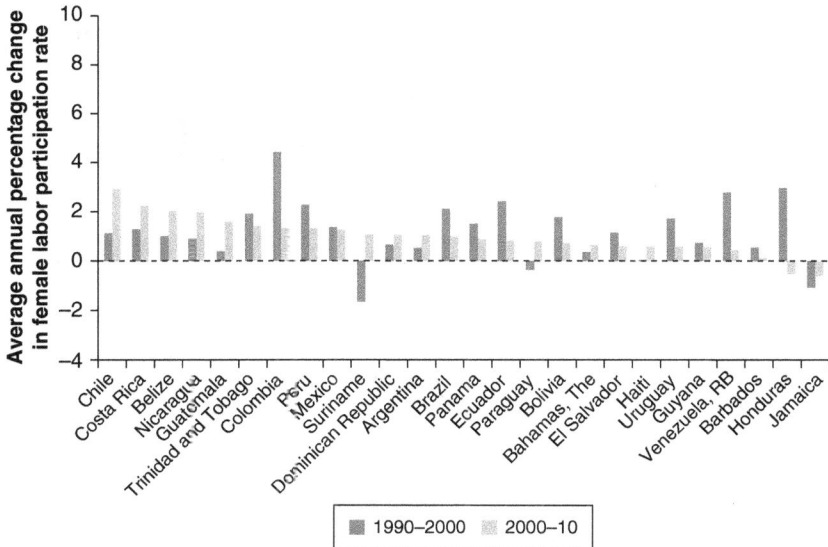

Source: World Development Indicators 2015.

Honduras started with one of the highest growth rates during the 1990s and had negative rates in the following period. It now has one of the lowest FLFP rates in LAC.

How do these growth rates compare with rates elsewhere in the world? Figure 3.11 compares 10 countries with relatively high current levels of FLFP (countries with a range of current FLFP levels for which comparable time series were available were chosen). The two countries with the lowest FLFP rates in this group are France and Italy (about 74 percent). All other countries have rates of 77–83 percent. Most countries had higher rates during the 1970s and 1980s. Norway, in particular, enjoyed a huge increase in FLFP during the 1970s, associated with the massive economic growth that accompanied the discovery of oil. It had an FLFP rate of just 22 percent in 1960.

FIGURE 3.11 Female labor force participation growth rates in selected high-income countries, 1960–2010

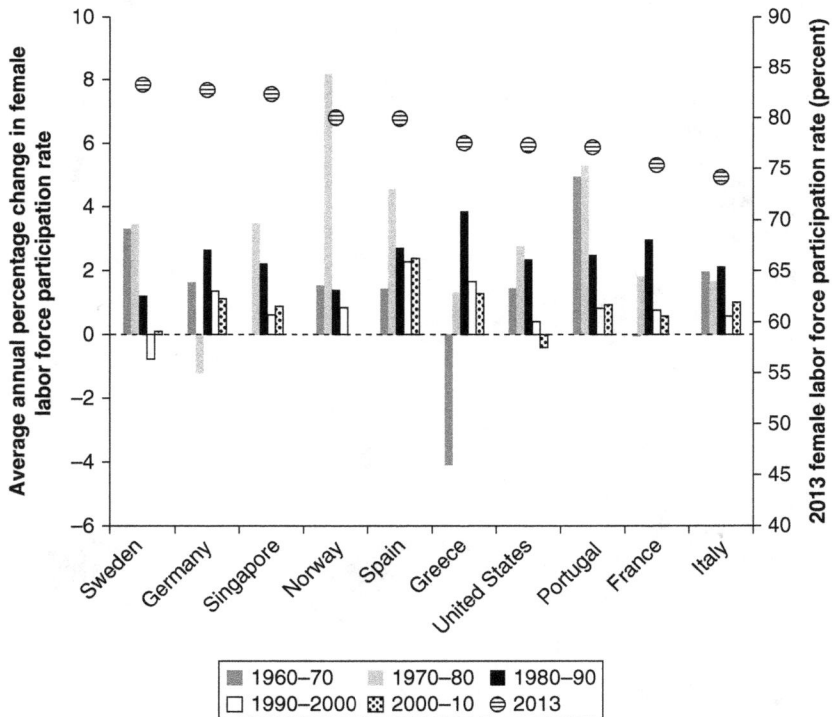

Source: World Development Indicators 2015.

Comparable data for LAC countries are not available for the period before 1990. However, among countries with similar levels of FLFP in 1990 (40–70 percent), FLFP in LAC grew at a slower pace than it did in countries outside the region.[2] Only Chile and Colombia had increases comparable to Greece, Norway, Portugal, Singapore, Spain, and Sweden (3–4 percent a year).

What would happen if LAC countries maintained the growth in FLFP rates they experienced over the past 10 years? Figure 3.12 shows the estimated number of years it would take each country to reach the current average FLFP rate in OECD countries of 62 percent. The Bahamas, Barbados, Bolivia, Brazil, Haiti,

FIGURE 3.12 Number of years needed to reach 2013 average female labor force participation rate in OECD if rate of increase observed in 2004–13 remains unchanged

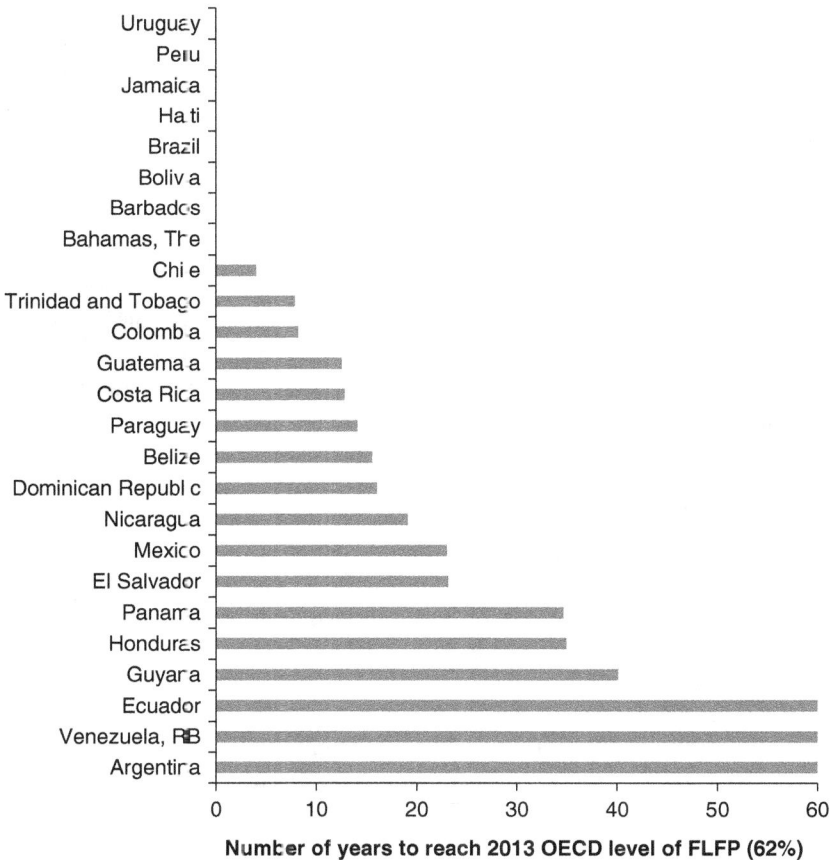

Number of years to reach 2013 OECD level of FLFP (62%)

Source: World Development Indicators 2015.
Note: FLFP = female labor force participation; OECD = Organisation for Economic Co-operation and Development.

Jamaica, Peru, and Uruguay have already reached or surpassed the 62 percent level. Chile and Colombia could soon reach the OECD average participation rate. In contrast, Argentina, Ecuador, and República Bolivariana de Venezuela—which had very slow or no annual growth during the period—would need more than 60 years to reach the benchmark. This exercise is particularly relevant in the context of the opportunity for some countries to capitalize on their favorable demographic situations (see the discussion of the demographic dividend in chapter 1).

Labor Market Outcomes of Women

Even countries that have made significant progress in economic participation for women have not achieved parity; millions of working women in LAC (and other regions) are still struggling for equality in the workplace. The gender gap in earnings remains significant, women continue to be more vulnerable to unemployment than men, women hold more informal and precarious jobs, and the jobs women hold are concentrated in lower-productivity sectors.

Gender Differences in Earnings

Despite higher enrollment rates and more schooling, women earn significantly less than men. LAC ranks third among the nine most inequitable regions in the world in terms of this gap (Ñopo 2012). Despite lower educational attainment, men in LAC earn on average 10 percent more than women (Atal, Ñopo, and Winder 2009). Between 1992 and 2007, the gender gap narrowed by about 7 percentage points (Hoyos and Ñopo 2010). Average differences in wages hide large heterogeneity, with gaps larger among poor and less educated women (Ñopo 2012).

Economists typically divide the gender gap in earnings into two components. One is explained by individual characteristics, such as education, experience, and sector. The other represents the unexplained variance, which may reflect discrimination.

Table 3.1 shows the gender wage gap after controlling for observable characteristics (age, education, and location). In every country, women earn less per hour than men with similar observable characteristics. In the Dominican Republic and Peru, women's hourly wages represent 70 percent of men's wages. Smaller gaps in earnings are observed in countries with fewer women in the labor market (Costa Rica, El Salvador, and Honduras). In the OECD countries, women's average hourly earnings are 85 percent of men's, with larger gaps in Estonia and the Republic of Korea (women in these countries with similar characteristics as men earn about 65 percent as much an hour). Gaps are smaller in Belgium, Luxembourg, and New Zealand (women in these

TABLE 3.1 Women's hourly wages as a percentage of men's in selected countries in Latin America and the Caribbean

Country/year	All workers	Adults 25–64
Honduras (2011)	98	99
El Salvador (2012)	96	94
Belize (1999)	96	93
Nicaragua (2009)	92	93
Costa Rica (2002)	90	89
Argentina (31 cities) (2013)	88	89
Mexico (2012)	84	86
Guatemala (2011)	87	85
Bolivia (2012)	82	82
Paraguay (2011)	82	82
Jamaica (1999)	80	81
Haiti (2001)	81	80
Ecuador (2012)	80	79
Colombia (2012)	79	79
Venezuela, RB (2006)	78	78
Uruguay (2012)	78	78
Panama (2012)	77	77
Suriname (1999)	78	77
Chile (2011)	77	76
Brazil (rural north) (2012)	75	74
Peru (2012)	73	73
Dominican Republic (2011)	72	70

Source: SEDLAC 2015.
Note: Table shows conditional wage gaps controlling for variables in a Mincer equation. Estimations for Panama used implicit rent to calculate hourly wages.

countries with similar characteristics as men earn about 94 percent as much an hour) (OECD 2014). The percentage of unexplained variance is even larger for women with children.[3]

With lower participation levels and wages than their male counterparts, women in LAC contribute an average of 37 percent of total adult household income (figure 3.13). They contribute about 35 percent to adult household labor income. Their contribution is lower among the poorest households and higher among the richest.

FIGURE 3.13 Average contribution of women to household labor income among all households, the richest and the poorest in selected countries in Latin America and the Caribbean, circa 2010

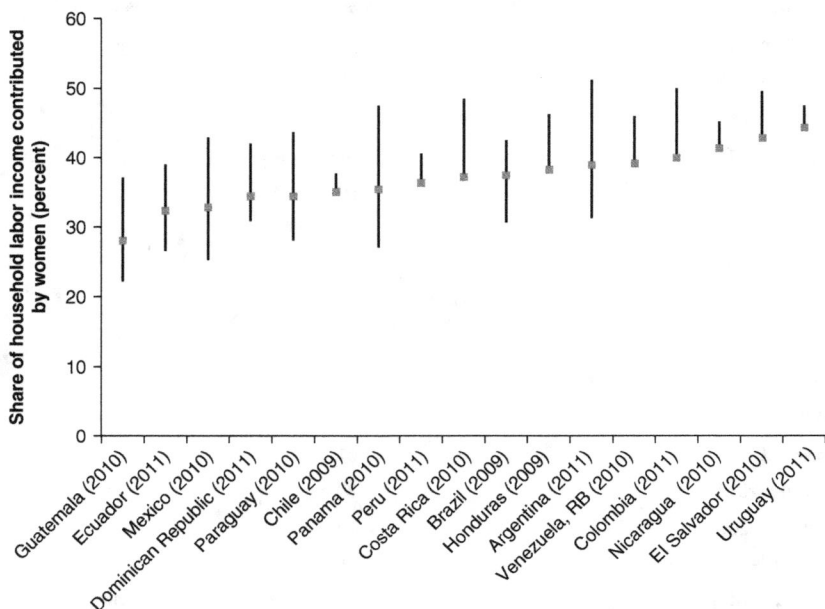

Source: CEDLAS and World Bank 2014.
Note: Dots indicate average of all households in the country. Tops of bars show contribution of women in households in top 20 percent of the income distribution. Bottoms of bars show contribution of women in households in bottom 20 percent.

Gender Differences in Unemployment and Informality

Women are more vulnerable than men to unemployment (figure 3.14), and are more likely to work in the informal and low-productivity sectors (World Bank 2012). Female-headed households, which account for 31 percent of all households in the region, are particularly vulnerable. Women often engage in informal or part-time jobs because they provide more flexibility. These jobs offer fewer (if any) benefits and protection than formal full-time employment. Indeed, 38 percent of female workers 25–45 receive no social security benefits.

Almost 60 percent of all employees working part-time are women (Pagés and Piras 2010). More women than men work part-time involuntarily (figure 3.15), and more men than women earn social security benefits (figure 3.16). Partly as a result, women's pensions are much smaller than men's. In Chile, for example,

FIGURE 3.14 Unemployment rates of men and women in selected countries in Latin America and the Caribbean, 2013

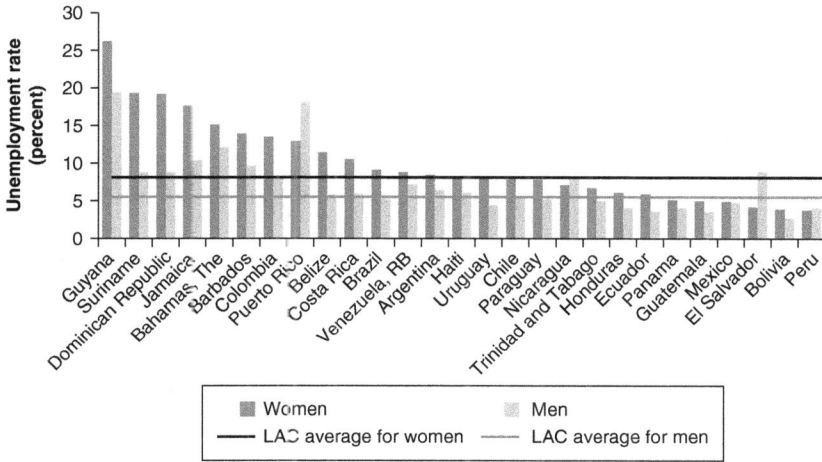

Source: World Development Indicators 2015.
Note: LAC = Latin America and the Caribbean.

FIGURE 3.15 Share of men and women in selected countries in Latin America and the Caribbean involuntarily working part-time, circa 2013

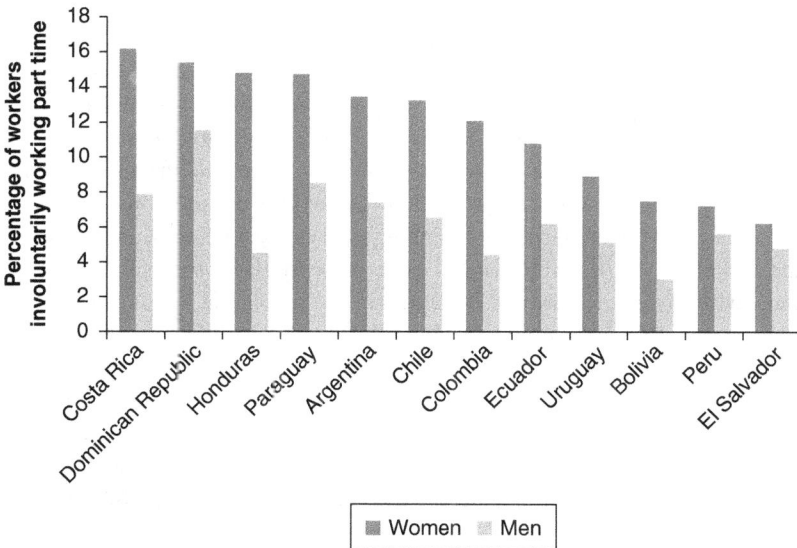

Source: IDB 2013.

FIGURE 3.16 Share of men and women in selected countries in Latin America and the Caribbean with jobs that provide social security benefits, circa 2013

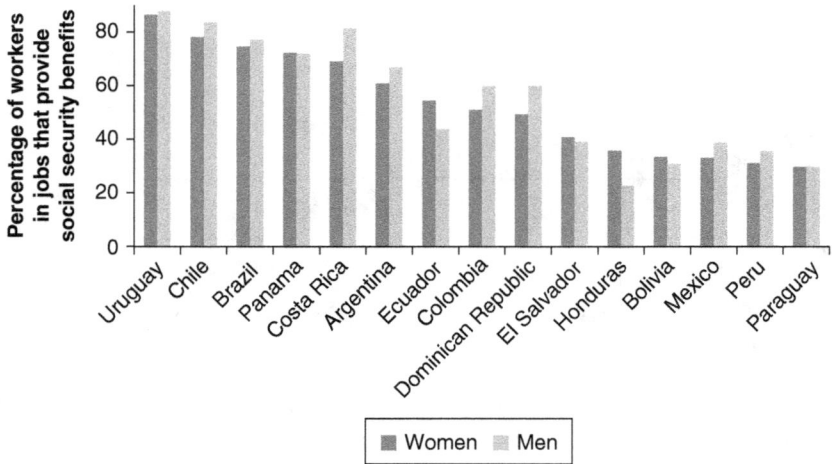

Source: IDB 2013.

the gross replacement rate (the total pension in retirement divided by earnings over the last 10 working years) is about 88 percent for men and just 64 percent for women (Paredes 2012).

Horizontal and Vertical Segregation by Gender

Occupational (horizontal) segregation is one source of the gender gap in earnings. Around the world, women are overrepresented in the service sector, which pays lower wages, and underrepresented in the industrial sector, which usually pays higher wages (figure 3.17). These patterns are consistent across LAC, showing variation only in financing, real estate, business, and the wholesale and retail sectors. Men tend to be more scattered across various occupations, whereas women are concentrated in the wholesale, retail, tourism, and social services sectors, which employ 60–80 percent of female workers in all countries in the region.

The hierarchical segregation of women is also pervasive, in both the labor market and politics. The Bahamas is the only country in LAC where the proportion of female legislators reaches 50 percent. The proportion of women in top management jobs is also very low, ranging from 4.5 percent in Chile to 33.2 percent in The Bahamas (table 3.2).

FIGURE 3.17 Sectoral distribution of male and female workers in selected countries in Latin America and the Caribbean, circa 2013

a. Men

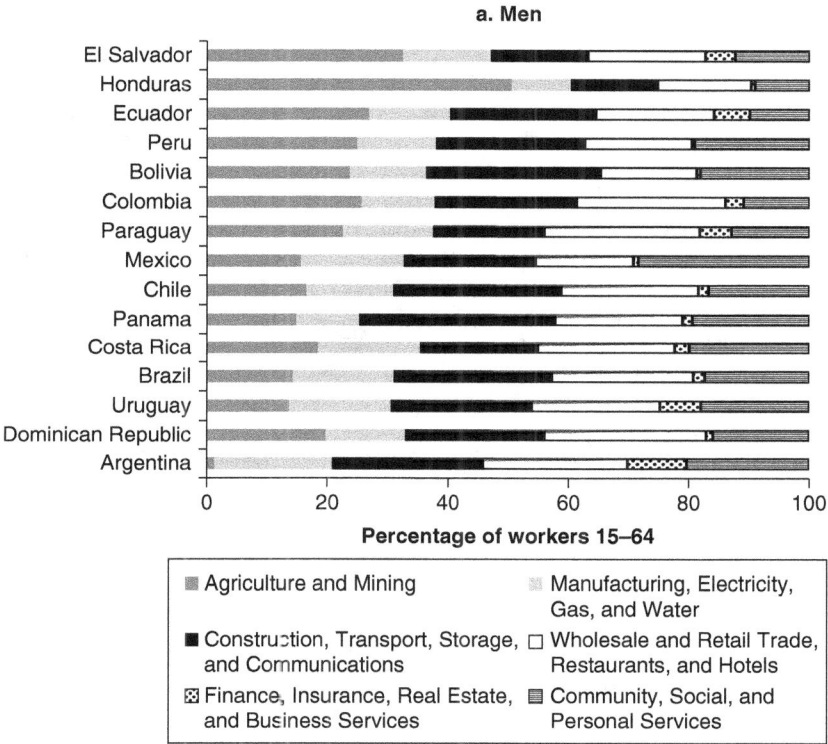

Percentage of workers 15–64

- ▦ Agriculture and Mining
- ▩ Manufacturing, Electricity, Gas, and Water
- ■ Construction, Transport, Storage, and Communications
- □ Wholesale and Retail Trade, Restaurants, and Hotels
- ⊠ Finance, Insurance, Real Estate, and Business Services
- ▤ Community, Social, and Personal Services

(continued on next page)

FIGURE 3.17 Sectoral distribution of male and female workers in selected countries in Latin America and the Caribbean, circa 2013 *(continued)*

b. Women

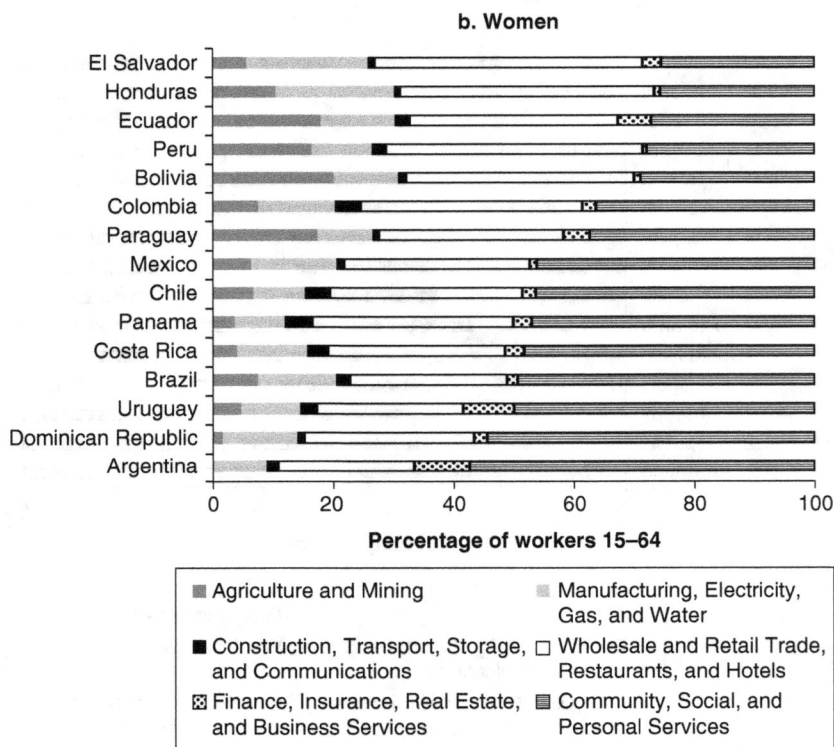

Percentage of workers 15–64

- ■ Agriculture and Mining
- ▨ Manufacturing, Electricity, Gas, and Water
- ■ Construction, Transport, Storage, and Communications
- □ Wholesale and Retail Trade, Restaurants, and Hotels
- ⊠ Finance, Insurance, Real Estate, and Business Services
- ▦ Community, Social, and Personal Services

Source: IDB 2013.

TABLE 3.2 Share of female legislators and senior officials, firm owners, and executive board members in Latin America and the Caribbean

Country	Government (legislators and senior officials)	Private companies	
		Owners	Executive board members
Argentina	23.1	38.0	9.2
Bahamas, The	51.7	58.3	33.2
Barbados	46.7	43.5	25.4
Belize	41.3	30.4	25.5
Bolivia	29.0	41.3	21.7

(continued on next page)

TABLE 3.2 Share of female legislators and senior officials, firm owners, and executive board members in Latin America and the Caribbean *(continued)*

Country	Government (legislators and senior officials)	Private companies	
		Owners	Executive board members
Brazil	36.0	59.3	17.9
Chile	32.7	29.6	4.5
Colombia	n.a.	35.3	12.1
Costa Rica	35.2	43.5	15.4
Dominican Republic	30.6	30.0	11.0
Ecuador	27.7	24.1	17.0
El Salvador	28.9	40.2	21.4
Guatemala	n.a.	44.2	15.7
Guyana	25.4	58.3	17.7
Honduras	n.a.	43.3	31.7
Jamaica	n.a.	38.2	24.1
Mexico	30.7	25.7	14.6
Nicaragua	41.0	61.9	32.3
Panama	46.0	24.7	23.5
Paraguay	34.0	51.6	22.8
Peru	19.4	28.7	14.1
Trinidad and Tobago	43.4	45.1	20.8
Uruguay	40.2	23.1	19.4
Venezuela, RB	n.a.	30.7	31.1

Source: World Bank 2015
Note: For the region as a whole, women own 39 percent of small firms, 38 percent of medium-size firms, and 29 percent of large firms.

Notes

1. Gender equality in economic participation and opportunity is captured by gender differences in labor force participation rates, remuneration, and advancement to managerial and professional positions. The Global Gender Gap Index comprises four component indexes: educational attainment, economic participation and opportunity, health and survival, and political empowerment (World Economic Forum 2015).

2. Countries with FLFP rates of 40–70 percent in the 1990s in LAC were (from lowest to highest) República Bolivariana de Venezuela, Ecuador, Guatemala, Panama, Trinidad and Tobago, El Salvador, Argentina, Dominican Republic, Suriname, Brazil, Peru, Bolivia, Uruguay, Paraguay, Haiti, The Bahamas, Barbados, and Jamaica. Countries

with FLFP rates of 40–70 percent in the 1990s outside LAC (from lowest to highest) were Spain, Greece, Italy, Singapore, Germany, France, Portugal, the United States, and Norway.

3. See, for example, evidence for the United States in Waldfogel (1998) and for other developed countries in Harkness and Waldfogel (2003).

References

Anxo, D., and J. Y. Boulin, eds. 2005. *Working Time Options over the Life Course: Changing Social Security Structures*. European Foundation for the Improvement of Living and Working Conditions, Dublin.

Atal, J. P., H. Ñopo, and N. Winder. 2009. "New Century, Old Disparities: Gender and Ethnic Wage Gaps in Latin America." Working Paper 109, Inter-American Development Bank, Washington, DC. Available at http://www.iadb.org/res/publications/pubfiles/pubIDB-WP-109.pdf.

CEDLAS (Centro de Estudios Distributivos Laborales y Sociales) and World Bank. 2014. Socio-Economic Database for Latin America and the Caribbean (SEDLAC). La Plata, Argentina, and Washington, DC: CEDLAS and the World Bank.

Choi, H-J., J. M. Joesch, and S. Lundberg. 2005. "Work and Family: Marriage, Children, Child Gender, and the Work Hours and Earnings of West German Men." IZA Discussion Paper 1761, Institute for the Study of Labor, Bonn.

Fagan, C., and B. J. Burchell. 2002. *Gender, Jobs and Working Conditions in the European Union*. European Foundation for the Improvement of Living and Working Conditions, Dublin.

Harkness, S., and J. Waldfogel. 2003. "The Family Gap in Pay: Evidence from Seven Industrialized Countries." In *Worker Well-Being and Public Policy*, Research in Labor Economics, Vol. 22, edited by S. Polachek. Bingley, United Kingdom: Emerald Group Publishing Limited.

Hoyos, A., and H. Ñopo. 2010. "Evolution of Gender Gaps in Latin America at the Turn of the Twentieth Century: An Addendum to 'New Century, Old Disparities.'" Working Paper 176, Inter-American Development Bank, Washington, DC.

IDB (Inter-American Development Bank). 2013. Sociometro-BID. Social Indicators Database. Washington, DC. Available at http://www.iadb.org/en/research-and-data//sociometro-bid,6981.html.

ILO (International Labour Organization). 2015. ILOSTAT Database. Geneva.

Lee, S., D. McCann, and J. C. Messenger. 2007. *Working Time around the World: Trends in Working Hours, Laws, and Policies in a Global Comparative Perspective*. New York and Geneva: Routledge and International Labour Office.

Lundberg, S., and E. Rose. 2002. "The Effects of Sons and Daughters on Men's Labor Supply and Wages." *Review of Economics and Statistics* 84 (2): 251–68.

Ñopo, H. 2012. *New Century, Old Disparities: Gender and Ethnic Earnings Gaps in Latin America and the Caribbean*. Washington, DC: Inter-American Development Bank.

OECD (Organisation for Economic Co-Operation and Development). 2014. OECD Family Database. Paris. Available at www.oecd.org/social/family/database.

Pagés, C., and C. Piras. 2010. *The Gender Dividend: Capitalizing on Women's Work*. Washington, DC: Inter-American Development Bank.

Paredes, R. 2012. "Las pensiones de vejez que genera el Sistema de AFP en Chile: Estimaciones de casas de remplazo." Working Paper, Department of Industrial Engineering. University of Chile, Santiago.

SEDLAC (Socio-Economic Database for Latin America and the Caribbean). 2015. Database for Latin America and the Caribbean (CEDLAS and World Bank). Available at http://sedlac.econo.unlp.edu.ar/eng/.

U.S. Bureau of Labor Statistics. 2014. "Stay-at-Home Mothers through the Years." *Monthly Labor Review*, September.

Waldfogel, J. 1998. "Understanding the 'Family Gap' in Pay for Women with Children." *Journal of Economic Perspectives* 12 (1): 137–56.

WHO (World Health Organization), UNICEF (United Nations Children's Fund), UNFPA (United Nations Population Fund), World Bank, and UNPD (United Nations Population Division). 2014. *Trends in Maternal Mortality: 1990 to 2013*. Geneva.

World Economic Forum. 2015. *The Global Gender Gap Index 2014*. Geneva.

World Bank. 2012. *World Development Report 2012: Gender Equality and Development*. Washington, DC: World Bank.

———. 2014. *Gender at Work. Emerging Messages: A Companion Report to the World Development Report on Jobs*. Washington, DC: World Bank.

World Development Indicators (database). World Bank, Washington, DC. http://data.worldbank.org/data-catalog/world-development-indicators.

CHAPTER 4

Use of Childcare Services in Latin America and the Caribbean

"Who's minding the kids?" is the subtitle of an influential work by Blau and Currie (2006) on childcare in the United States and the title of a series of reports by Laughlin (2013) describing characteristics of children in different types of childcare arrangements. The question is difficult to answer in Latin America and the Caribbean (LAC), where little is known about the share of children participating in nonparental childcare arrangements or demand for formal childcare.

This chapter identifies the prevailing care arrangements in the region and explores potential differences in the use of formal childcare services among households with different income levels and sociodemographic characteristics. It presents for the first time comparable statistics on the use of childcare services for a large number of LAC countries (see Vegas and Jaimovich 2016 for a discussion of the state of the art in measures of attendance and access to early childhood education in LAC).

This chapter is organized as follows: The first section identifies the main childcare arrangements used in LAC. The second section examines factors that influence enrollment in and describes the features of formal childcare. The third section provides data on household expenditures on formal childcare. The last section shows that use of childcare is segmented by socioeconomic and demographic characteristics. Annex 4A provides details on the methodological aspects of measurement of the use of the childcare. Annex 4B presents an estimation of the probability of using different care arrangements by households with different socioeconomic characteristics.

Childcare Arrangements Used

Only a few household surveys in LAC include childcare-related questions. Surveys in Colombia, Ecuador, Guatemala, Honduras, Mexico, and Trinidad and Tobago include information about who stays with a child most of the time during the week. Given the different composition and wording of each questionnaire, however, it is possible to compare statistics on care arrangements for only three of these countries: Colombia, Ecuador, and Honduras (figure 4.1). (For details on sources of information and comparability, see annex 4A.)

Parental care is the predominant childcare arrangement for young children in LAC. Informal care arrangements are used more frequently than formal ones in all countries for which data are available except Colombia. Grandmothers are frequently the main caregivers when mothers work. Mexico's household survey reveals

FIGURE 4.1 Main childcare provider in Colombia, Ecuador, and Honduras, by child's age

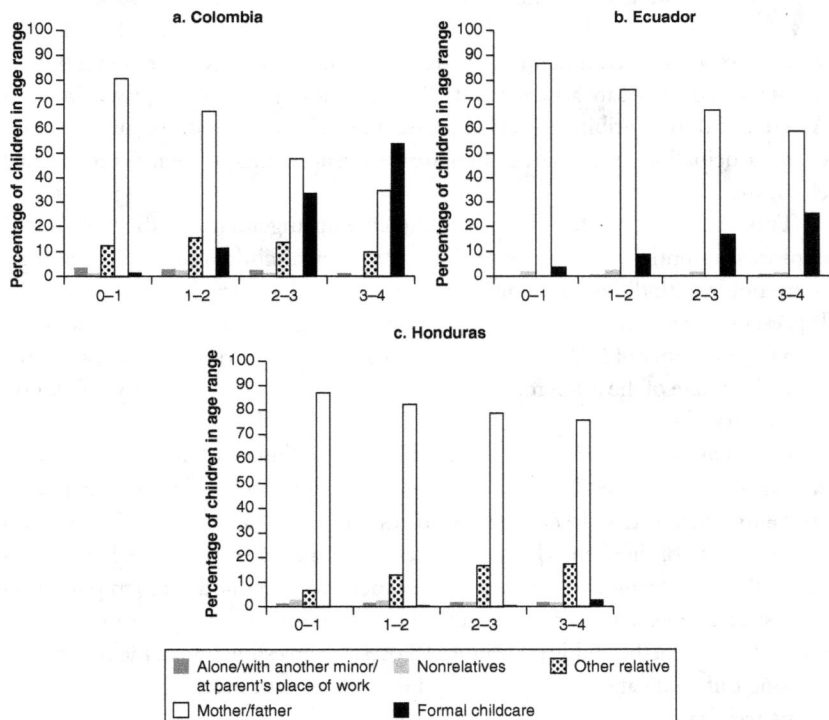

Sources: Colombia: ENCV 2011; Ecuador: ECV 2006; Honduras: ENCOVI 2004 (see table 4.1 for names of surveys).

that 12 percent of children younger than 5 are cared for by their grandmothers, and 4 percent attend a formal childcare center. As children get older, nonparental care is more frequent; in Colombia, however, care by family members is still more common than formal childcare. Use of precarious care arrangements for young children is nonnegligible in some countries, with the share of children cared for by another minor, left alone, or taken to the mother's workplace ranging from 2.5 to 5 percent in the three countries shown in figure 4.1.

Public childcare is the main type of formal service used by children 0–5 in every country for which information was available. Although the data sources are not completely comparable, the answers in the surveys were aggregated to estimate the share of users by type of provision. The results show that at least 60 percent of childcare users in all countries send their children to public facilities (figure 4.2). In Bolivia, Brazil, El Salvador, and Uruguay, 30–40 percent of users use private childcare services. Use of private childcare also reaches 30 percent in Chile, but half of these private centers receive some kind of public subsidy. Guatemala has the smallest share of users of private services.

FIGURE 4.2 Use of public and private childcare services in selected countries in Latin America and the Caribbean, circa 2012

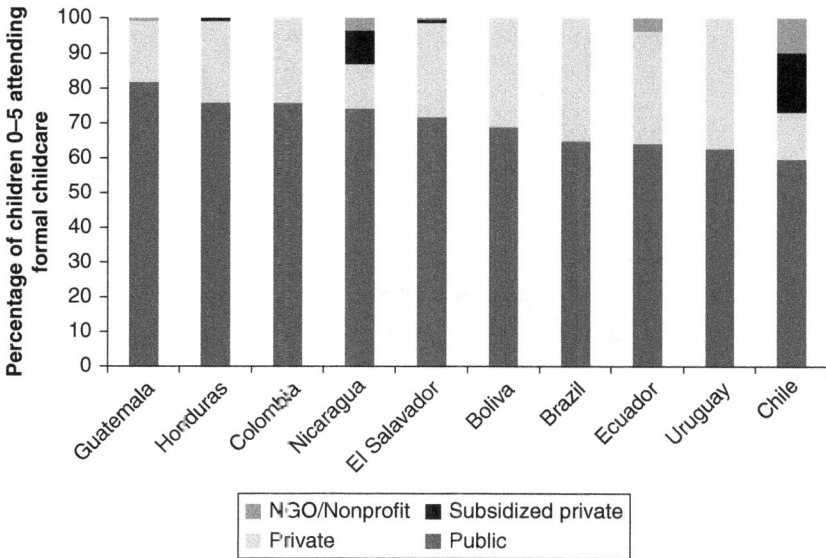

Source: Mateo Díaz and Rodriguez-Chamussy 2015.
Note: Survey answer options included nongovernmental organization (NGO)/nonprofit and subsidized private only in Chile, El Salvador, and Nicaragua. These services may be available in the other countries but were not picked up by their surveys.

Factors Affecting Use of Formal Childcare

Use of formal childcare can be compared in 16 countries, based on data from a decade of household surveys and other specialized longitudinal surveys in LAC (table 4.1).

TABLE 4.1 Surveys in Latin America and the Caribbean that include information on use of childcare services

Country	Survey	Year	Children's age for questionnaire application
Households surveys with information on children from birth			
Bolivia	Encuesta de Hogares (EH)	2012	0–6
Brazil	Pesquisa Nacional por Amostra de Domicilios (PNAD)	2012	All ages
Chile	Encuesta de Caracterización Socioeconómica Nacional (CASEN)	2011	0–6
Colombia	Encuesta Nacional de Calidad de Vida (ENCV)	2011, 2013	0–5
Ecuador	Encuesta de Condiciones de Vida (ECV)	2006	All ages
El Salvador	Encuesta de Hogares de Propósitos Múltiples (EHPM)	2012	0–3
Guatemala	Encuesta Nacional de Condiciones de Vida (ENCOVI)	2011	0–7
Honduras	Encuesta Nacional de Condiciones de Vida (ENCOVI)	2004	0–7
Nicaragua	Encuesta Nacional de Hogares sobre Medición del Nivel de Vida (EMNV)	2009	All ages
Trinidad and Tobago	Survey of Living Conditions (SLC)	2005	All ages
Uruguay	Encuesta Continua de Hogares (ECH)	2013	All ages
Household surveys with information on older children			
Argentina	Encuesta Permanente de Hogares Continua (EPH)	2013	2+
Costa Rica	Encuesta Nacional de Hogares (ENAHO)	2012	2+
Mexico	Encuesta Nacional sobre Ingresos y Gastos de los Hogares (ENIGH)	2012	3+
Peru	Encuesta Nacional de Hogares (ENAHO)	2012	3+
Venezuela, RB	Encuesta de Hogares por Muestreo (EHM)	2013	3+
Specialized longitudinal household surveys			
Chile	Encuesta Longitudinal de la Primera Infancia (ELPI)	2012	All ages
Colombia	Encuesta Longitudinal Colombiana de la Universidad de los Andes (ELCA)	2010, 2013	0–4
Mexico	Encuesta Nacional de Empleo y Seguridad Social (ENESS)	2009	0–5

Source: Mateo Díaz and Rodriguez-Chamussy 2015.

Surveys collect information on childcare in two ways. The most common approach is to ask about attendance at early childhood education or childcare centers within the education section of the survey. The second approach is to include a module on childcare. Some questionnaires, such as the Encuesta de Condiciones de Vida (ECV) 2006 in Ecuador or the Encuesta Nacional de Calidad de Vida (ENCV) 2004 in Honduras, include a stand-alone question within the dedicated section; others, such as the ENCV 2011 in Colombia, ask more generally about the main care arrangements used, with attendance at childcare centers included as one possible answer (see Mateo Díaz and Rodriguez-Chamussy 2013 for the survey questions on childcare).

The history and purposes of childcare policies in different countries influence the process of information gathering. The way in which surveys ask questions may reflect some features of the existing childcare supply and may be indicative of the magnitude of public investment. For instance, formal childcare in Mexico has long been conceptualized as a social security benefit for working mothers (Myers and others 2012). Half of the public supply of childcare is provided by the two institutions in charge of the social security of workers (Instituto Mexicano del Seguro Social [IMSS] and Instituto de Seguridad y Servicios Sociales de los Trabajadores del Estado [ISSSTE]) and financed through a payroll tax. It is not then a coincidence that the only source of information about the use of formal childcare for children 0–6 in Mexico (the Encuesta Nacional de Empleo y Seguridad Social [ENESS]) is gathered through a special module on social security benefits applied immediately after the questionnaire of the National Survey on Employment (ENOE) in 2004 and 2009. The increased emphasis on early childhood education in LAC countries calls for the expansion and improvement of data gathering.

Female Labor Force Participation

Subsidizing childcare appears to increase child enrollment, which in turn increases female labor supply (see chapter 2 and Mateo Díaz and Rodriguez-Chamussy 2013). The proportion of children 0–3 attending childcare and rates of female labor force participation (FLFP) are strongly correlated in both Europe and LAC (see chapter 2). The relationship is stronger for children 0–3 than for children 3–5, suggesting that easing barriers to FLFP is strongly related to the competing demands for mothers' time (figure 4.3).

Children's Age

Use of formal childcare in LAC is limited, especially for younger children. Estimates for 16 LAC countries show that enrollment in formal childcare ranges from less than 1 percent to 26 percent for children 0–3 and from 10 percent to 75 percent for children 3–5.[1] The share of children in formal childcare is highest in Uruguay, where rates are comparable to rates in Canada (OECD 2014). Countries in Central America have the lowest rates of childcare use in the region (figure 4.4).

FIGURE 4.3 Female labor force participation and use of formal childcare for children ages 0–3 and 3–5 in selected countries in Latin America and the Caribbean, circa 2012

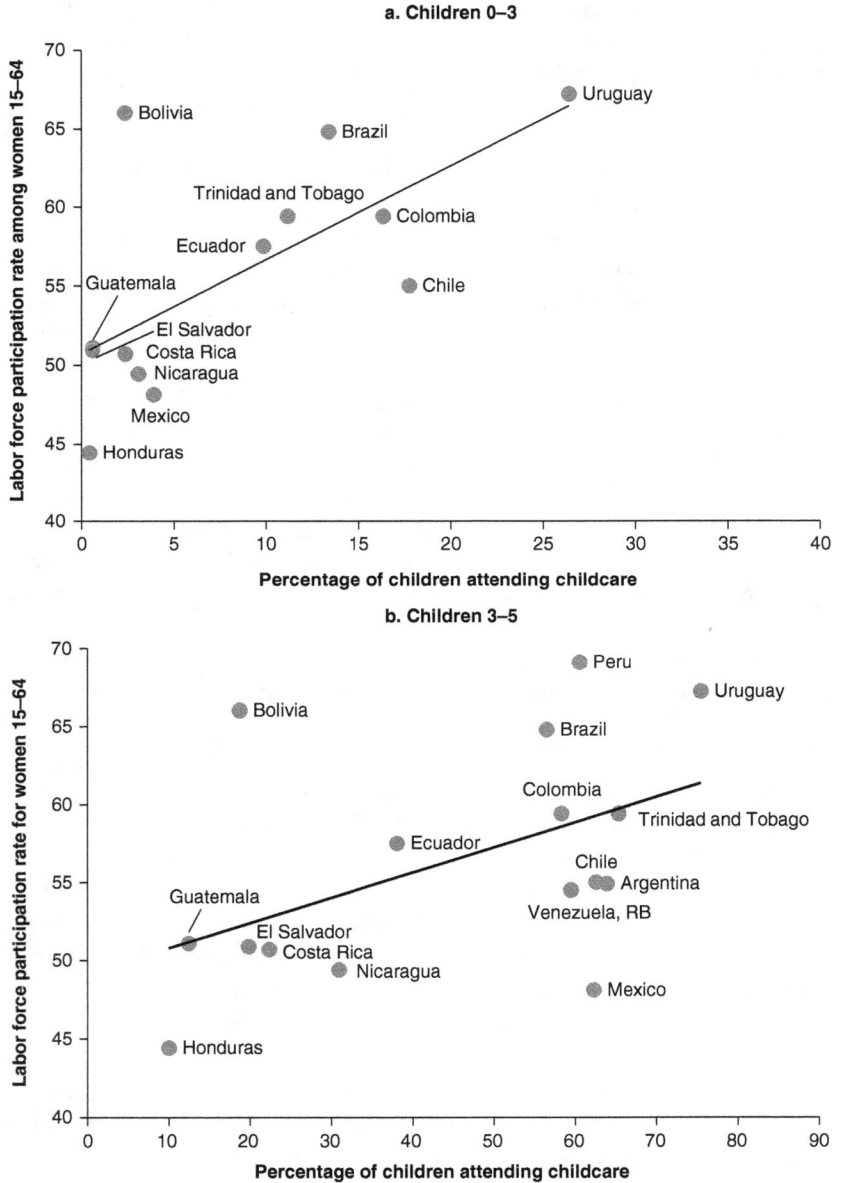

a. Children 0–3

b. Children 3–5

Sources: World Development Indicators 2015 and national household surveys.
Note: See Mateo Díaz and Rodriguez-Chamussy (2015) for methodology.

FIGURE 4.4 Use of formal childcare in selected countries in Latin America and the Caribbean, by children's age

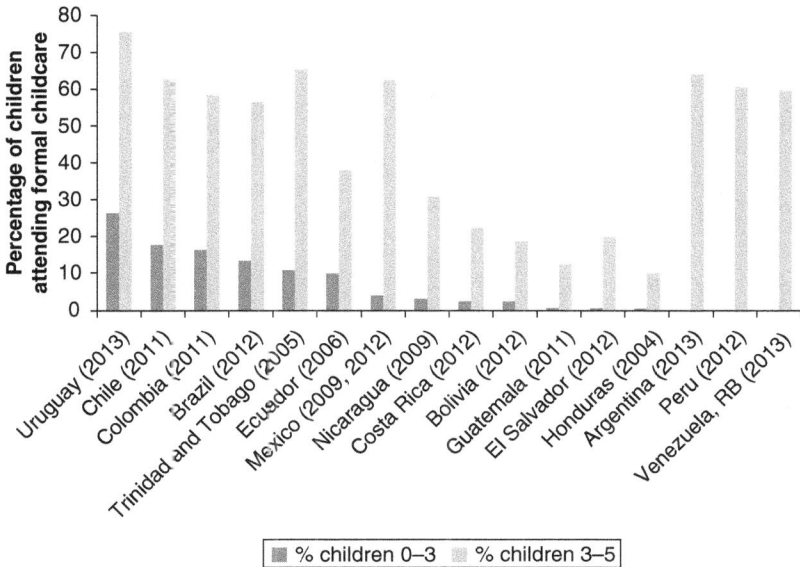

Compared with developed countries, enrollment rates in LAC countries are extremely low (figure 4.5). In the European Union (EU 27), 30 percent of children 0–3 attend formal childcare. No LAC country has rates this high. In about two-thirds of Organisation for Economic Co-operation and Development (OECD) countries, at least 70 percent of children 3–5 are enrolled in formal childcare or preschool; coverage is near universal in many European countries. In LAC, Uruguay has the highest rates, comparable to Finland and Romania; Brazil, Chile, Colombia, Mexico, Peru, and República Bolivariana de Venezuela have rates similar to EU countries with the lowest rates. Rates in Bolivia, Costa Rica, El Salvador, Guatemala, Honduras, and Nicaragua are very low.

Childcare Schedules

Very limited information is available on the frequency and intensity of use of childcare, and the data that do exist are not comparable. However, some examples are illustrative. In Ecuador children enrolled in daycare attend 3.5 days a week,

FIGURE 4.5 Enrollment in childcare programs in selected high-income countries and countries in Latin America and the Caribbean, by GDP per capita, circa 2012

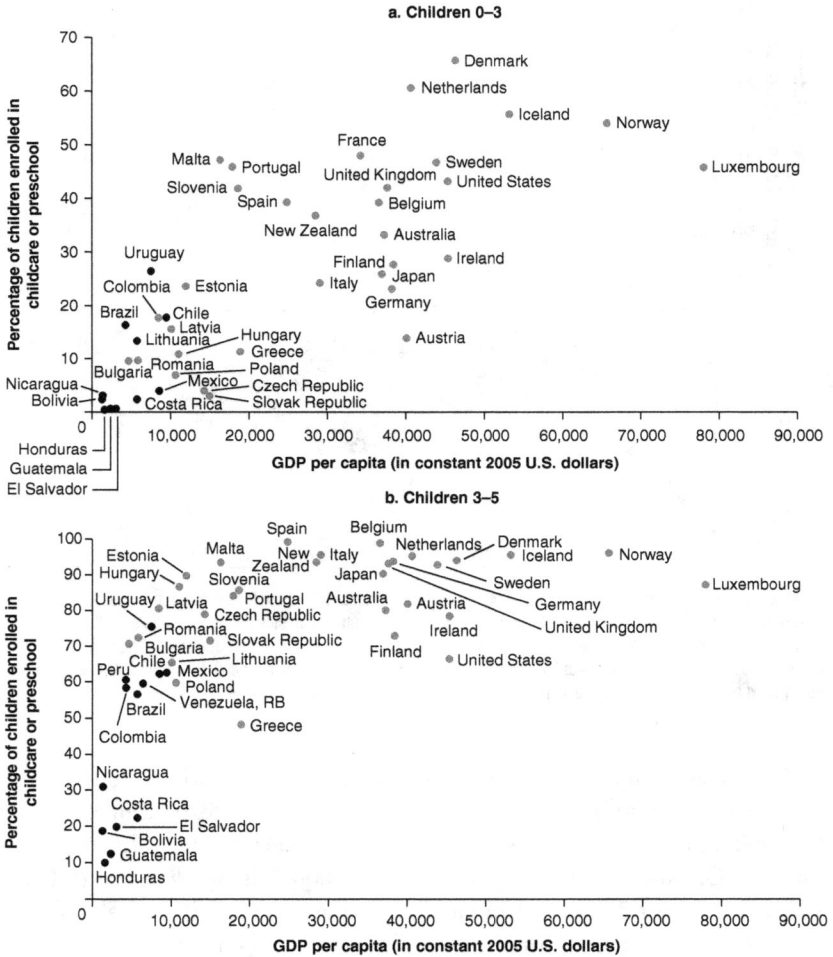

a. Children 0–3

Percentage of children enrolled in childcare or preschool

Denmark
Netherlands
Iceland
Norway
France
Malta • Portugal
Slovenia
Spain
New Zealand
Uruguay
Colombia • Estonia
Brazil • Chile
Latvia
Lithuania — Hungary
Greece
Bulgaria
Romania — Poland
Nicaragua
Bolivia
Costa Rica — Slovak Republic
Honduras
Guatemala
El Salvador
United Kingdom • United States
Sweden
Belgium
Australia
Finland • Ireland
Italy • Japan
Germany
Austria
Mexico — Czech Republic
Luxembourg

GDP per capita (in constant 2005 U.S. dollars)

b. Children 3–5

Percentage of children enrolled in childcare or preschool

Spain
Belgium
Estonia
Malta
New
Zealand
Italy
Netherlands — Denmark
Iceland
Norway
Hungary
Slovenia
Japan
Uruguay • Latvia
Slovenia
Portugal
Australia
Austria
Germany
Sweden
Romania
Czech Republic
Bulgaria
Slovak Republic
Ireland
United Kingdom
Peru
Chile
Mexico
Lithuania
Finland • United States
Brazil
Poland
Venezuela, RB
Colombia
Greece
Nicaragua
Costa Rica
El Salvador
Bolivia
Guatemala
Honduras
Luxembourg

GDP per capita (in constant 2005 U.S. dollars)

Sources: Enrollment rates for Organisation for Economic Co-operation and Development (OECD) countries: OECD 2014; GDP per capita: World Development Indicators 2014; enrollment rates for Latin America and the Caribbean (LAC) countries: Household surveys described in table 4.1.

for about 4.9 hours a day. In Honduras formal arrangements are used 3.6 hours a day. In Uruguay average attendance is 4.7 days a week for 4.6 hours a day. Limited hours of operation require mothers who work full-time to combine formal childcare with other arrangements.

Use of informal care arrangements is frequently complementary to use of formal childcare when working hours exceed the service hours of daycare.

In the United States, for example, children of working mothers who attend formal childcare centers (nursery school or preschool) are more likely to be in multiple arrangements than children whose mothers are not employed; parents with children in daycare centers that are open the entire working day are less likely to use multiple arrangements than parents with children in nursery schools or preschools (Laughlin 2013). Plantenga and Remery (2009) find similar results in European countries: When formal services are lacking, mothers often combine various informal arrangements to cover a full working day.

Distance from Mother's Place of Work

Distance can make formal childcare impractical for many households. Black, Kolesnikova, and Taylor (2014) find that FLFP rates of married women in the United States, particularly women with young children, are negatively correlated with the average commuting time in the metropolitan area.

In their study of Buenos Aires, Peralta Quiros, Mehndiratta, and Ochoa (2014) find that inadequate transportation options constrain women, particularly women with children, who are not able to access the same range of work opportunities as men as a result. They show that trips made by women, particularly women with children, were made at significantly lower travel speeds. As there was no difference found in travel times between men and women, their findings suggest that working mothers had shorter commutes. The authors suggest that if average travel speeds for women become equal to those of men, the range of job opportunities would open up significantly for them.

Surveys from Colombia, Honduras, and Nicaragua include information about the main mode of transportation used to travel between home and the place of childcare (figure 4.6). In all three countries, the majority of families using formal childcare walk to the center. These data and other evidence suggest that distance to the childcare center is a crucial element in the enrollment decision (Attanasio and Vera-Hernandez 2004; Mateo Díaz and Rodriguez-Chamussy 2013; Urzúa and Veramendi 2011).

Household Expenditure on Formal Childcare

Estimates of outlays on formal childcare could be made for six countries in the region (table 4.2). In view of the scant sources of information on spending, these data are valuable.

Among childcare users in the six countries, only about one-third pay some fees; the other two-thirds pay nothing for the services they receive. Among households that pay for childcare, the average out-of-pocket expenditure on childcare ranges from 11 percent of household per capita income (in Nicaragua) to 26 percent (in Guatemala).

FIGURE 4.6 Transportation used to take children from home to childcare center in Colombia, Honduras, and Nicaragua

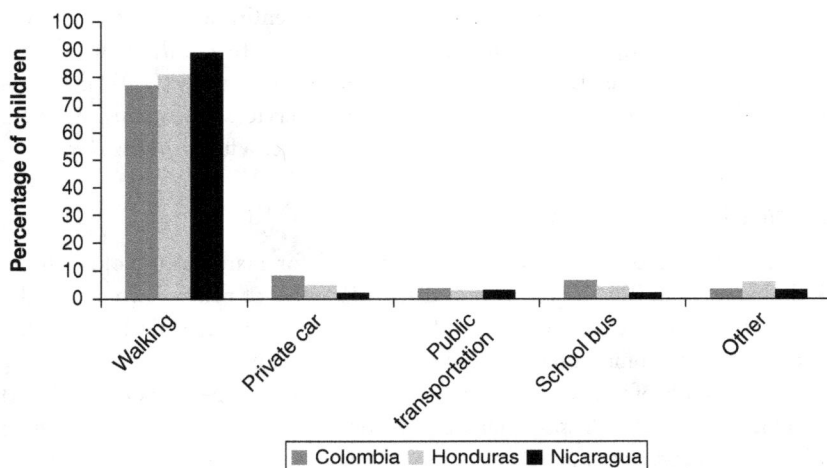

Source: Mateo Díaz and Rodriguez-Chamussy 2015.
Note: "Other" includes bicycle, motorcycle, and horse or other riding animal.

Fees for private childcare as a proportion of per capita household income are highest in Mexico (35 percent), followed by Honduras (31 percent), Guatemala (30 percent), Colombia (26 percent), Ecuador (19 percent), and Nicaragua (14 percent). Beyond fees, other costs (such as transportation), may be crucial in women's decisions to enter the labor force and use nonparental childcare.

Segmented Demand for Formal Childcare

This section shows how the use of formal childcare is remarkably different for segments of the population with different socioeconomic characteristics. It then models the importance of the various factors associated with childcare decisions.

Who Uses Formal Childcare?

In almost all of the countries analyzed, use of formal childcare for children 0–5 is higher among richer households (figure 4.7). Use of services by households in the richest quintile is more than twice that of households in the poorest quintile in Brazil, El Salvador, and Honduras. Use among wealthier households is also higher in Bolivia, Ecuador, and Nicaragua, although the difference between the top and bottom quintiles is smaller.

TABLE 4.2 Average out-of-pocket household expenditure on childcare fees in selected countries in Latin America and the Caribbean

Country/ survey/year	Percentage of households using childcare that pay no fees	Percentage of households using childcare that pay some fees	Average monthly out-of-pocket expenditure per child in childcare		Average monthly out-of-pocket expenditure per child in private childcare	
			Local currency unit	Percentage of household per capita income	Local currency unit	Percentage of household per capita income
Colombia (ENCV 2011)	37	63	63,662	13	132,510	26
Ecuador (ECV 2006)	65	36	30	15	37	19
Guatemala (ENCOVI 2011)	81	19	270	26	307	30
Honduras (ENCOVI 2004)	76	24	504	19	832	31
Mexico (ENESS 2009)	57	44	716	23	1,098	35
Nicaragua (EMNV 2009)	80	21	198	11	250	14
Average	65.3	34.2		18		26

Source: Household surveys; see table 4.1 for names of surveys.
Note: Average monthly out-of-pocket expenditures include both outlays in public and private childcare.

Vegas and Jaimovich (2016) estimate that in 44 of 49 countries for which data on income inequality are available, the rate of childcare center attendance by children from the richest 20 percent of households is twice that of the poorest 20 percent. Chile, where childcare use appears to be equal across income levels, is an outlier.

Use of childcare is greater in urban areas than in rural areas in all 10 countries analyzed (figure 4.8). Fewer childcare services are available in rural areas, centers are more dispersed, social norms about maternal care are stronger, and extended families are more prevalent.

In every country studied except Chile, the share of children attending childcare is much lower in households in which the household head has no education (figure 4.9, panel a). The share of children attending formal childcare correlates positively with the mother's education as well (figure 4.9, panel b). In Brazil, for example, 26 percent of children of mothers with no completed education, 34 percent of children of mothers who completed intermediate education, and

FIGURE 4.7 Use of formal childcare in selected countries in Latin America and the Caribbean, by household income quintile, circa 2012

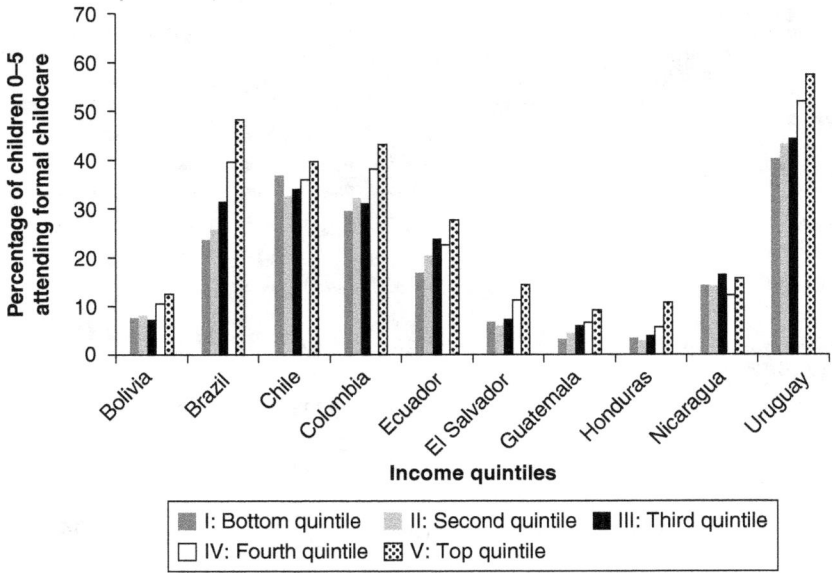

FIGURE 4.8 Use of formal childcare in rural and urban areas of selected countries in Latin America and the Caribbean, circa 2012

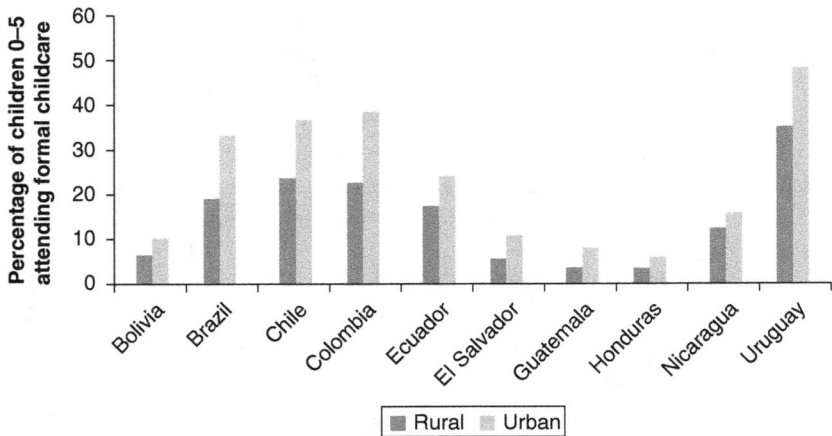

FIGURE 4.9 Use of formal childcare in selected countries in Latin America and the Caribbean, by education of household head and mother, circa 2012

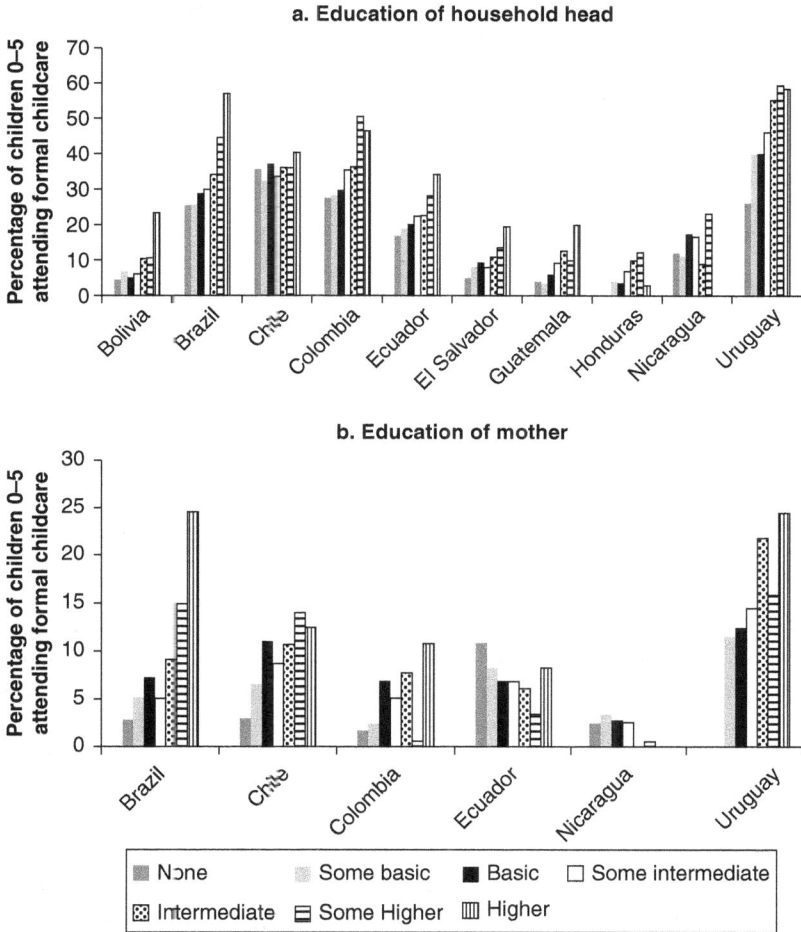

a. Education of household head

b. Education of mother

Legend: ■ None ▨ Some basic ■ Basic □ Some intermediate ⊠ Intermediate ☰ Some Higher ▥ Higher

Source: Mateo Díaz and Rodriguez-Chamussy 2015.

54 percent of children of mothers who completed higher education attend formal childcare.

Children whose mothers are in the labor market are more likely to attend formal childcare than children with nonworking mothers in all countries studied (figure 4.10). In Brazil and Chile, the difference is about 10 percentage points.

FIGURE 4.10 Use of formal childcare in selected countries in Latin America and the Caribbean, by mother's labor participation status, circa 2012

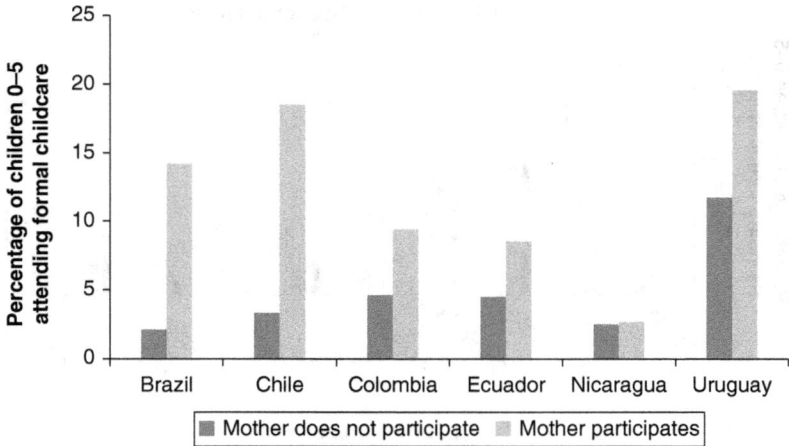

Source: Mateo Díaz and Rodriguez-Chamussy 2015.

Modeling the Use of Childcare with Data from Colombia

This section uses data from Colombia's ENCV 2013 to explore the importance of various factors in a household's decision to use formal childcare or an alternative arrangement. The analysis highlights the importance of the marginal effects of sociodemographic characteristics. It confirms that the use of childcare is segmented, and that decisions regarding maternal labor force participation and the use of formal childcare often coincide. For instance, a child with no younger siblings from a poor rural family in Colombia headed by the father in which the mother does not participate in the labor market and has no formal education has a 12 percent probability of attending formal childcare. The probability of a child with the same characteristics attending formal childcare doubles if the mother works (table 4.3). (These probabilities are estimated using the probit model described in annex 4B.)

The marginal effects of the mother's education and being at the top of the income distribution are also positive and significant: An urban family in the middle quintile of the income distribution in which the mother completed intermediate education and is in the labor market has a 43 percent probability of sending a child to formal childcare. This probability increases to 51 percent if the mother completed higher education and to 72 percent if the family has similar characteristics but is in the top income quintile and there is a younger sibling.

TABLE 4.3 Probability of attending formal childcare in Colombia, by household characteristics

Profile	Probability of child attending early childhood education center (percent)
• Household is in bottom quintile of income distribution • Father is household head • Mother has no education • Mother is out of the labor market • Household is rural • There are no alternative caregivers at home • There are no younger siblings	12.9
• Household is in bottom quintile of income distribution • Father is household head • Mother has no education • Mother participates in the labor market • Household is rural • There are no alternative caregivers at home • There are no younger siblings	24.8
• Household is in bottom quintile of income distribution • Father is household head • Mother has no education • Mother participates in the labor market • Household is urban • There are no alternative caregivers at home • There are no younger siblings	36.6
• Household is in third quintile of income distribution • Father is household head • Mother has intermediate education • Mother participates in the labor market • Household is urban • There are no alternative caregivers at home • There are no younger siblings	43.1
• Household is in third quintile of income distribution • Father is household head • Mother has tertiary education • Mother participates in the labor market • Household is urban • There are no alternative caregivers at home • There are no younger siblings	50.9
• Household is in richest quintile of income distribution • Father is household head • Mother has tertiary education • Mother participates in the labor market • Household is urban • There are no alternative caregivers at home • There are younger siblings	72.0

Source: Estimation of probit model with data from Encuesta Nacional de Calidad de Vida (ENCV) 2013.

Table 4.4 presents estimates of the probabilities that a child stays home with his or her parents instead of using other types of childcare arrangements. Children 0–5 who come from households with higher income, live in urban areas, and have mothers with higher educational attainment are more likely to be in childcare than to stay home with parents or other caregivers, even after controlling for other factors, such as household head, presence of younger siblings, and presence of other potential caregivers in the household. Several interesting points emerge from table 4.4:

- Use of public childcare increases with income before falling, showing a reverse *U*-shape type of relationship.

- The main substitute for parental care seems to be care by other relatives or a third person. The probability of a child staying at home under parental care decreases sharply in households with higher income and higher education of the mother. However, only the probability of using private childcare or

TABLE 4.4 Probability of using various childcare arrangements in Colombia, by household characteristics

Profile	Probability of using different childcare arrangements				
	Staying at home with mother/ father	Public formal childcare	Private formal childcare	At home with another person	At work with mother/father; at home cared for by another child; home alone
• Household is in bottom quintile of income distribution • Father is household head • Mother has no education • Mother is out of the labor market • Household is rural • There are no alternative caregivers at home • There are no younger siblings	85.4	12.1	0.0	0.6	2.0
• Household is in third quintile of income distribution • Father is household head • Mother has intermediate education • Mother participates in the labor market • Household is urban • There are no alternative caregivers at home • There are no younger siblings	53.9	35.6	7.7	2.4	0.5

(continued on next page)

TABLE 4.4 Probability of using various childcare arrangements in Colombia, by household characteristics *(continued)*

Profile	Probability of using different childcare arrangements				
	Staying at home with mother/ father	Public formal childcare	Private formal childcare	At home with another person	At work with mother/father; at home cared for by another child; home alone
• Household is in richest quintile of income distribution • Father is household head • Mother has tertiary education • Mother participates in the labor market • Household is urban • There are no alternative caregivers at home • There are younger siblings	28.4	20.3	45.4	5.7	0.3

Source: Estimation of multinomial logit model with data from Encuesta Nacional de Calidad de Vida (ENCV) 2013 in Colombia.
Note: For the estimated relative log odds of using different childcare arrangements, see annex 4B in this chapter.

a caregiver at home increases significantly; the probability of using public formal childcare does not increase.

- An estimated 2 percent of households with the most vulnerable socioeconomic family profile are likely to leave their children in a precarious care arrangement (alone or in the care of another minor, for example).

Annex 4A: Methodological Issues in Estimating the Use of Childcare

This annex examines the main methodological issues encountered in estimating the use of childcare services (see Mateo Díaz and Rodríguez-Chamussy 2015 for more details).

Content and Scope of Questionnaires

The topics covered in each survey vary, but they generally focus on enrollment in and attendance at childcare and on household expenditure on tuition and fees for childcare programs. Tables 4A.1 and 4A.2 summarize the information included in each survey; the appendix to Mateo Díaz and Rodriguez-Chamussy (2015) provides the list of questions (in Spanish) included in all questionnaires.

Only a few questions about childcare are included. In Mexico they are administered only to working mothers. In five countries they are administered to

(continued on next page)

TABLE 4A.1 Summary of information collected by surveys in Latin America and the Caribbean in which questions on childcare apply to children from birth

Topic	Household surveys												Longitudinal surveys		
	Bolivia (EH 2012)	Brazil (PNAD 2012)	Chile (CASEN 2011)	Colombia (ENCV 2011)	Colombia (ENCV 2013)	Ecuador (ECV 2006)	El Salvador (EHPM 2012)	Guatemala (ENCOVI 2011)	Honduras (ENCOVI 2004)	Nicaragua (EMNV 2009)	Trinidad and Tobago (SLC 2005)	Uruguay (ECH 2013)	Chile (ELPI 2012)	Colombia (ELCA 2010)	Mexico (ENESS 2009)
Attendance to childcare	Yes	Yes	Yes	Yes[a]	Yes	Yes	Yes	Yes	Yes	Yes	Yes	Yes	Yes	Yes	Yes[a]
Type of institution attended	Yes	Yes	Yes	Yes	Yes	Yes	Yes	Yes	Yes	Yes	Yes	Yes	Yes	Yes	Yes[a]
Hours of attendance						Yes			Yes		Yes	Yes	Yes	Yes	Yes[a]
Days of attendance						Yes						Yes	Yes		
Monthly fee payments (last month)			Yes	Yes		Yes		Yes	Yes	Yes				Yes	Yes[a]
Other payments (last month)			Yes	Yes		Yes		Yes	Yes	Yes				Yes	
Tuition payments (last school year)			Yes	Yes		Yes		Yes	Yes	Yes					

104

TABLE 4A.1 Summary of information collected by surveys in Latin America and the Caribbean in which questions on childcare apply to children from birth *(continued)*

Topic	Household surveys												Longitudinal surveys		
	Bolivia (EH 2012)	Brazil (PNAD 2012)	Chile (CASEN 2011)	Colombia (ENCV 2011)	Colombia (ENCV 2013)	Ecuador (ECV 2006)	El Salvador (EHPM 2012)	Guatemala (ENCOVI 2011)	Honduras (ENCOVI 2004)	Nicaragua (EMNV 2009)	Trinidad and Tobago (SLC 2005)	Uruguay (ECH 2013)	Chile (ELPI 2012)	Colombia (ELCA 2010)	Mexico (ENESS 2009)
Other payments (last school year)				Yes		Yes			Yes	Yes					
Service includes food				Yes	Yes				Yes			Yes			
Program has a curriculum															
Mean of transportation to childcare				Yes		Yes			Yes	Yes					
Time of transportation to childcare				Yes		Yes			Yes						
Reasons for not attending			Yes	Yes	Yes	Yes			Yes	Yes	Yes		Yes	Yes	Yes[a]
Reasons for attending													Yes		

(continued on next page)

105

TABLE 4A.1 Summary of information collected by surveys in Latin America and the Caribbean in which questions on childcare apply to children from birth *(continued)*

Topic	Household surveys												Longitudinal surveys		
	Bolivia (EH 2012)	Brazil (PNAD 2012)	Chile (CASEN 2011)	Colombia (ENCV 2011)	Colombia (ENCV 2013)	Ecuador (ECV 2006)	El Salvador (EHPM 2012)	Guatemala (ENCOVI 2011)	Honduras (ENCOVI 2004)	Nicaragua (EMNV 2009)	Trinidad and Tobago (SLC 2005)	Uruguay (ECH 2013)	Chile (ELPI 2012)	Colombia (ELCA 2010)	Mexico (ENESS 2009)
Child's main caregiver				Yes	Yes	Yes		Yes	Yes		Yes		Yes	Yes	Yes
Childcare facilities at parents' work place								Yes					Yes		
Availability of childcare near home													Yes		
Availability of childcare near work													Yes		
Identification of child's mother	Yes		Yes	Yes	Yes	Yes		Yes				Yes	Yes	Yes	

Note: Table includes both the 2011 and 2013 editions of the ENCV in Colombia because they contain different information, and the 2013 edition is less complete than the 2011 one. See table 4.1 for the names of each survey.

a. Questions were administered only to working mothers.

TABLE 4A.2 Summary of information collected by household surveys in Latin America and the Caribbean in which questions on childcare apply only to children who are at least 2 or 3 years old

Topic	Argentina (EPH 2013)	Costa Rica (ENAHO 2012)	Mexico (ENIGH 2012)	Peru (ENAHO 2012)	Venezuela, RB (EHM 2013)
Attendance in childcare	Yes	Yes	Yes	Yes	Yes
Type of institution attended	Yes	Yes	Yes	Yes	
Hours of attendance					
Days of attendance					
Monthly fee payments (last month)				Yes	
Other payments (last month)				Yes	
Tuition payments (last school year)				Yes	
Other payments (last school year)				Yes	
Service includes food					
Program has a curriculum					
Means of transportation to childcare					
Time of transportation to childcare					
Reasons for NOT attending		Yes		Yes	Yes
Reasons for attending					
Child's main caregiver					
Childcare facilities at parents' work place					
Identification of child's mother			Yes		

respondents only when their children are at least 2 (Argentina and Costa Rica) or 3 (Mexico, Peru, and República Bolivariana de Venezuela) (table 4A.2).

Participation Rates in Formal Childcare

The most comparable statistics on the use of formal childcare for children 0–5 are based on household surveys for 10 countries: Bolivia (2012), Brazil (2012), Chile (2011), Colombia (2011), Ecuador (2006), El Salvador (2012), Guatemala (2011), Honduras (2004), Nicaragua (2009), and Uruguay (2013). This selection was made based on the analysis of differences in questions, sampling, and units of observation explained in the chapter.

Childcare included nursery school, daycare, preschool, and all other forms of nonparental childcare outside the home. The estimate is the number of children attending childcare programs as a percentage of the total number of children in the age group. To confirm the validity of this approach, we also estimate a measure at the household level, using households with children in the age group as the unit of analysis. Results were very similar.

Some surveys include just one question on school attendance, which applies to all members of the household regardless of their age. If the child was 5 or younger, attendance at some childcare program or initial education was assumed. Another set of surveys divides attendance questions by age. For the youngest children, they ask about attendance at kindergarten, nursery school, or an initial education center. For older children, they ask about school attendance. A variable of attendance for children 0–5 was constructed, in which 1 is assigned if the child attends any kind of care or educational institution and 0 is assigned otherwise. This variable may be a combination of two or three original variables depending on how the attendance questions were split in the questionnaire.

Primary sources of data for Argentina, Costa Rica, Mexico, Peru, and República Bolivariana de Venezuela do not cover very young children. Where possible, we used additional sources of information to construct the indicator for the missing age range. For Costa Rica the indicator includes only children attending centers from the Centros de Educación y Nutrición y de Centros Infantiles de Atención Integral (CEN-CINAI), a public institution whose main objective is to improve the nutritional status of mothers and children and child development by providing daycare to poor and at-risk children. For Mexico the design of the questionnaire limits the estimated indicator to children of working mothers. For both countries the estimates of children 0–3 attending formal childcare need to be interpreted as minimums.

Type of institution or program

We grouped early childhood care and education institutions and programs into four categories depending on their financing source: public, private subsidized, and nonprofit (including community daycare, foundations, and nongovernmental organizations [NGOs]). Surveys in Chile, Colombia, Ecuador, El Salvador, Guatemala, Mexico, and Uruguay ask directly about attendance at specific programs and institutions. Table 4A.3 shows the categories in which these programs were classified, based on information from national experts and the managerial staffs of the institutions. In Colombia, the classification is based on two original variables: One classified the institution as public or private, the other classified public institutions as subsidized or not subsidized (see the questionnaires in Mateo Díaz and Rodriguez-Chamussy 2015). For the other surveys, the classification is apparent from the options in the questionnaire.

TABLE 4A.3 Classification of early childhood care and education institutions and programs in selected countries in Latin America and the Caribbean

Country	Public	Private	Private subsidized	Community daycare/ foundation/NGO
Chile	Junta Nacional de Jardines Infantiles (JUNJI)			Fundación Integra
Colombia	Hogares comunitarios, Instituto Colombiano de Bienestar Familiar (ICBF) institutions	Daycare		
Ecuador	Ministerio de Bienestar Social (MES)/Operacion Rescate Infantil (ORI)			
El Salvador			Centros de Desarrollo Integral (CDI ISNA)	
Guatemala	Ministry of Education: Programa Nacional de Autogestion para el Desarrollo Educativo (PRONADE)/New unitary schools			Cooperatives
Mexico, Encuesta Nacional de Empleo y Seguridad Social (ENESS)	Desarrollo Integral de la Familia (DIF)		Estancias Infantiles, Secretaría de Desarrollo Social (SEDESOL), Guarderias del Instituto Mexicano del Seguro Social (IMSS), Guarderias del Instituto de Seguridad y Servicios Sociales para los Trabajadores del Estado (ISSSTE)	
Uruguay	Plan Centros de Atención a la Infancia y la Familia (CAIF)			

Informal childcare arrangements

Surveys in Colombia, Ecuador, Guatemala, Honduras, Mexico, and Trinidad and Tobago include information about who stays with the child most of the time on weekdays. This information is available only for children in the age groups covered by these surveys (see table 4.1).

Each of the surveys includes different answer options. Three (Ecuador, Guatemala, and Honduras) do not include a specific question about informal childcare arrangements. Information about use of informal arrangements had to be constructed from the question about the child's main caregiver (see table 4A.4). To compare the results, we created a new variable, which applies only to children not attending formal childcare (table 4A.4).

Differences by household characteristics

To explore potential differences in the use of formal childcare services among households with different characteristics, it was necessary to construct a number of variables and harmonize them across countries when possible. We constructed the most important variables—income quintiles and level of education—as follows:

- *Income quintiles:* We first calculated household monetary labor and non-labor income (the sums of the individual incomes of household members). We then summed those two components to obtain total household income. (We used this process when total household income was not available from the raw database. When it was, we used the original variable. The original variable was available only for Mexico and Honduras.) After defining household income, we ordered households, ranking from the lowest to the highest income and divided the sample into five equal parts (quintiles). Appropriate expansion factor is used to represent the entire population.

- *Level of education:* We constructed two category variables defined for the head of the household and the mother of each child. Seven dichotomous variables indicated the level of education: none, some basic, basic, some intermediate, intermediate, some superior, and superior. A four-category variable (constructed from the seven-category variable) indicates the level of education that the individual did or did not complete: no education, basic education, intermediate education, and higher education. In surveys that are not harmonized or that did not include information on the seven dichotomous variables (Bolivia, Colombia, Guatemala, Honduras, Mexico, and Nicaragua), we used the reported years of education in each survey.

Missing values

Some surveys include many missing values (nonresponses or invalid answers). Only 15 percent of responses to the question about the use of formal childcare were valid in the Mexican survey (ENESS), for example. In Ecuador information on the reasons for nonattendance was available for only 7.6 percent of children who do not attend childcare; the number of valid responses was also very low in El Salvador and Mexico. Response rates to the question about the use of informal arrangements for children not attending formal centers are much higher (the average is more than 92 percent for the five surveys that include this information). Table 4A.5 shows the percentage of nonmissing response rates for each of these variables.

Children and their mothers

To calculate the proportion of children attending childcare centers and link that information to their mothers' characteristics (participation in the labor market, level of education), it was first necessary to associate each child with his or her mother. Only six surveys had a variable allowing this connection to

TABLE 4A.4 Classification of nonformal caregivers

Caregiver	Description of categories included as they appear in surveys
Mother or father	Mother at home, parents at home, mother, father at home, father
Other relative	Household member, household member 15 or older, household member 10 or older, grandmother
Nonrelative at home	Nursemaid, nanny, nurse, neighbors and friends, other relatives, relative not living in the household relative 18 or older
Precarious arrangement	Father or mother at place of work, no caregiver (child left alone), household member younger than 10, relative younger than 18

TABLE 4A.5 Nonmissing response rates on childcare information in selected surveys

Country (survey)	Percentage of responses on children attending formal daycare that include information about the nature of the institution	Percentage of responses on children not attending formal daycare that include information about reasons for not attending	Percentage of responses on children not attending formal daycare that include information about main caregiver
Bolivia (EH 2012)	100.0	—	—
Brazil (PNAD 2012)	100.0	—	—
Chile (CASEN 2011)	98.8	100.0	—
Colombia (ENCV 2013)	100.0	100.0	92.7
Ecuador (ECV 2006)	100.0	7.6	92.4
El Salvador (EHPM 2012)	99.9	25.1	—
Guatemala (ENCOVI 2011)	83.9	—	94.7
Honduras (ENCOVI 2004)	71.3	100.0	100.0
Mexico (ENESS 2009)	15.1	28.2	99.9
Nicaragua (EMNV 2009)	75.6	100	—
Uruguay (ECH 2013)	99.8	—	—

Note: See table 4.1 for names of surveys — = Information not collected in survey.

be made. The variable used asked if the mother of the person being interviewed lived in the household and, if so, what her relation was to the household head. Tables 4A.1 and 4A.2 indicate which surveys included a question identifying the mother among the household members.

Surveys in Chile (Encuesta de Caracterización Socioeconómica Nacional [CASEN]), El Salvador, and Nicaragua did not include a question that allowed direct tracking of the mother and her children. To link children's information with their mothers' in these cases, we had to restrict the analysis to children whose mother could be identified through their reported relationship to the household head. This decision resulted in the loss of data on children living in households headed by a grandfather, grandmother, uncle, aunt, or other relative or nonrelative. The data lost represented about 38 percent of the total in the three surveys (32 percent in El Salvador, 38 percent in Chile's CASEN, and 43 percent in Nicaragua).

The Mexican ENESS survey posed a similar but more complicated data problem. Because the link between the child and mother could not be directly established, we had to use only data from children who were born to household heads and their partners, which meant losing about 32 percent of all children. In addition, the survey design asked questions about childcare use only of working mothers.

Although the Uruguayan survey does ask about the mother of every person living in the household and identifies the mother with a number, the variable coding had a problem: Zero was not included in the questionnaire options, and 96 percent of the sample had a zero value for this variable. This survey was therefore treated like the surveys that did not include a mother question that associated each child with his or her mother.

Annex 4B: Estimating the Probability of Using Formal Childcare versus Other Care Arrangements

To explore the marginal effect of factors associated with the probability of using formal childcare and different childcare arrangements for their children 0–5, we estimated a probit (table 4A.6) and a multinomial logit model (table 4A.7) using the Colombian Encuesta Nacional de Calidad de Vida (ENCV) 2011 survey. We chose the ENCV because it is one of the most complete surveys available.

In the probit model, the dependent variable indicates whether or not the child attends formal daycare; the independent variables include household characteristics (urban/rural, income quintile, head of household); individual characteristics of the head of the household (level of education); individual characteristics of the mother of the child (level of education, participation in the labor market); and the composition of the household (at least one adult older than 15 other than the parents of the child lives in the household, at least one younger child lives in the household).

TABLE 4A.6 Probit results on use of childcare in Colombia

Item	Coefficient	Marginal effect
Second income quintile	−0.0299	−0.00620
	(0.0733)	(0.0151)
Third income quintile	−0.0845	−0.0170
	(0.0720)	(0.0144)
Fourth income quintile	0.00745	0.00158
	(0.0830)	(0.0176)
Fifth income quintile	−0.00168	−0.00035
	(0.0940)	(0.0198)
Head of household completed basic education	−0.0162	−0.00339
	(0.0662)	(0.0138)
Head of household completed intermediate education	−0.0379	−0.00781
	(0.0835)	(0.0170)
Head of household completed higher education	−0.0138	−0.00289
	(0.124)	(0.0257)
Urban	0.339***	0.0851***
	(0.0530)	(0.0165)
Household headed by mother	−0.00683	−0.00143
	(0.0696)	(0.0146)
Household headed by grandparent	−0.202**	−0.0378***
	(0.0825)	(0.0139)
Household headed by other	−0.207	−0.0386*
	(0.130)	(0.0214)
Mother participates in labor market	0.449***	0.119***
	(0.0520)	(0.0171)
Mother completed basic education	0.125	0.0282
	(0.0813)	(0.0184)
Mother completed intermediate education	0.251***	0.0606***
	(0.0902)	(0.0227)
Mother completed higher education	0.448***	0.119***
	(0.116)	(0.0348)

(continued on next page)

TABLE 4A.6 Probit results on use of childcare in Colombia *(continued)*

Item	Coefficient	Marginal effect
At least one adult (older than 15) in household other than parents	0.0595	0.0130
	(0.0680)	(0.0151)
At least one younger child in household	0.475***	0.127***
	(0.0672)	(0.0214)
Constant	−1.130***	
	(0.0810)	

Note: Robust standard errors are in parentheses. Number of observations is 5,350.
*** $p < 0.01$, ** $p < 0.05$, * $p < 0.1$

TABLE 4A.7 Multinomial logit results on use of childcare in Colombia

Item	Private daycare	Parent at home	Nanny or relative 18 or older at home	Precarious form of care
Second income quintile	0.461***	1.019	0.945	0.936
	(0.123)	(0.108)	(0.197)	(0.255)
Third income quintile	0.957	1.049	1.734***	1.065
	(0.203)	(0.106)	(0.326)	(0.276)
Fourth income quintile	1.195	0.993	1.509**	0.232***
	(0.241)	(0.109)	(0.289)	(0.0959)
Fifth income quintile	3.302***	1.311**	3.251***	0.446*
	(0.673)	(0.181)	(0.656)	(0.186)
Head of household completed basic education	0.892	1.044	0.945	0.869
	(0.190)	(0.103)	(0.156)	(0.224)
Head of household completed intermediate education	1.360	1.166	1.401*	0.324***
	(0.308)	(0.139)	(0.262)	(0.124)
Head of household completed higher education	2.204***	1.118	2.212***	2.523**
	(0.603)	(0.206)	(0.549)	(1.085)
Urban	4.712***	0.575***	1.315	1.084
	(1.540)	(0.0504)	(0.223)	(0.264)
Household headed by mother	0.862	0.824*	1.495***	1.306
	(0.147)	(0.0814)	(0.218)	(0.349)

(continued on next page)

TABLE 4A.7 Multinomial logit results on use of childcare in Colombia *(continued)*

Item	Private daycare	Parent at home	Nanny or relative 18 or older at home	Precarious form of care
Household headed by grandparent	1.142	1.312**	2.284***	1.220
	(0.216)	(0.149)	(0.393)	(0.388)
Household headed by other	0.869	1.028	3.027***	1.497
	(0.284)	(0.188)	(0.732)	(0.689)
Mother participates in labor market	1.719***	0.348***	3.932***	1.773***
	(0.239)	(0.0251)	(0.571)	(0.381)
Mother completed basic education	1.276e+07	0.892	0.850	0.402***
	(1.301e+10)	(0.113)	(0.220)	(0.127)
Mother completed intermediate education	1.623e+07	0.676***	0.914	0.669
	(1.654e+10)	(0.0926)	(0.241)	(0.223)
Mother completed higher education	3.022e+07	0.521***	1.282	0.194***
	(3.081e+10)	(0.0907)	(0.377)	(0.101)
At least one adult (older than 15) in household other than parents	1.021	0.848*	1.135	1.151
	(0.159)	(0.0781)	(0.166)	(0.295)
At least one younger child in household	1.014	0.452***	0.507***	0.372***
	(0.167)	(0.0417)	(0.0813)	(0.117)
Constant	2.13e–09	7.042***	0.0453***	0.161***
	(2.17e–06)	(0.921)	(0.0132)	(0.0518)

Note: Standard errors in parentheses. Number of observations is 5,327. Precarious arrangements include leaving the child in the care of another minor, leaving the child alone, and bringing the child to work.
*** $p < 0.01$, ** $p < 0.05$, * $p < 0.1$

The reference household for both estimates is a poor (bottom 20 percent of the income distribution) rural household headed by the child's father in which the mother does not participate in the labor market and has no formal education, there are no younger children, and the only adults (people over 15) living in the household are the child's parents.

To model the probabilities of using different childcare arrangements, we estimated a multinomial logit (table 4A.7). The dependent variable is a five-category variable that indicates the type of childcare arrangement used by the family: formal public services (base category); formal private services; parental care at home; nonparental care at home (relative or nonrelative); and precarious forms of care such as leaving the child alone, in the care of another minor, or at work with the mother or father. The regressors used in the multinomial logit regression are the same as the ones included in the probit model.

The multinomial logit model assumes the independence of irrelevant alternatives (IIA), which means that the odds for any pair of outcomes are determined without reference to the other available outcomes. Under the IIA assumption, one would expect no systematic change in the coefficients if the outcomes from the model were excluded. Either the Hausman or the Small-Hsiao test can be used to test this assumption. The null hypothesis of both tests is that the odds are independent of other alternatives. The desirable scenario is to find evidence not to reject the null hypothesis, which is the case for the multinomial logit estimated for Colombia (tables 4A.8 and 4A.9). In this exercise, we omit the base category of the original estimation (public daycare) by reestimating the model using the largest remaining category as the base category.

TABLE 4A.8 Small-Hsiao tests of independence of irrelevant alternatives (IIA) assumption

Omitted variable	lnL(full)	lnL(omit)	Chi^2	Degrees of freedom	$P > $ Chi^2
Mother or father at home	−664.69	−649.18	31.03	36	0.704
Nanny or relative older than 18	−1,496.89	−1,529.99	−66.20	36	1.000
Mother or father at work, no caregiver (child remains alone), or relative younger than 18	−1,865.49	−1,978.04	−225.09	36	1.000
Private daycare	−739.51	−818.47	−157.92	36	1.000

Note: The null hypothesis is that the odds of one outcome versus another is independent of other alternatives. (Outcome J versus Outcome K) are independent of other alternatives. Number of observations is 5,028.

TABLE 4A.9 Hausman tests of independence of irrelevant alternatives (IIA) assumption

Omitted variable	Chi^2	Degrees of freedom	$P > $ Chi^2
Mother or father at home	−24.46	36	—
Nanny or relative older than 18	1.27	36	1.000
Mother or father at work, no caregiver (child remains alone), or relative younger than 18	2.46	36	1.000
Private daycare	20.62	36	0.981

Note: The null hypothesis is that the odds of one outcome versus another is independent of other alternatives. (Outcome J versus Outcome K) are independent of other alternatives. Number of observations is 5,028. If Chi$^2 < 0$, the estimated model does not meet the asymptotic assumptions of the test. Hausman and McFadden (1984) note the possibility of obtaining negative test statistics and conclude that a negative result is evidence that IIA has not been violated.

Note

1. Analysis is based on individuals (the number of children enrolled in childcare programs as a percentage of the total number of children in the age group). Using households with children in the age group as the unit of analysis yielded similar results. See Mateo Díaz and Rodriguez-Chamussy (2015) for details on methodology and sources of information.

References

Attanasio, O., and M. Vera-Hernandez. 2004. "Medium and Long Run Effects of Nutrition and Child Care: Evaluation of a Community Nursery Programme in Rural Colombia." IFS Paper EWP04/06, Institute for Fiscal Studies, London.

Black, D. A., N. Kolesnikova, and L. J. Taylor. 2014. "Why Do So Few Women Work in New York (and So Many in Minneapolis)? Labor Supply of Married Women across U.S. Cities." *Journal of Urban Economics* 79: 59–71.

Blau, D. M., and J. Currie. 2006. "Pre-School, Day Care and After-School Care: Who's Minding the Kids?" In *Handbook of the Economics of Education*, Vol. 2, edited by E. A. Hanushek and F. Welch. Amsterdam: North-Holland.

Hausman, J., and D. McFadden. 1984. "Specification Test for the Multinomial Logit Model." *Econometrica* 52 (5):1219–240.

Laughlin, L. 2013. *Who's Minding the Kids? Child Care: Arrangements: Spring 2011.* Household Economics Study, U.S. Census Bureau, Washington, DC.

Mateo Díaz, M. and L. Rodriguez-Chamussy. 2013. "Childcare and Women's Labor Participation: Evidence for Latin America and the Caribbean." Technical Note IDB-TN-586, Inter-American Development Bank, Washington, DC. Available at https://publications.iadb.org/handle/11319/6493.

———. 2015. "Who Cares about Childcare? Estimations of Childcare Use in Latin America and the Caribbean." Technical Note IDB-TN-815, Inter-American Development Bank, Washington, DC. Available at https://publications.iadb.org/handle/11319/6941.

Myers, R. G., A. Martínez, M. A. Delgado, J. L. Fernández, and A. Martínez. 2012. "Desarrollo infantil temprano en México: diagnóstico y recomendaciones." Monograph 144 Inter-American Development Bank, Washington, DC.

OECD (Organisation for Economic Co-operation and Development). 2014. OECD Family Database. Paris: OECD.

Peralta Quiros, T., S. R. Mehndiratta, and M. C. Ochoa. 2014. "Gender, Travel and Job Access: Evidence from Buenos Aires." World Bank, Washington, DC. Available at http://siteresources.worldbank.org/INTURBANTRANSPORT/Resources/2014-Feb-5-Gender-and-Mobility.pdf.

Plantenga, J., and C. Remery. 2009. *The Provision of Childcare Services: A Comparative Review of 30 European Countries.* Luxembourg: Office for Official Publications of the European Communities.

Urzúa, S., and G. Veramendi. 2011. "The Impact of Out-of-Home Childcare Centers on Early Childhood Development." Working Paper 240, Inter-American Development Bank, Washington, DC. Available at http://www.iadb.org/en/research-and-data/publication-details,3169.html?pub_id=IDB-WP-240.

Vegas, E., and A. Jaimovich. 2016. "The Importance of Early Childhood for Education and Development." In *Routledge Handbook on International Education and Development*, edited by S. McGrath and Q. Gu. New York: Routledge.

World Development Indicators (database). World Bank, Washington, DC. http://data.worldbank.org/data-catalog/world-development-indicators.

CHAPTER 5

Features of Formal Childcare in Latin America and the Caribbean

This chapter represents a major effort of collection, systematization, and analysis of information about the supply and operation of childcare services in Latin America and the Caribbean (LAC).[1] The first section maps 40 childcare programs in 21 LAC countries.[2] The second section examines public sector programs.[3] The third section looks at private provision.

Features of Formal Childcare Programs

Differences in the institutional architecture and entities responsible for early childhood programs reflect the different objectives behind public policies on childcare. Tension always exists between the components of education and care; the degree of emphasis depends on the age of the children and whether the main objective is to support labor participation by parents or support child development. Enrollment criteria reflect these decisions. If, for example, one of the objectives of the program is to support working families, only working parents may be eligible.

In the description of features of childcare programs, the focus is on program features that make childcare a viable and convenient option for working parents. They include the population targeted (working families, vulnerable households, all children); age requirements for children; schedules; coverage and location of programs; models of operation (home-based or center-based); prices and fees; and transitions between programs (parental leave, childcare, school) (table 5.1; for figures on coverage, monthly costs per child, and private childcare centers, see annex 5A).

119

TABLE 5.1 Number of "convenience" features of childcare programs in selected countries in Latin America and the Caribbean

Country	Program	Number of convenience factors						
		1	2	3	4	5	6	7
Bahamas, The	Day Care Services, Early Childhood Development Centre (ECDC)							
Costa Rica	Centros de Educación y Nutrición y Centros Infantiles de Atención Integral (CEN-CINAI)							
Ecuador	Centros Infantiles del Buen Vivir, Ministerio de Inclusión Económica y Social (MIES)							
Honduras	Centros de Atención Integral, Instituto Hondureño de la Niñez y la Familia (IHNFA)							
Bolivia	Programa de Desarrollo Inicial, Servicio Departamental de Gestión Social (SEDEGES), La Paz							
Chile	Fundación Integra							
Chile	Junta Nacional de Jardines Infantiles (JUNJI)							
Dominican Republic	Estancias Infantiles, Instituto Dominicano de Seguros Sociales (IDSS)							
Guatemala	Hogares Comunitarios, Secretaría de Obras Sociales de la Esposa del Presidente (SOSEP)							
Mexico	Centros de Desarrollo Infantil Distrito Federal (CENDI DF), Secretaría de Educación Pública Distrito Federal (SEP-DF)							
Mexico	Estancias Infantiles del Instituto de Seguridad y Servicios Sociales de los Trabajadores del Estado (ISSSTE)							
Mexico	Guarderías, Instituto Mexicano del Seguro Social (IMSS)							
Peru	Cuna Más							
Paraguay	Programa Nacional Abrazo, Centros de Protección							
Uruguay	Plan Centros de Atención a la Infancia y a la Familia (CAIF)							
Argentina	Centros de Primera Infancia (CPI), Buenos Aires							
Chile	Programa de Mejoramiento a la Infancia, JUNJI							
Dominican Republic	Programa de Atención Integral a la Primera Infancia, Consejo Nacional para la Niñez y la Adolescencia (CONANI)							

(continued on next page)

TABLE 5.1 Number of "conven ence" features of childcare programs in selected countries in Latin America and the Caribbean *(continued)*

Country	Program	Number of convenience factors						
		1	2	3	4	5	6	7
El Salvador	Centros de Bienestar Infantil, Instituto Salvadoreño para el Desarrollo Integral de la Niñez y la Adolescencia (CBI ISNA)							
Guatemala	Programa de Atención Integral al Niño Menor de Seis Años (PAIN)							
Mexico	Estancias Infantiles, Secretaría de Desarrollo Social (SEDESOL)							
Nicaragua	Centros de Desarrollo Infantil (CDI)							
Panama	Centro de Orientación Infantil y Familiar (COIF)							
Argentina	Jardines Infantiles, Buenos Aires							
Barbados	Day Care Centre, Child Care Board							
Brazil	Centros de Educação Infantil, Fortaleza							
Chile	Centros Educativo, Culturales de Infancia, JUNJI							
Colombia	Hogares Comunitarios, Instituto Colombiano de Bienestar Familiar (ICBF)							
Colombia	Modalidad Institucional, Instituto Colombiano de Bienestar Familiar (ICBF)							
Nicaragua	Centros Infantiles Comunitarios (CICO)							
Paraguay	Programa Nacional Abrazo, Centros Comunitarios							
Brazil	Espaço de Desenvolvimento Infantil, Rio de Janeiro							
El Salvador	Centros de Desarrollo Integral, Instituto Salvadoreño para el Desarrollo Integral de la Niñez y la Adolescencia (CDI ISNA)							
Jamaica	Early Childhood Commission (ECC)							
Mexico	Centros de Educación Inicial, Secretaría de Educación Pública Distrito Federal (SEP-DF)							
Panama	Centros de Educación Inicial Comunitarios (CEIC), Ministerio de Educación (MEDUCA)							
Panama	Centros Familiares y Comunitarios de Educación Inicial (CEFACEI), MEDUCA							

(continued on next page)

TABLE 5.1 Number of "convenience" features of childcare programs in selected countries in Latin America and the Caribbean *(continued)*

Country	Program	Number of convenience factors						
		1	2	3	4	5	6	7
Trinidad and Tobago	Early Childhood Care and Education Centers (ECCEC)							
Mexico	Jardines Infantiles, SEP-DF							
Number of programs		1	7	8	8	11	3	1

Source: Authors' elaboration based on administrative data.
Note: Features include parents' occupational status; age at which children are accepted; schedules (full day); schedules (extended day); schedules (full year); distribution of centers; and fees. Each feature was coded as a dummy variable (0 if the feature was absent, 1 if it was present). For occupational status, a value of 1 was given if parents' occupational status was part of the targeting criteria, and 0 otherwise. For age, a value of 1 was given if the program accepts children younger than six months; a value of 0 was given otherwise. For schedules, a value of 1 was given if programs run full day, extended day, or full year, and 0 otherwise (three variables). The distributions of centers was calculated as the ratio between the number of children enrolled and the number of centers in the program. A value of 1 was given if value was below average (80.5 children/center); a value of 0 was given if the value was above average. A value of 1 was given to programs without fees; and value of 0 was given to programs with fees.

The number of convenience factors ranges from one to seven. Most programs include three to five.

Most the programs (29 of 40) emphasize early childhood development in their mission. Programs whose objective was to support parents' labor market decisions tend to accept children at an earlier age, to focus more on care than educational aspects, and to be open longer hours (usually matching parents' work schedules). Programs that were conceived and designed with a particular emphasis evolved during implementation, however, mainly as a result of changes in supply and demand: Some programs conceived to focus on stimulation progressively incorporated features to respond to working families' needs, and some programs with a strong emphasis on supporting female labor force participation (FLFP) incorporated or strengthened stimulation components.

Target Population

Of the 40 programs analyzed, 12 (30 percent) admit all children who meet the age requirements. Of the programs that include targeting criteria, more than half have an income/vulnerability criteria, and 12 (30 percent) include criteria targeting working parents (5 of those programs are counted twice, as they have both vulnerability and occupational status criteria).[4]

Of the 28 programs with targeting criteria, 16 apply specific instruments to identify the target population (for example, a poverty line or exclusion/inclusion criteria used in other social programs already recorded in a government's database). Most programs that seek to facilitate FLFP use specific instruments (such as introducing a clear targeting instrument (such as proof of working status of parents), offering longer service hours, or placing fewer restrictions on age for eligibility) to reach the target population.

Age Requirements

Most programs accept children from 3 months old; particularly programs with an emphasis on FLFP. Almost 70 percent of programs with an emphasis on early child development but just 55 percent of FLFP programs have a curriculum (measured by looking at the presence or absence in the description and program requirements for the operation of childcare centers). A qualitative study by Harris-Van Keuren and Rodríguez Gómez (2013) compares 19 learning guidelines from a selected number of programs in LAC for infants and toddlers younger than 3.

Schedules

Programs can be divided into three groups: part-day programs, full-day programs, and programs that include an extended day program that goes beyond normal service hours (both part-day and full-day programs can offer extended-day options). Of the 40 programs examined, 80 percent offer full-day services. Of the remaining 20 percent, only one targets working families; the emphasis of these programs is on child development and stimulation. Almost a third of all childcare programs have some kind of extended-day option. The proportion of such programs is higher among programs supporting FLFP.

In addition to opening hours, year-round availability is an important component of support for working families. Twenty-four programs (60 percent) offer services 12 months a year; the other 40 percent close for certain periods of the year.

Scale and Location

The scale of childcare programs varies widely (table 5.2). Among national programs, small programs (such as the Centros Educativos Culturales de Infancia [CECI]—a modality of the Junta Nacional de Jardines Infantiles [JUNJI] in Chile, the Centros Infantiles Comunitarios [CICO] in Nicaragua, and the Centros de Desarrollo Integral Instituto Salvadoreño para el Desarrollo Integral de la Niñez y la Adolescencia [CDI ISNA] in El Salvador) serve about 1,500 children. Larger programs, such as Hogares Comunitarios in Colombia, serve more than a million children. The average number of children per center varies greatly. Programs in The Bahamas, Chile, Colombia, Panama, and Peru have fewer than 25 children per center; the Programa Nacional Abrazo in Paraguay has more than 250.

TABLE 5.2 Numbers of centers and children served by selected childcare programs in Latin America and the Caribbean

Program	Country	Number of centers	Number of children enrolled
National programs			
Hogares Comunitarios	Colombia	65,550	1,058,593
Modalidad Institucional, Instituto Colombiano de Bienestar Familiar (ICBF)	Colombia	8,343	701,961
Estancias Infantiles, Secretaría de Desarrollo Social (SEDESOL)	Mexico	9,410	268,577
Jardines, Secretaría de Educación Pública (SEP)	Mexico	2,661	237,643
Guarderias, Instituto Mexicano del Seguro Social (IMSS)	Mexico	1,418	209,056
Junta Nacional de Jardines Infantiles (JUNJI)	Chile	2,498	168,883
Centros Asistenciales de Desarrollo Infantil (CADI) y Centros de Atención Infantil Comunitarios (CAIC), Desarrollo Integral de la Familia (DIF)	Mexico	—	133,911
Early Childhood Commission (ECC)	Jamaica	1784	107,691
Centros Infantiles del Buen Vivir	Ecuador	2,349	93,226
Fundación Integra	Chile	1,046	73,185
Cuna Más	Peru	5,732	56,766
Plan Centros de Atención a la Infancia y a la Familia (CAIF)	Uruguay	347	45,549
Estancias Infantiles, Instituto de Seguridad y Servicios Sociales de los Trabajadores del Estado (ISSSTE)	Mexico	242	34,318
Centros Familiares y Comunitarios de Educación Inicial (CEFACEI)	Panama	1,100	22,226
Programa de Atención Integral al Niño Menor de Seis Años (PAIN)	Guatemala	340	22,011
Centros de Educación y Nutrición y Centros Infantiles de Atención Integral (CEN-CINAI)	Costa Rica	625	19,100
Hogares Comunitarios, Secretaría de Obras Sociales de la Esposa del Presidente (SOSEP)	Guatemala	795	16,024
Estancias Infantiles (EI)	Dominican Republic	114	8,325
Consejo Nacional para la Niñez y la Adolescencia (CONANI)	Dominican Republic	52	7,910
Centros de Desarrollo Infantil (CDI)	Nicaragua	62	7,800
Early Childhood Care and Education Centers (ECCEC)	Trinidad and Tobago	193	7,224
Daycare Centre, Child Care Board (CCB)	Barbados	82	7,032

(continued on next page)

TABLE 5.2 Numbers of centers and children served by selected childcare programs in Latin America and the Caribbean *(continued)*

Program	Country	Number of centers	Number of children enrolled
National programs			
Centros de Bienestar Infantil (CBI ISNA)	El Salvador	191	5,854
Programa de Desarrollo Inicial (PDI)	Bolivia	127	5,353
Centros de Desarrollo Infantil (CENDI DF)	Mexico	29	5,311
Programa Nacional Abrazo, Centros de Protección	Paraguay	14	3,813
Centro de Orientación Infantil y Familiar (COIF)	Panama	102	3,574
Junta Nacional de Jardines Infantiles, Programa de Mejoramiento a la Infancia (JUNJI, PMI)	Chile	136	2,352
Programa Nacional Abrazo, Centros Comunitarios	Paraguay	20	2,246
Instituto Hondureño de la Niñez y la Familia (IHNFA)	Honduras	34	1,997
Centros de Educación Inicial Comunitarios (CEIC)	Panama	222	1,776
Day Care Services	Barbados	250	1,700
JUNJI, Centro Educativo Cultural de Infancia (CECI)	Chile	115	1,697
Centros Infantiles Comunitarios (CICC)	Nicaragua	20	1,549
Centros de Desarrollo Integral (CDI ISNA)	El Salvador	15	1,428
Centros de Educación Inicial (CEI)	Mexico	2	199
Subnational programs			
Creche Pública Rio de Janeiro	Brazil	1,269	130,006
Jardines Infantiles	Argentina	383	46,818
Creches Públicas Fortaleza	Brazil	135	32,232
Centros de Primera Infancia (CPI)	Argentina	50	6,400
Total		107,857	3,561,316

Source: Authors' elaboration based on administrative data.
Note: — = Not available.

For programs for which there is an estimate of the eligible population (The Bahamas, Barbados, Chile, Colombia, Costa Rica, the Dominican Republic, Ecuador, Jamaica, Mexico, Nicaragua, Peru, Trinidad and Tobago), rates of coverage range from 3 percent (Estancias Infantiles in the Dominican Republic) to 85 percent (Early Childhood Commission [ECC] in Jamaica) (see annex 5A). Some very large programs, such as Hogares Comunitarios in Colombia, leave a large part of the eligible population (more than 60 percent) unserved, and some small programs, such as ECC in Jamaica, have almost full coverage (more than 80 percent).

Figure 5.1 shows the percent of all children in the covered age group each program reaches. These figures range from less than 5 percent to more than 50 percent.

The location of centers is also important in determining the use of childcare. For a given number of centers, take-up will be greater if they are located closer to workplaces.

Center-Based and Home-Based Models of Operation

There are two main operation models, center-based and home-based. Center-based programs function in licensed premises, sometimes used exclusively as childcare centers, sometimes part of community spaces with multipurpose use. Home-based programs care for children in homes. The only purely home-based programs are Hogares Comunitarios in Guatemala and Hogares Comunitarios in Colombia (see annex 5A for details).

FIGURE 5.1 Shares of all children in eligible age group that are enrolled in formal childcare programs in selected countries in Latin America and the Caribbean

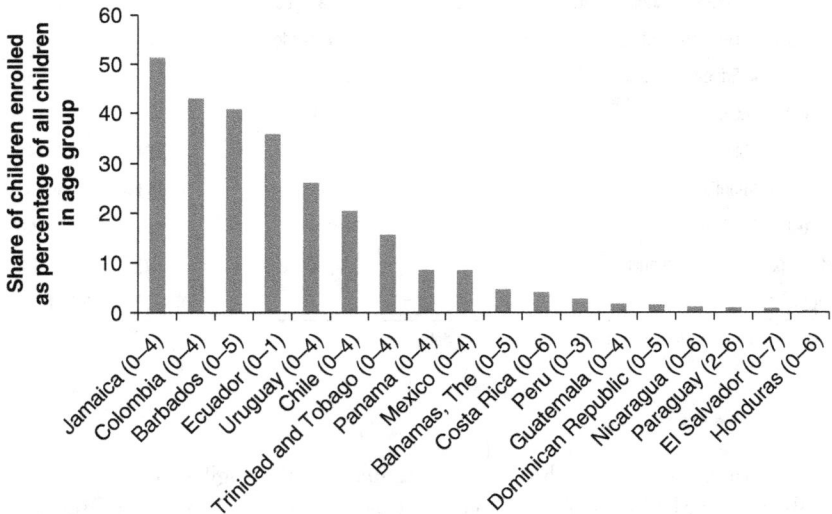

Source: Authors' elaboration based on administrative data.
Note: Data on coverage of programs are based on administrative data provided by program directors. Numbers of children in age group come from census data for 2012 in Chile; 2011 in Costa Rica, Jamaica, Trinidad and Tobago, and Uruguay; 2010 in The Bahamas, Barbados, Dominican Republic, Ecuador, Mexico, and Panama; 2007 in El Salvador and Peru; 2005 in Colombia and Nicaragua; 2002 in Paraguay; and 2001 in Honduras. Data for Guatemala are from Population Prospects from the Instituto Nacional de Estadística (INE) Guatemala 2013.

The vast majority of programs are provided at dedicated centers. The second-most common arrangement is the use of community spaces, such as libraries or community centers.

A few programs combine center-based and home-based operations. Examples include the Day Care Centre/Child Care Board program in Barbados; the Early Childhood Commission (ECC) program in Jamaica; Estancias Infantil, Secretaría de Desarrollo Social (SEDESOL) in Mexico; and Cuna Más in Peru.

Prices and Fees

Seventy percent of the public childcare programs studied (28 of 40) do not charge parents fees (table 5.3). Programs that do require some monetary contribution charge monthly fees that represent 2–16 percent of monthly household per capita income.

TABLE 5.3 Fees charged by selected childcare programs in Latin America and the Caribbean

Program	Country	Monthly fee (US dollars)	Percentage of average household per capita income
Programs that charge fees			
Centros de Desarrollo Infantil (CDI)	Nicaragua	12.0	16.1
Estancias Infantiles, Secretaría de Desarrollo Social (SEDESOL)	Mexico	34.0	13.1
Centros de Educación Inicial, Secretaría de Educación Pública Distrito Federal (SEP-DF)	Mexico	27.0	10.3
Estancias Infantiles, Instituto Dominicano de Seguros Sociales (IDSS)	Dominican Republic	19.0	10.0
Jardines Infantiles (SEP-DF)	Mexico	25.0	9.6
Centros de Desarrollo Integral Instituto Salvadoreño para el Desarrollo Integral de la Niñez y la Adolescencia, Instituto Salvadoreño para el Desarrollo Integra de la Niñez y la Adolescencia (CDI ISNA)	El Salvador	1.5	9.0
Programa de Desarrollo Inicial, Servicio Departamental de Gestión Social La Paz (SEDEGES)	Bolivia	14.5	8.8
Centro de Orientación Infantil y Familiar (COIF)	Panama	25.6	7.2
Centros de Primera Infancia (CPI)	Argentina	29.3	4.4
Hogares Comunitarios, Instituto Colombiano de Bienestar Familiar (ICBF)	Colombia	6.3	2.2

(continued on next page)

TABLE 5.3 Fees charged by selected childcare programs in Latin America and the Caribbean *(continued)*

Program	Country	Monthly fee (US dollars)	Percentage of average household per capita income
Programs that charge no fees (100% publicly funded)			
Jardines Infantiles	Argentina		
Day Care Services, Early Childhood Development Centre (ECDC)	Bahamas, The		
Espaços de Desarrollo Infantil	Brazil		
Atención en Educación Infantil	Brazil		
Fundación Integra	Chile		
Junta Nacional de Jardines Infantiles (JUNJI)	Chile		
Programa de Mejoramiento a la Infancia (PMI) (JUNJI)	Chile		
Centro Educativo Cultural de Infancia (CECI) (JUNJI)	Chile		
Modalidad Institucional (ICBF)	Colombia		
Centros de Educación y Nutrición y Centros Infantiles de Atención Integral (CEN-CINAI)	Costa Rica		
Programa de Atención Integral a la Primera Infancia, Consejo Nacional para la Niñez y la Adolescencia (CONANI)	Dominican Republic		
Centros Infantiles del Buen Vivir, Ministerio de Inclusión Económica y Social (MIES)	Ecuador		
Centros de Bienestar Infantil, Instituto Salvadoreño para el Desarrollo Integral de la Niñez y la Adolescencia (CBI ISNA)	El Salvador		
Hogares Comunitarios, Secretaría de Obras Sociales de la Esposa del Presidente (SOSEP)	Guatemala		
Programa de Atención Integral al Niño Menor de Seis Años (PAIN)	Guatemala		
Centros de Atención Integral, Instituto Hondureño de la Niñez y la Familia (IHNFA)	Honduras		
Centros de Desarrollo Infantil Distrito Federal (CENDI DF) (SEP-DF)	Mexico		
Guarderías, Instituto Mexicano del Seguro Social (IMSS)	Mexico		
Estancias Infantiles, Instituto de Seguridad y Servicios Sociales de los Trabajadores del Estado (ISSSTE)	Mexico		
Centros Infantiles Comunitarios (CICO)	Nicaragua		
Centros Familiares y Comunitarios de Educación Inicial (CEFACEI), Ministerio de Educación (MEDUCA)	Panama		
Centros de Educación Inicial Comunitarios (CEIC) (MEDUCA)	Panama		

(continued on next page)

TABLE 5.3 Fees charged by selected childcare programs in Latin America and the Caribbean *(continued)*

Program	Country	Monthly fee (US dollars)	Percentage of average household per capita income
Programs that charge no fees (100% publicly funded)			
Programa Nacional Abrazo, Centros Comunitarios	Paraguay		
Programa Nacional Abrazo, Centros de Protección	Paraguay		
Cuna Más	Peru		
Early Childhood Care and Education Centers (ECCEC)	Trinidad and Tobago		
Plan Centros de Atención a la Infancia y a la Familia (CAIF)	Uruguay		

Source: Authors' elaboration based on administrative data and Household Survey data.
Note: Information on average fees was not available for Barbados or Jamaica.

The programs in Jamaica (Early Childhood Commission) and Mexico (SEDESOL) are exceptional in that centers can charge fees that exceed the subsidy. These prices are unregulated. The variation can be as extreme as setting different prices for children within the same center. In the case of SEDESOL, an average price estimated from surveys is reflected in the table (Ángeles and others 2011).

Transitions between Parental Leave, Childcare, and Compulsory Education

When should childcare start? How long should parental, maternity, and paternity leave be? Evidence from advanced economies finds a consistent relationship between maternity leave entitlements and the probability of mothers returning to the labor market (see chapter 2). Extending those benefits for too long may be counterproductive for FLFP, however.

All countries in LAC provide maternity leave, and most offer women leave during pregnancy (table 5.4). Less than half of the countries studied (11) offer paternity leave. The duration of maternity leave ranges from 30 days in Bolivia to 24 weeks in Chile and 26 weeks in República Bolivariana de Venezuela for mothers, and from 2 to 14 days for fathers.

In the 11 countries that offer paternity leave, social security pays for benefits in only 3; the employer is liable for benefits in the other 8, probably making it harder for fathers to take advantage of the benefit. In contrast, social security covers 100 percent of the benefit in 15 of the 25 countries that offer maternity leave (60 percent). One-third of countries have a mixed system, in which the cost is shared (in varying proportions) by social security and the employer, with the

TABLE 5.4 Duration and benefits of maternity and paternity leave in selected countries in Latin America and the Caribbean

Country	Maternity leave		Paternity leave	
	Duration	Benefit	Duration	Benefit
Argentina	45–90 days	100% of salary	2 days; 5 days for some public sector workers	100% of salary
Bahamas, The	At least 8 weeks	100% of salary	7 days	Unpaid
Barbados	6 weeks	100% of salary	No paternal leave	None
Belize	7 weeks	100% of salary	No paternal leave	None
Bolivia	30 days	100% of national minimum wage; 75% if more than minimum wage	2 days in public sector; 3 days in private sector	—
Brazil	91 days	100% of salary	5 consecutive days	100% of salary
Chile	24 weeks (following childbirth or adoption)	100% of salary (up to a ceiling)	5 days (following childbirth or adoption)	100% of salary
Colombia	12 weeks (following childbirth or adoption)	100% of salary	8 days (following childbirth or adoption)	100% of salary
Costa Rica	12 weeks (following childbirth or adoption)	100% for 9 months or more of Social Security contributions,75% for 6–9 months of Social Security contributions, 50% for 3–6 months of Social Security contributions	1 week for childbirth	—
Dominican Republic	6 weeks	100% of salary	2 days	100% of salary
Ecuador	10 weeks	100% of salary	10 days; 15 days for multiple births or cesarean; 8 additional days if baby is premature or needs special care; 25 days if child is born with degenerative or terminal illness or severe disability	100% of salary

(continued on next page)

130

TABLE 5.4 Duration and benefits of maternity and paternity leave in selected countries in Latin America and the Caribbean *(continued)*

Country	Maternity leave		Paternity leave	
	Duration	Benefit	Duration	Benefit
El Salvador	6–12 weeks	75% of salary	3 days	100% of salary
Guatemala	54–84 days	100% of salary	2 days	100% of salary
Guyana	7–13 weeks	70% of salary	No paternal leave	None
Haiti	6 weeks	100% of salary	No paternal leave	None
Honduras	12 weeks	100% of salary for 10 weeks	No paternal leave	None
Jamaica	12 weeks	100% of salary for 8 weeks	No paternal leave	None
Mexico	6 weeks (following childbirth or adoption)	100% of salary	5 days for birth or adoption	—
Nicaragua	8–12 weeks (10 weeks in case of multiple births)	100% of salary	No paternal leave	None
Panama	8 weeks	100% of salary	No paternal leave	None
Paraguay	6 weeks	50% of salary for 9 weeks	3 days	100%
Peru	45–90 days; 30 additional days following multiple births	100% of salary	4 days	—
Suriname	12 weeks	—	—	—
Trinidad and Tobago	7–13 weeks	100% of salary	No paternal leave	None
Uruguay	6–13 weeks	100% of salary	3 days in the public sector; 10 days in the private sector	100% of salary

Source: National legislation; Addati, Cassirer, and Gilchrist 2014.
Note: — = Not available.

131

employer shouldering 25–50 percent. In only two countries, Haiti and Jamaica, is the employer liable for 100 percent of these benefits (these calculations exclude Suriname, for which very limited information was available).

In many countries, public childcare is not available right after maternity leave ends. Belize has no public childcare program, creating a gap of almost five years (after seven weeks of maternity leave) to be bridged by working parents alone. Brazil's two subnational public programs accept children from seven months or one year of age; maternity leave grants three months, creating a gap of several months. Maternity leave in Colombia is 12 weeks. The Modalidad Institucional of the Instituto Colombiano de Bienestar Familiar (ICBF) accepts children from six months; its other national program (Hogares Comunitarios) covers the gap. The publicly subsidized program in Ecuador accepts children from age 1, but maternity leave covers only 10 weeks. In Barbados, El Salvador, and Peru, the uncovered period is three months.[5] Public childcare in Jamaica and Trinidad and Tobago starts only at age 3.[6]

The second transition is the passage between childcare and formal education. Figure 5.2 maps the childcare, preschool, and compulsory school programs in each country by age group. The only country offering extended hours at all centers is The Bahamas. Centros de Primera Infancia (CPI) in Argentina; Fundación Integra in Chile; Centros de Educación y Nutrición y Centros Infantiles de Atención Integral (CEN-CINAI) in Costa Rica; Centros Infantiles del Buen Vivir in Ecuador; Early Childhood Commission in Jamaica; Estancias Infantiles (SEDESOL) and Guarderias (Instituto Mexicano del Seguro Social [IMSS]) in Mexico; Programa Nacional Abrazo, Centros de Protección in Paraguay; and Plan Centros de Atención a la Infancia y a la Familia (CAIF) in Uruguay offer extended hours at some but not all centers.

The trend in LAC has been a move toward universal schooling for 5-year-olds and in some cases to include one or two years of initial education (figure 5.3), as in Organisation for Economic Co-operation and Development (OECD) countries. Compulsory education starts at age 5 in ten countries and at or after age 6 in nine countries (age 7 in El Salvador and Suriname). Education is mandatory for children 3 or 4 in Bolivia, Brazil, Ecuador, Mexico, Panama, Uruguay, and República Bolivariana de Venezuela. Compulsory school tends to be part-time, although several countries (Argentina, Chile, Colombia, Mexico, Uruguay, and República Bolivariana de Venezuela) have progressively extended the school day.[7] The duration of the day and of extended days differs across countries. In some countries, a full school day is six or seven hours; extended days in some countries add about 10 percent.

Families of children enrolled in three-quarters of all programs could face difficult transitions. The most difficult transitions exist where childcare stops before the compulsory school age (Cuna Más in Peru and Early Childhood Care and Education Centers [ECCEC] in Trinidad and Tobago) and the childcare program is full-time but the school day is part-time or does not completely cover the working schedule.

FIGURE 5.2 Integration of childcare, preschool, and compulsory education programs in selected countries in Latin America and the Caribbean

	Childcare				Preschool		Compulsory school	
Country	0	1	2	3	4	5	6	7
Argentina	Centros de Primera Infancia (CPI)							
	Jardines Infantiles							
Bahamas, The	Day Care Services, Early Childhood Development Centre (ECDC)							
Barbados	Day Care Centre, Child Care Board (CCB)							
Belize								
Bolivia	Programa de Desarrollo Inicial (Servicio Departamental de Gestión Social [SEDEGES]) La Paz							
Brazil	Espaço de Desenvolvimento Infantil, Rio de Janeiro							
	Centros de Educação Infantil, Fortaleza							
Chile	Fundación Integra							
	Junta Nacional de Jardines Infantiles (JUNJI)							
	Programa de Mejoramiento a la Infancia (PMI) (JUNJI)							
	Centro Educativo Cultural de Infancia (CECI) (JUNJI)							
Colombia	Hogares Comunitarios (Instituto Colombiano de Bienestar Familiar [ICBF])							
	Modalidad Institucional (ICBF)							
Costa Rica	Centros de Educación y Nutrición y Centros Infantiles de Atención Integral (CEN-CINAI)							
Dominican Republic	Estancias Infantiles (Instituto Dominicano del Seguro Social [IDSS])							
	Programa de Atención Integral a la Primera Infancia (Consejo Nacional para la Niñez y la Adolescencia [CONANI])							
Ecuador	Centros Infantiles del Buen Vivir							
El Salvador	Centros de Desarrollo Integral (Instituto Salvadoreño para el Desarrollo Integral de la Niñez y la Adolescencia [CDI ISNA])							
	Centros de Bienestar Infantil (CBI ISNA)							
Guatemala	Hogares Comunitarios (Secretaría de Obras Sociales de la Esposa del Presidente [SOSEP])							
	Programa de Atención Integral al Niño Menor de Seis Años (PAIN)							
Honduras	Centros de Atención Integral (Instituto Hondureño de la Niñez y la Familia [IHNFA])							
Jamaica	Early Childhood Commission (ECC)							
Mexico	Guarderías (Instituto Mexicano del Seguro Social [IMSS])							
	Estancias Infantiles (Instituto de Seguridad y Servicios Sociales de los Trabajadores del Estado [ISSSTE])							
	Estancias Infantiles (Secretaría de Desarrollo Social [SEDESOL])							
	Centros de Desarrollo Infantil (CENDI SEP)							
	Jardines (SEP)							
	Centros de Educacion Inicial (CEI SEP)							
	Centros de Asistencia Infantil Comunitarios (CAIC) (Desarrollo Integral de la Familia [DIF])							
	Centros Asistenciales de Desarrollo Infantil Comunitario (CADI) (DIF)							
Nicaragua	Centros de Desarrollo Infantil (CDI)							
	Centros Infantiles Comunitarios (CICO)							
Panama	Centro de Orientación Infantil y Familiar (COIF)							
	Centros de Educación Inicial Comunitarios (CEIC)							
	Centros Familiares y Comunitarios de Educación Inicial (CEFACEI)							
Paraguay	Programa Nacional Abrazo, Centros de Protección							
	Programa Nacional Abrazo, Centros Comunitarios							
Peru	Cuna Más							
Trinidad and Tobago	Early Childhood Care and Education Centers (ECCEC)							
Uruguay	Plan Centros de Atención a la Infancia y a la Familia (CAIF)							

▨ Full-time (5–8 hours)   ▨ Part time (up to 5 hours)   ☐ Extended hours (more than 8 hours)

Note: Figures at top of figure indicate age of children. Information was not available for Guyana, Haiti, Suriname, or República Bolivariana de Venezuela.

FIGURE 5.3 Starting age of compulsory education in selected countries in Latin America and the Caribbean

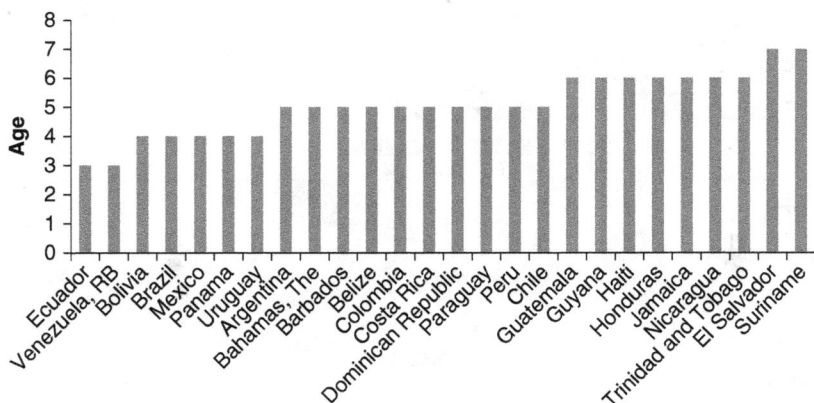

Source: National legislation; UNESCO (http://data.un.org/); administrative data.

After-school programs are not widespread in LAC. A qualitative study in Mexico based on focus group interviews with mothers of young children in four cities revealed that some private childcare centers offer before- and after-school care for children attending public preschool:

> There are seven teachers in my son's childcare center . . . (one takes care of) the youngest children; (another takes care of) 1-year-olds; (then another takes care of) 2-year-olds; and then one for the 3- and 4-year-olds and someone else to take the children to kindergarten, because they also have kindergarten-aged children . . . and the teachers take them there . . . So, for example, if you start work at 8 and drop off your child at this time, they take the children to kindergarten at 9. At 2 they pick the children up from kindergarten, and at 5 you go to the center to take your child home.

Public Supply of Childcare

History of Formal Childcare in Latin America and the Caribbean

Early childhood care and education began in the region at different points. The creation of establishments for young children was initially part of public programs for children from families that were unable to take care of them, primarily because of poverty (UNESCO 2010). The first early education centers in the region were created at the end of the 19th and beginning of the 20th centuries.[8] Known as *jardines infantiles, escuelas para parvulos,* or kindergartens, they were aimed at

5-year-olds and were generally incorporated into primary schools. The objectives of these programs were diverse. Some public programs targeted children from families without sufficient means to raise them at home. Many private programs sought to provide early stimulation for children from families that could afford it (UNESCO 2010).

The number of childcare and early education programs expanded in the 1970s, in some cases accompanied by an increase in FLFP. In Colombia, preschool centers for children 0–6 of public employees and working parents in the formal private sector were created in 1974. In Mexico, childcare centers for working mothers in the formal sector began operating in the 1970s (the Instituto de Seguridad y Servicios Sociales de los Trabajadores del Estado [ISSSTE] was established in 1970; the Instituto Mexicano del Seguro Social [IMSS]) in 1973).[9] Chile developed the National Childcare Center Board (Junta Nacional de Jardines Infantiles [JUNJI]) in 1970; its emphasis was on child well-being and development rather than support of working families.

The 1980s and 1990s were characterized by an expansion of coverage in response to the increasing demand and growing needs of working mothers. During the 1990s, new modalities of provision were established in order to expand enrollment. In Mexico, for example, direct public provision by IMSS and ISSSTE was complemented with outsourced centers.[10]

Description of Current Programs

The public childcare programs examined are administered at the national level in 17 countries. Although partnerships and cooperation with local governments may exist, all the programs are under the administration of a national public entity.[11] In Argentina and Brazil, childcare programs are under the local administration of municipalities; in Bolivia the program is run by the departmental government through the Servicio Departamental de Gestión Social (SEDEGES). Of the seven programs identified in Mexico, three are administered nationally, three are managed by the Ministry of Education of each of the 32 states, and one is managed by local chapters (municipal presidents and state governors) of the National System for Integral Family Development (Sistema Nacional para el Desarrollo Integral de la Familia [DIF]).

Figure 5.4 presents selected examples of decentralized interventions by nationally operated programs. (Given their dispersion in different geographical units and administrative bodies, it would have been very difficult to obtain information on locally run programs. It is often hard for local governments to allocate time and resources to answer information requests, and there are no national registries for these programs.)

Figure 5.4 shows wide dispersion in the allocation of responsibilities for these programs, not only between but also within countries. Five ministries (education,

FIGURE 5.4 Selected publicly supported childcare programs in Latin America and the Caribbean, by year of implementation and institution in charge

Year of implementation: 1920, 1930, 1940, 1950, 1960, 1970, 1980, 1990, 2000, 2010, 2014

Program (year of implementation)	Institution in charge of program's operation
Mexico: Jardines Secretaría de Educación Pública (SEP) 1928	Ministry of Education
Mexico: Centros de Desarrollo Infantil (CENDI) 1976	
Trinidad and Tobago: Early Childhood Care and Education Centers (ECCEC) 1974	
Guatemala: Programa de Atención Integral al Niño Menor de Seis Años (PAIN) 1984	
Panama: Centro Familiar y Comunitario de Educación Inicial (CEFACEI) 1997	
Panama: Centros de Educación Inicial Comunitario (CEIC) 2006	
Jamaica: Early Childhood Commission (ECC) 2003	
The Bahamas: Day Care Services, 1998	
El Salvador: Centros de Desarrollo Instituto Salvadoreño para el Desarrollo Integral de la Niñez y la Adolescencia (CDI ISNA), 1904	Government institution with budget from Ministry of Education
Chile: Junta Nacional de Jardines Infantiles (JUNJI) 1970	
El Salvador: Centros de Bienestar Infantil (CBI ISNA) 1993	
Chile: Programa de Mejoramiento a la Infancia (PMI) (JUNJI) 2007	
Chile: Centro Educativo Cultural de Infancia (CECI) (JUNJI) 2011	Nongovernment institution with budget from Ministry of Education
Chile: Fundación Integra 1979	Ministry of Social Development (inclusion)
Panama: Centro de Orientación Infantil y Familiar (COIF) 1980	
Mexico: Estancias Infantiles (Secretaría de Desarrollo Social [SEDESOL]) 2007	
Ecuador: Centros Infantiles Buen Vivir, 2010	
Peru: Cuna Más, 2012	
Nicaragua: Centros de Desarrollo Infantil (CDI) 1980	Ministry of Family, Childhood and Adolescence
Nicaragua: Centros Infantiles Comunitarios (CICO) 2013	
Costa Rica: Centros de Educación y Nutrición y Centros Infantiles de Atención Integral (CEN-CINAI) 1971	Government institution with budget from Ministry of Health
Barbados: Daycare Centre, Child Care Board (CCB) 1978	Government institution with budget from Ministry of Labor
Colombia: Modalidad Institucional, Instituto Colombiano de Bienestar Familiar (ICBF) 1974	Autonomous government institutions
Mexico: Estancias Infantiles (Instituto de Seguridad y Servicios Sociales de los Trabajadores del Estado [ISSSTE]) 1970	
Mexico: Guarderías, Instituto Mexicano del Seguro Social (IMSS) 1973	
Dominican Republic: Consejo Nacional para la Niñez y la Adolescencia (CONANI) 1980	
Colombia: Hogares Comunitarios (ICBF) 1984	
Uruguay: Plan Centros de Atención a la Infancia y a la Familia (CAIF) 1988	
Dominican Republic: Estancias Infantiles 1990	
Honduras: Instituto Hondureño de la Niñez y la Familia (IHNFA) 1997	
Guatemala: Hogares Comunitarios 1991	Office of the President or the Office of the First Lady
Paraguay: Centros de Protección Programa Abrazo 2009	
Paraguay: Centros Comunitarios Programa Abrazo 2011	
Argentina: Jardines Infantiles, 1940	Local (state/municipal) ministries of education, social development, or decentralized government institution
Mexico: Centros de Asistencia Infantil Comunitarios (CAIC), Desarrollo Integral de la Familia (DIF) 1972	
Mexico: Centros Asistenciales de Desarrollo Infantil (CADI) (DIF) 1991	
Brazil: Centros de Educação Infantil, Fortaleza, 2002	
Argentina: Centros de Primera Infancia (CPI), Buenos Aires 2009	
Brazil: Creches, Rio de Janeiro 2009	
Bolivia: Programa de Desarrollo Inicial (PDI), La Paz 2013	

social development, family, health, and labor) are in charge of programs. The first programs were to some extent dependent on the Ministry of Education (at the national or local level or via a government institution with a budget from the Ministry of Education). This ministry continues to be in charge of more programs than any other ministry. Programs run by autonomous government institutions (institutions that are administratively and financially autonomous and headed by a director and a board) were initiated mainly during the late 1970s and the 1980s. In some cases these institutions were created to coordinate policies specifically for child welfare, including adoptions and children's rights (an example is the Consejo Nacional para la Niñez y la Adolescencia [CONANI] in the Dominican Republic). In other cases they were created to coordinate family welfare, including antipoverty programs (ICBF in Colombia, for example) or to manage social security and employment benefits (IMSS and ISSSTE in Mexico).

Management and Funding of Childcare Programs

Five provision models can be distinguished: unsubsidized private provision, subsidized private provision, subsidized community provision, outsourced public provision, and direct public provision (figure 5.5). Unsubsidized private childcare is provided entirely by a private operator; the public sector has only a regulatory role. Subsidized private childcare is also provided by a private operator but receives financial support from the government. Subsidized community-managed childcare includes programs in which centers that are run by the community and provide formal services receive public funding. Outsourced public childcare is financed entirely by the public sector, but the government pays private operators to run the centers. Public childcare includes programs that are both financed and managed directly by the government.

All the programs included in this study have some public sector involvement. Nationally, 8 percent of public support for childcare programs in LAC is provided through subsidized private childcare, 34 percent through subsidized community management, 29 percent through outsourced public services, and 18 percent through direct public service (figure 5.6). Programs that are administered at the local level (in Argentina, Bolivia, and Brazil) are not included in these figures.

Of the programs analyzed, outsourced public childcare seems to be the most efficient. The range of costs across programs and countries is also the narrowest. The range of costs of entirely publicly provided programs is very wide.

The percentage of total costs covered by public and private sources differs across programs, although most receive most of their funding from the general (national) budget (table 5.5).[12] The other two financing mechanisms are tax revenues from individual income taxes and payroll taxes.

In 2013 Colombia imposed a special tax on individual income (*impuesto sobre la renta para la equidad* [CREE]), known as the fairness tax. Among other items,

FIGURE 5.5 Models of formal childcare

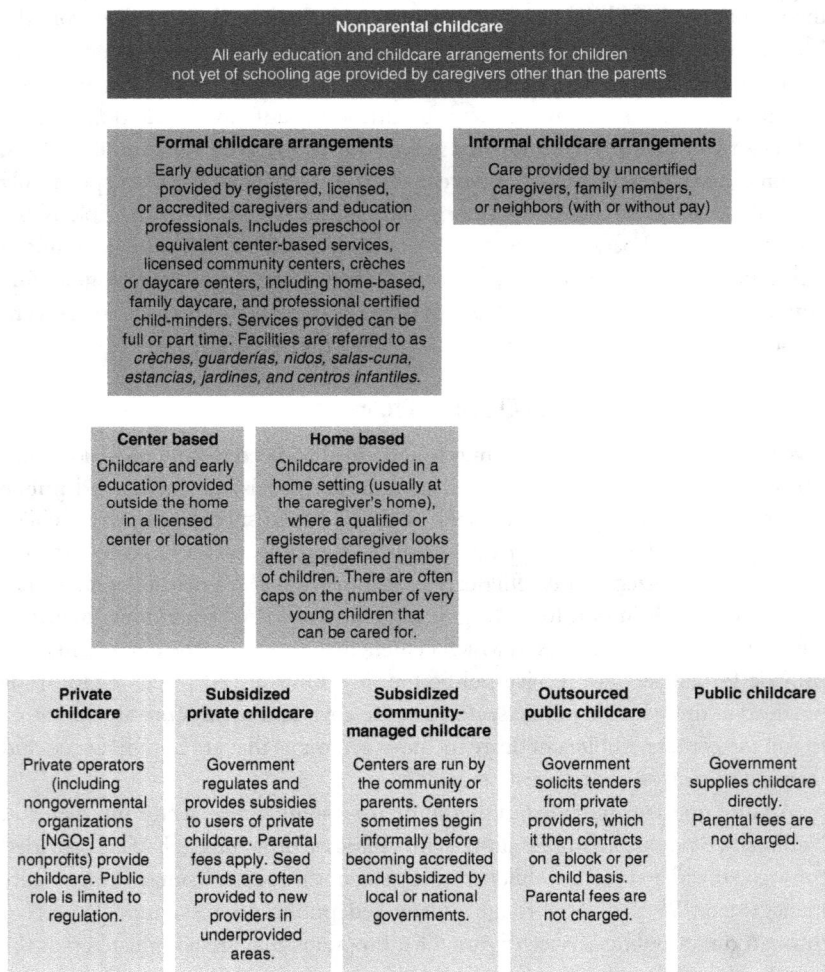

Nonparental childcare
All early education and childcare arrangements for children not yet of schooling age provided by caregivers other than the parents

Formal childcare arrangements	Informal childcare arrangements
Early education and care services provided by registered, licensed, or accredited caregivers and education professionals. Includes preschool or equivalent center-based services, licensed community centers, crèches or daycare centers, including home-based, family daycare, and professional certified child-minders. Services provided can be full or part time. Facilities are referred to as *crèches, guarderías, nidos, salas-cuna, estancias, jardines,* and *centros infantiles.*	Care provided by uncertified caregivers, family members, or neighbors (with or without pay)

Center based	Home based
Childcare and early education provided outside the home in a licensed center or location	Childcare provided in a home setting (usually at the caregiver's home), where a qualified or registered caregiver looks after a predefined number of children. There are often caps on the number of very young children that can be cared for.

Private childcare	Subsidized private childcare	Subsidized community-managed childcare	Outsourced public childcare	Public childcare
Private operators (including nongovernmental organizations [NGOs] and nonprofits) provide childcare. Public role is limited to regulation.	Government regulates and provides subsidies to users of private childcare. Parental fees apply. Seed funds are often provided to new providers in underprovided areas.	Centers are run by the community or parents. Centers sometimes begin informally before becoming accredited and subsidized by local or national governments.	Government solicits tenders from private providers, which it then contracts on a block or per child basis. Parental fees are not charged.	Government supplies childcare directly. Parental fees are not charged.

such as health insurance and national technical education, the CREE pays for family welfare and childcare programs under the Instituto Colombiano de Bienestar Familiar (ICBF), which were previously funded by a payroll tax. Guatemala uses a consumption tax to pay for public childcare. In Mexico IMSS programs are funded by a 0.8 percent payroll tax paid by all employees affiliated with the social security system; these taxes cover 100 percent of the program. For ISSSTE programs, employees contribute 0.5 percent of their base salaries and employers contribute another 0.5 percent.

FIGURE 5.6 Model of childcare provision in countries with nationally administered programs in selected countries in Latin America and the Caribbean

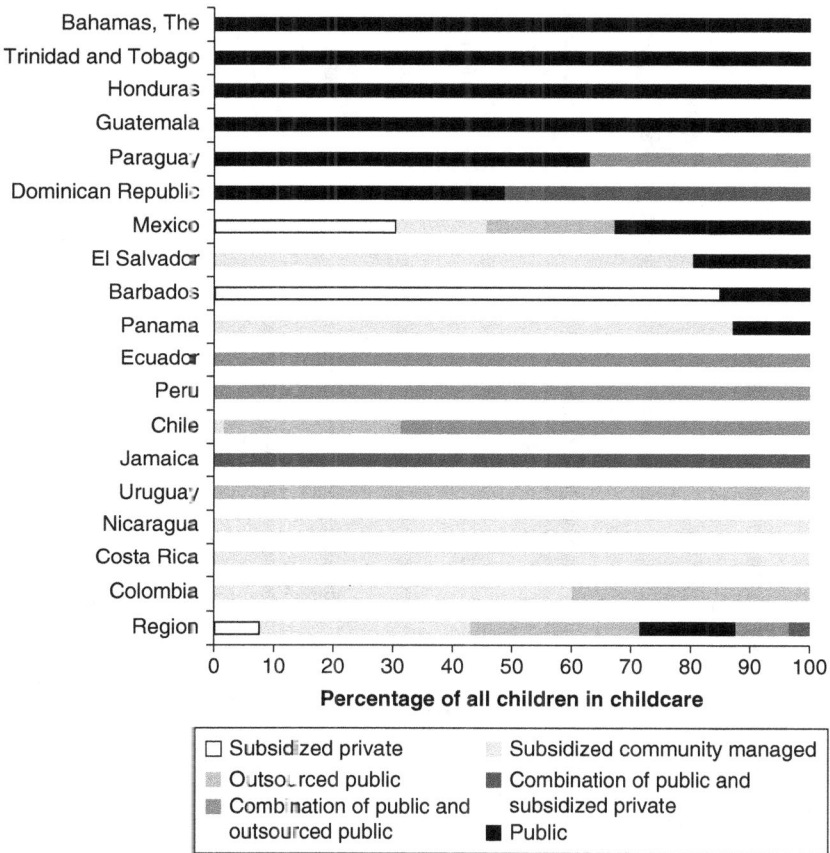

Percentage of all children in childcare

Legend:
- ☐ Subsidized private
- Subsidized community managed
- Outsourced public
- ■ Combination of public and subsidized private
- Combination of public and outsourced public
- ■ Public

More than half of the programs seek to reach the most vulnerable people. Good intentions sometimes translate into bad outcomes, however, to paraphrase the title of a book by Santiago Levy (2008) on social policy, informality, and growth. When unevenly distributed across income levels, differences in take-up can skew the allocation of resources in an undesirable direction.

The quasi-Lorenz curves in figure 5.7 show the distributional outcome of public spending on childcare programs in four countries (Chile, Colombia, Mexico, and Uruguay).[13] Curves above the 45° line indicate disproportionately high spending on lower-income populations; curves below the 45° line indicate disproportionately high spending on higher-income populations. The results show

TABLE 5.5 Funding sources of childcare programs in selected countries in Latin America and the Caribbean

Country/program	Public		Private	
	Percentage of total	Funding source	Percentage of total	Funding source
Bolivia				
Programa de Desarrollo Inicial, Servicio Departamental de Gestión Social (SEDEGES)	—	Federal budget transfer to local government	—	Parental fees
Chile				
Fundación Integra	90	Federal budget	10	Self-administered and private resources
Junta Nacional de Jardines Infantiles (JUNJI)	100	Federal budget	0	n.a.
Colombia				
Hogares Comunitarios, Instituto Colombiano de Bienestar Familiar (ICBF)	—	Tax revenue from individual income tax	—	Parental fees
Modalidad Institucional (ICBF)	100	Tax revenue from individual income tax	0	Parental fees
Costa Rica				
Centros de Educación y Nutrición y Centros Infantiles de Atención Integral (CEN–CINAI)	85	Federal budget	15	Voluntary contributions of families and community
Dominican Republic				
Programa de Atención Integral a la Primera Infancia, Consejo Nacional para la Niñez y la Adolescencia (CONANI)	100	Federal budget	0	n.a.

(continued on next page)

TABLE 5.5 Funding sources of childcare programs in selected countries in Latin America and the Caribbean *(continued)*

Country/program	Public		Private	
	Percentage of total	Funding source	Percentage of total	Funding source
Ecuador				
Centros Infantiles del Buen Vivir, Ministerio de Inclusión Económica y Social (MIES)	85–90	Federal budget	10–15	NGOs, religious associations
El Salvador				
Centros de Bienestar Infantil, Instituto Salvadoreño para el Desarrollo Integral de la Niñez y la Adolescencia (CBI ISNA)	100	Federal budget	0	n.a.
Centros de Desarrollo Integral (CDI ISNA)	—	Federal budget	—	Parental fees
Guatemala				
Hogares Comunitarios, Secretaría de Obras Sociales de la Esposa del Presidente (SOSEP)	100	Federal budget (35%) and consumption tax (65%)	0	n.a.
Programa de Atención Integral al Niño Menor de Seis Años (PAIN)	100	Federal budget	0	n.a.
Jamaica				
Early Childhood Commission (ECC)	—	Federal budget	—	Parental fees

(continued on next page)

TABLE 5.5 Funding sources of childcare programs in selected countries in Latin America and the Caribbean *(continued)*

Country/program	Public		Private	
	Percentage of total	Funding source	Percentage of total	Funding source
Mexico				
Estancias Infantiles, Instituto de Seguridad y Servicios Sociales de los Trabajadores del Estado (ISSSTE)	100	Payroll tax	0	n.a.
Estancias Infantiles, Secretaría de Desarrollo Social (SEDESOL)	67.3	Federal budget	32.7	Parental fees
Guarderías, Instituto Mexicano del Seguro Social (IMSS)	100	Payroll tax	0	n.a.
Nicaragua				
Centros de Desarrollo Infantil (CDI)	75	Federal budget to local government and local	25	
Centros Infantiles Comunitarios (CICO)	100	Federal budget	0	n.a.
Panama				
Centros de Educación Inicial Comunitarios (CEIC), Ministerio de Educación (MEDUCA)	100	Federal budget	0	n.a.
Centros Familiares y Comunitarios de Educación Inicial (CEFACEI) (MEDUCA)	100	Federal budget	0	n.a.

(continued on next page)

TABLE 5.5 Funding sources of childcare programs in selected countries in Latin America and the Caribbean *(continued)*

Country/program	Public		Private	
	Percentage of total	Funding source	Percentage of total	Funding source
Paraguay				
Programa Nacional Abrazo, Centros Comunitarios	100	Federal budget	0	n.a.
Programa Nacional Abrazo, Centros de Protección	100	Federal budget	0	n.a.
Peru				
Cuna Más	100	Federal budget	0	n.a.
Trinidad and Tobago				
Early Childhood Care and Education Centers (ECCEC)	100	Federal budget	0	n.a.
Uruguay				
Plan Centros de Atención a la Infancia y a la Familia (CAIF)	100	Federal budget	0	n.a.

Source: Authors' elaboration based on administrative data.
Note: NGO = Nongovernmental organization; — = Not available; n.a. = Not applicable.

143

FIGURE 5.7 Distributional effect of public spending on childcare programs in Chile, Colombia, Mexico, and Uruguay, 2009

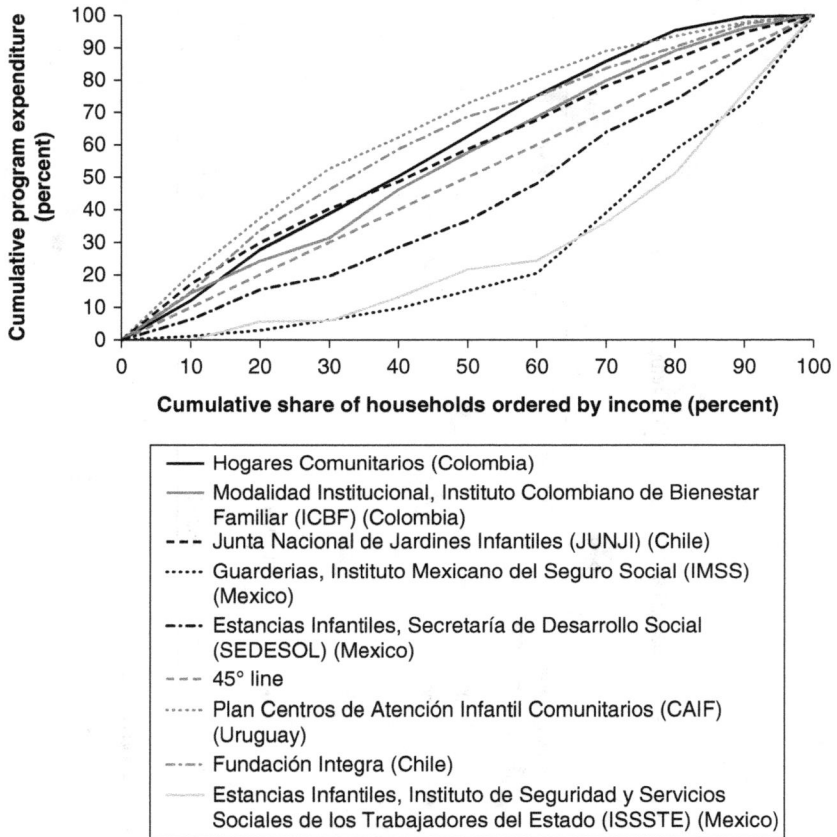

Legend:
- Hogares Comunitarios (Colombia)
- Modalidad Institucional, Instituto Colombiano de Bienestar Familiar (ICBF) (Colombia)
- Junta Nacional de Jardines Infantiles (JUNJI) (Chile)
- Guarderias, Instituto Mexicano del Seguro Social (IMSS) (Mexico)
- Estancias Infantiles, Secretaría de Desarrollo Social (SEDESOL) (Mexico)
- 45° line
- Plan Centros de Atención Infantil Comunitarios (CAIF) (Uruguay)
- Fundación Integra (Chile)
- Estancias Infantiles, Instituto de Seguridad y Servicios Sociales de los Trabajadores del Estado (ISSSTE) (Mexico)

Source: Authors' elaboration based on household surveys.

consistency between the targeting objectives of the programs and their actual spending distribution across income deciles, as the curves for all programs except the Mexican programs (two of which do not include a target criterion based on income or vulnerability) lie above the 45° line.

Mothers of children enrolled in Mexico's ISSSTE and IMSS programs, which do not include an income criterion, are formally employed and tend to be in the upper income quintiles. More problematic is the case of Estancias Infantiles (SEDESOL). Although the program reports targeting the vulnerable, the poorest 50 percent of the population receives less than 40 percent of total public spending on the program.[14]

Private Supply of Childcare

The numbers for private providers of childcare in LAC are unknown, as there is no consolidated registry. According to the surveys and the data on the use of childcare reported in chapter 4, private providers play a secondary role in the provision of services. Out of 10 countries studied, Chile and Nicaragua have the smallest shares of children attending private centers (about 13 percent); Ecuador (32 percent) and Uruguay (37 percent) have the largest shares. The probability of a child attending private childcare is directly associated with household income, according to data from Colombia's 2013 National Quality of Life Survey (Encuesta Nacional de Calidad de Vida [ENCV]).

Table 5.6 summarizes regulations for private provision. Countries in the first group (Argentina, Colombia, the Dominican Republic, Honduras, Panama, and Peru) have specific regulations for private providers of both childcare and preschool. The areas regulated for childcare are very different from the areas regulated for preschool. For the second group of countries (The Bahamas, Belize, Brazil, Chile, Costa Rica, Ecuador, Jamaica, Mexico, Trinidad and Tobago, and Uruguay), specific regulations are evident only for private providers of childcare; legislation for preschool was not found. In Barbados, Bolivia, El Salvador, Guatemala, and Nicaragua, only general regulations for preschool programs cover private childcare; no special regulations govern childcare.

Most countries regulate the age of children; require centers to be registered; and impose safety, infrastructure, and curriculum requirements. Some countries also regulate opening hours and days, group size, and prices. Only three countries (Chile, Costa Rica, and the Dominican Republic) accredit private childcare providers, and only one (the Dominican Republic) requires accreditation.

The differences between daycare and preschool services are reflected mainly in the level of clarity and precision of standards, the diffusion or concentration of regulations in different documents, and the level of consistency between regulations for public and private providers. Educational standards and obligations for private providers are much clearer at the preschool level, with higher consistency between public and private provision guidelines and requirements. In contrast, norms for private providers of childcare in nurseries, crèches, and daycare centers are not integrated within a consistent framework. Regulations for childcare tend to be more scattered across laws, decrees, acts, agreements, and norms than regulations for preschool. Sometimes one aspect of regulation, such as infrastructure, is covered in one legal document while other aspects, such as staff-child ratios, are covered in different ones. In addition, some aspects are regulated at the national level and others at the

TABLE 5.6 Regulations governing private childcare programs in selected countries in Latin America and the Caribbean

Country	Type of regulation											Accreditation	
	Child's age	Registration	Safety	Infrastructure	Curricula	Training of staff	Health	Staff-child ratios	Opening hours/ days	Group size	Price	Exists	Compulsory
Countries that regulate both childcare and preschool													
Argentina	✓	✓	✓	✓	✓	✓	✓	✓					
Colombia	✓	✓	✓	✓		✓		✓					✓
Dominican Republic	✓	✓		✓	✓							✓	
Honduras	✓	✓			✓								
Panama	✓	✓		✓	✓	✓	✓						
Peru	✓	✓	✓	✓	✓	✓		✓	✓	✓	✓		
Countries that regulate childcare but not preschool													
Bahamas, The[a]	✓	✓	✓	✓		✓	✓	✓	✓				
Belize	✓	✓	✓	✓	✓	✓	✓	✓	✓				
Brazil[a]	✓	✓	✓	✓	✓	✓	✓	✓	✓	✓			
Chile[a]	✓	✓	✓	✓	✓	✓		✓	✓			✓	
Costa Rica[a]	✓	✓	✓	✓	✓	✓	✓		✓			✓	
Ecuador[a]	✓	✓	✓	✓	✓	✓	✓		✓	✓			

(continued on next page)

TABLE 5.6 Regulations governing private childcare programs in selected countries in Latin America and the Caribbean *(continued)*

Country	Type of regulation											Accreditation	
	Child's age	Registration	Safety	Infrastructure	Curricula	Training of staff	Health	Staff-child ratios	Opening hours/ days	Group size	Price	Exists	Compulsory
Jamaica[a]	✓	✓	✓	✓	✓	✓	✓	✓	✓				
Mexico[a]	✓	✓	✓	✓		✓		✓	✓	✓			
Trinidad and Tobago[a]	✓	✓	✓	✓	✓	✓	✓	✓					
Uruguay[a]	✓	✓	✓	✓	✓	✓	✓	✓					
Countries in which regulations for preschools cover childcare													
Barbados	✓			✓									
Bolivia	✓	✓	✓	✓	✓	✓		✓		✓			
El Salvador	✓	✓	✓			✓			✓	✓	✓		
Guatemala	✓	✓			✓					✓	✓		
Nicaragua	✓	✓			✓		✓						

Source: Authors' elaboration based on national regulations.

Note: Screened cells indicate that aspect is regulated for preschool. Information on Guyana, Haiti, Paraguay, Suriname, and República Bolivariana de Venezuela was not available.

a. Regulations for private sector are included as part of general legislation for initial education and preschool.

147

local level. The lack of integration reflects the different institutions involved in the provision of services.

It is not possible to draw general conclusions about whether broader regulations should be introduced in the region. Countries need more information about how private supply is structured (the number of centers, their geographic distribution, the size and type of the population served, interactions between public and private supply) to make decisions about regulation. It could be argued that for aspects directly related to the quality of services, there is no reason for different standards between public and private provision; for other aspects (such as fees), the private sector logic will be very different from that of the public sector.

Regulations for social services in general and education in particular should set the conditions required for the private sector to operate efficiently while ensuring the delivery of quality education. Doing so entails establishing clear criteria to open and register private centers. Regulations should be accompanied by an effective quality assurance system based on the disclosure of information about fees, programs, the quality of infrastructure and facilities, curriculum, teacher qualifications, and group sizes that allows consumers and regulators to fully assess each program (Patrinos, Barrera-Osorio, and Guáqueta 2009; Roth 1987). Imposing very restrictive regulations on private providers could reduce supply, especially to the most vulnerable populations. It is therefore important to calibrate the scope of regulations without compromising the quality of services (Bastos and Cristia 2012; Hotz and Xiao 2011; Mateo Díaz, Rodriguez-Chamussy and Grafe 2014).

Several countries have attempted to integrate program regulations or synchronize the operation of diverse institutions in one all-encompassing regulation. Uruguay has integrated childcare center legislation in the Education Law. Three countries have single pieces of legislation concerning early childhood education and care: the Early Childhood Act in The Bahamas; the *Ley General para las Guarderías Infantiles y Hogares Escuela* (General Law for Childcare and Schooling Homes) in Costa Rica; and the 2014 Acuerdo 0024 in Ecuador, which regulates education services (public, private, and mixed) for children 0–5. In 2012 Mexico published a regulatory framework for all nursery schools and childcare centers (private, public, and mixed). The law, which creates a unified information registry for all centers providing care and education services for children between the ages of 43 days and 4 years, came in response to the need to ensure safety. It faces implementation challenges, especially effective interinstitutional coordination (Mateo Díaz, Rodriguez-Chamussy, and Grafe 2014).

Annex 5A: Descriptions of Childcare Programs in Latin America and the Caribbean

FIGURE 5A.1 Coverage of selected childcare programs in Latin America and the Caribbean

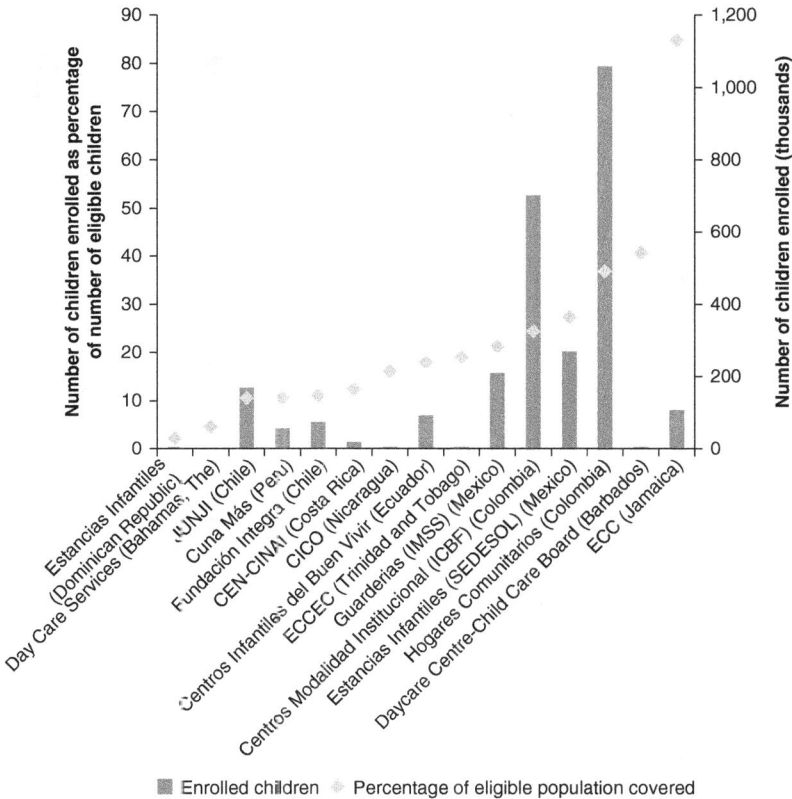

■ Enrolled children ◈ Percentage of eligible population covered

Source: Authors' elaboration based on administrative data and Household Survey data.
Note: Figure includes only countries for which estimates of target population were available. CEN-CINAI: Centros de Educación y Nutrición y Centros Infantiles de Atención Integral; CICO: Centros Infantiles Comunitarios; ECC: Early Childhood Commission; ECCEC: Early Childhood Care and Education Centers; ICBF: Instituto Colombiano de Bienestar Familiar; IMSS: Instituto Mexicano del Seguro Social; JUNJI: Junta Nacional de Jardines Infantiles; SEDESOL: Secretaría de Desarrollo Social.

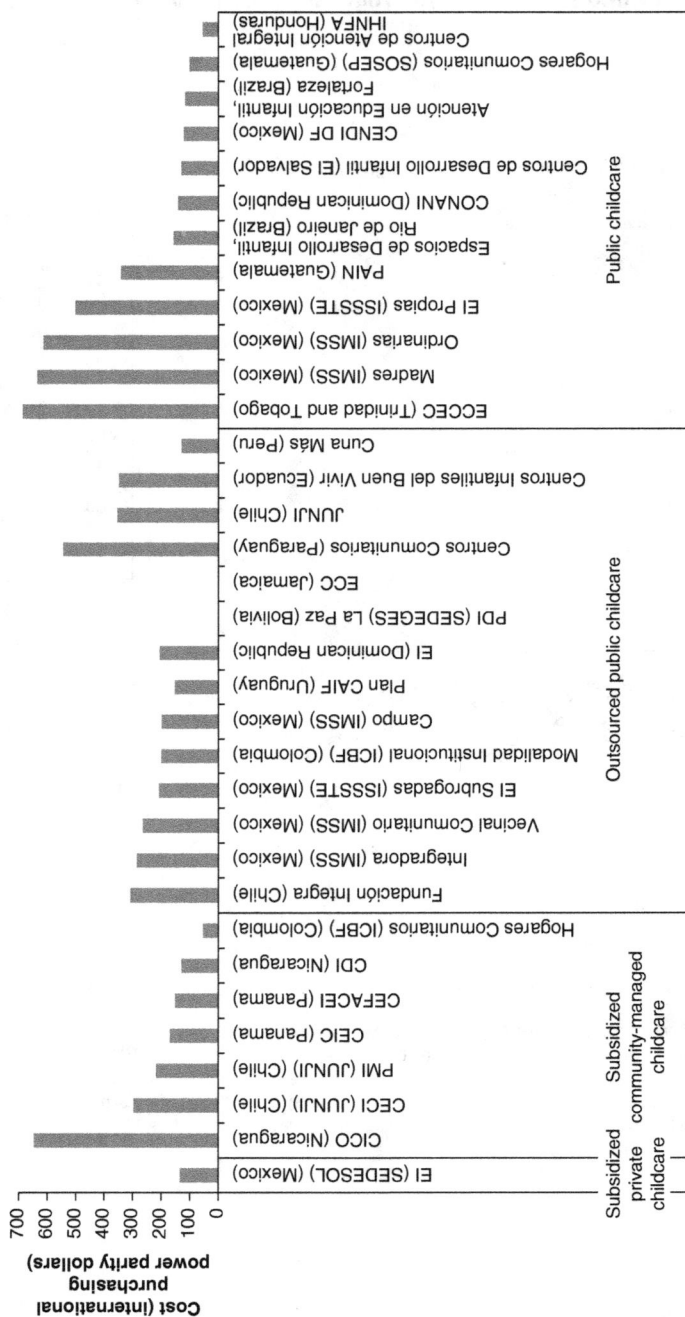

FIGURE 5A.2 Average monthly cost per child of selected childcare programs in Latin America and the Caribbean

Source: Authors' elaboration based on administrative data.

Note: CANF: Centros de Atención a la Infancia y a la Familia; CDI: Centros de Desarrollo Infantil; CECI: Centro Educativo Cultural de Infancia; CEFACE: Centro Familiar y Comunitario de Educación Inicial; CEIC: Centros de Educación Inicial Comunitarios; CENDI DF: Centros de Desarrollo Infantil Distrito Federal; CICO: Centros Infantiles Comunitarios; CONANI: Consejo Nacional para la Niñez y la Adolescencia; ECC: Early Childhood Commission; ECCEC: Early Childhood Care and Education Centers; ICBF: Instituto Colombiano de Bienestar Familiar; IHNFA: Instituto Hondureño de la Niñez y la Familia; EI: Estancias Infantiles; ICBF: Instituto Colombiano de Bienestar Familiar; IHNFA: Instituto Hondureño de la Niñez y la Familia; IMSS: Instituto Mexicano del Seguro Social; ISSSTE: Instituto de Seguridad y Servicios Sociales de los Trabajadores del Estado; JUNJI: Junta Nacional de Jardines Infantiles; PAIN: Programa de Atención Integral al Niño Menor de Seis Años; PDI: Programa de Desarrollo Inicial; SEDEGES: Servicio Departamental de Gestión Social; SEDESOL: Secretaría de Desarrollo Social; SOSEP: Secretaría de Obras Sociales de la Esposa del Presidente.

TABLE 5A.1 Number of private childcare centers in selected countries in Latin America and the Caribbean

Country	Type of center	Number of centers	Source
Bolivia	Childcare	676	Dirección Educación Inicial, Ministerio de Educación Bolivia
Chile	—	1,311	Secretaria Ejecutiva de Primera Infancia, Ministerio de Educación
Colombia	Preschool	10,420	Dirección de Primera Infancia, Ministerio de Educación de Colombia
Costa Rica	Preschool	281	Ministerio de Educación, Dirección de Centros Privados
Ecuador	Preschool	2,130	Dirección Nacional de Educación Inicial y Básica
El Salvador	Childcare/preschool	969	Dirección Nacional de Educación, Ministerio de Educación
Guatemala	Childcare/preschool	2,448	Dirección de Educación Preprimaria, Ministerio de Educación de Guatemala
Honduras	Preschool	1,122	Secretaria de Educación, Coordinación de Educación Preescolar.
Jamaica	Childcare/preschool	2,530	Early Childhood Commission
Mexico	Preschool	14,866	Sistema Educativo de los Estados Unidos Mexicanos principales cifras, ciclo escolar 2011–2012
Nicaragua	Preschool	568	Politica Nacional de Primera Infancia Amor por los más Chiquitos y Chiquitas
Panama	—	456	Dirección Educación Inicial, Ministerio de Educación Panamá
Paraguay	Childcare/preschool	616	Dirección General de Educación Inicial y Escolar Básica, Ministerio de Educación de Paraguay
Peru (Lima only)	—	9,108	Dirección de Educación Inicial, Ministerio de Educación del Perú
Trinidad and Tobago	Childcare/preschool	882	Early Childhood Care and Education Centers
Uruguay	—	462	Dirección de Educación, Ministerio de Educación y Cultura

Source: Authors' elaboration based on administrative data.
Note: Figures are approximations. — = Not available.

Notes

1. During 2013 we contacted specialists and directors of publicly supported childcare programs to gather information about programs' operation, structure, financing, and coverage. We distributed a questionnaire and followed up with telephone calls and emails to obtain and validate information. We also created a database on the legislation framework in which early childhood care and education policies operate in each country, available at http://www.iadb.org/en/research-and-data/female-labor-force /list-laws,8525.html.

2. The countries are Argentina, The Bahamas, Barbados, Bolivia, Brazil, Chile, Colombia, Costa Rica, the Dominican Republic, Ecuador, El Salvador, Guatemala, Honduras, Jamaica, Mexico, Nicaragua, Panama, Paraguay, Peru, Trinidad and Tobago, and Uruguay.

3. Preschool programs that are part of the education system (within schools) are not included.

4. Thirty percent of have no selection criteria, 40 percent have only income-based criteria, 18 percent have only employment criteria, and 13 percent have both income and employment criteria.

5. In Barbados the government childcare program starts at three months, and maternity leave covers six weeks. However, women can accumulate untaken pregnancy leave after the birth of the child. A woman who takes no pregnancy leave could take up to three months off after the birth.

6. Data on publicly supported programs in Belize, Guyana, Haiti, Suriname, and República Bolivariana de Venezuela were not available.

7. Extended day programs have been progressively implemented in the following countries: Argentina: Programa de Extensión Horaria (2002); Chile: Jornada Escolar Completa Diurna (1997); Colombia: Law to end school "shifts" and require a minimum number of teaching hours (1996); Mexico: *Programa de escuelas de tiempo completo* (2007); Uruguay: *Escuelas de Tiempo Completo* (1998); República Bolivariana de Venezuela: *Programa Simoncito y Escuela Bolivariana* (1999).

8. The first early education centers in the region were created in Argentina in 1823, in Brazil in 1875, in Mexico in 1883, in El Salvador in 1886, in Uruguay in 1892, in Cuba in 1889, in Ecuador in 1900, in Peru in 1902, in Bolivia in 1906, and in Panama in 1908 (Peralta and Gómez 1998).

9. For Chile, see Ley 17.301; for Colombia, see Ley 27 de 1974, published in Diario Oficial No 34.244; for Mexico, see Ley Federal del Trabajo. Relevant laws and regulations are available at http://www.iadb.org/en/research-and-data/female-labor -force/list-laws,8525.html.

10. The expansion was especially significant at Guarderias (IMSS), where the number of children served rose from 82,870 children at 692 centers in 1999 to 190,057 children at 1,516 centers in 2005, and Estancias Infantiles (ISSSTE), where the number rose from 28,329 children at 135 centers in 1999 to 37,313 children at 265 centers in 2008 (INEGI 2013).

11. Countries with nationally administered programs include The Bahamas, Barbados, Chile, Colombia, Costa Rica, the Dominican Republic, Ecuador, El Salvador, Guatemala, Honduras, Jamaica, Nicaragua, Panama, Paraguay, Peru, Trinidad and Tobago, and Uruguay.

12. The general federal budget, also referred to as federal funds, comprises tax revenue collected by the federal government for general purposes.

13. Data on the budget for each program were gathered through questionnaires and follow-ups with specialists and directors of the programs in the region (for the list of people contacted, see the appendix). Data on usage were taken from surveys that asked about the type of institution children attended. Data on both the budget and usage were available on 11 programs in 6 countries. In two of those countries (Honduras and Nicaragua), the surveys were not representative; therefore, data on those countries are not presented.

14. Rules of operation for Estancias Infantiles (SEDESOL) have changed over the past few years; the program now targets households below the poverty line. It is uncertain whether these changes alone can move the incidence curve. The other relevant factor would be program take-up, which is correlated with income and other socioeconomic variables (see chapter 4).

References

Addati, L., N. Cassirer, and K. Gilchrist. 2014. *Maternity and Paternity at Work: Law and Practice across the World*. Geneva: International Labor Office.

Ángeles, G., P. Gadsen, S. Galiani, P. Gertler, A. Herrera, P. Kariger, and E. Seira. 2011. *Evaluación de impacto del Programa Estancia Infantiles para Apoyar a Madres Trabajadoras: informe final de la evaluación de impacto*. (Impact Evaluation of the Program "Estancias Infantiles para Apoyar a Madres Trabajadoras": Final Report) Cuernavaca, Morelos, Mexico: National Institute of Public Health.

Bastos, P., and J. Cristia. 2012. "Supply and Quality Choices in Private Childcare Markets: Evidence from São Paulo." *Journal of Development Economics* 98 (2): 242–55.

Harris-Van Keuren, C., and D. Rodríguez Gómez. 2013. "Early Childhood Learning Guidelines in Latin America and the Caribbean." Monograph 142, Inter-American Development Bank, Washington, DC. Available at https://publications.iadb.org /handle/11319/6350?locale-attribute=en.

Hotz, J. V., and M. Xiao. 2011. "The Impact of Regulations on the Supply and Quality of Care in Child Care Markets." *American Economic Review* 101 (5): 1775–805.

INEGI (Instituto Nacional de Estadística y Geografía). 2013. "Estadísticas sobre salud, discapacidad y seguridad social." (Statistics on Health, Disabilities and Social Assistance). Aguacalientes, Mexico. Available at http://www3.inegi.org.mx/sistemas /sisept/default.aspx?t=mso213&s=est&c=27730.

Levy, S. 2008. *Good Intentions, Bad Outcomes: Social Policy, Informality, and Economic Growth in Mexico*. Washington, DC: Brookings Institution Press.

Mateo Díaz, M., L. Rodriguez-Chamussy, and F. Grafe. 2014. "Ley de Guarderías in México y los desafíos institucionales de conectar familia y trabajo." (Law on Childcare in Mexico and the Challenges Connecting Family and Work.) Policy Brief 219, Inter-American Development Bank, Washington, DC. Available at http://publications.iadb .org/handle/11319/6650.

Patrinos, H., F. Barrera-Osorio, and J. Guáqueta. 2009. *The Role and Impact of Public-Private Partnerships in Education.* Washington, DC: World Bank.

Peralta, M. V., and G. Fujimoto Gómez. 1998. *La atención integral de la primera infancia en América Latina: ejes centrales y los desafíos para el Siglo XXI.* Organization of American States, Santiago, Chile.

Roth, G. 1987. *The Private Provision of Public Services in Developing Countries.* EDI Series in Economic Development. Oxford: Oxford University Press.

UNESCO (United Nations Educational, Scientific and Cultural Organization). 2010. *Early Childhood Care and Education Regional Report, Latin America and the Caribbean.* Report prepared for the UNESCO World Conference on Early Childhood Care and Education (ECCE), held in Moscow, September 27–29.

PART III

What Do We Know?
Policy Recommendations

CHAPTER 6

Childcare outside Latin America and the Caribbean

How does childcare in Latin America and the Caribbean (LAC) compare with childcare in other regions of the world? What can be learned from countries with more consolidated systems of childcare? How do countries reduce inequality in access to childcare? How do they handle the trade-offs between investments that support female labor force participation (FLFP) and investments that boost child development? Are there ways to ease transitions from parental leave to early care systems and then to early education? Does money make a difference?

To answer these questions, this chapter considers four aspects of early childhood care and education and describes how countries in the Organisation for Economic Co-operation and Development (OECD), in particular in Europe and the United States, approach them:

- How are childcare systems organized?
- How do childcare systems interact with complementary policies?
- How are certain structural and program requirements applied to ensure quality in service delivery?
- How much do other countries spend on early childhood care and education, and how affordable is childcare for families?

Use of Formal Childcare

Expanding access to childcare, in particular in early childhood (0–3), is a challenge in both developed and developing countries (EACEA 2009). As part of their economic and social strategies, some countries have set targets for enrollment and the use of formal childcare for different age groups. For instance, in 2002 the European

Council established a target stipulating that 90 percent of children 3–5 and at least 33 percent of children younger than 3 have access to childcare (European Council 2002).[1] In setting these targets, European Union (EU) countries recognized high-quality, affordable childcare from birth to compulsory school age as a critical action reinforcing their employment strategies, with a commitment to removing disincentives to female labor force participation.

Figure 6.1 presents enrollment rates in formal childcare by children 0–3 and 3–5 in OECD and EU countries. The average enrollments in the OECD are about 30 percent for children 0– 3 and 80 percent for children 3–5.

Based on a review of 30 European countries, the Education, Audiovisual and Culture Executive Agency (EACEA 2009) identifies two main organizational

FIGURE 6.1 Average enrollment rates in formal childcare in selected OECD and EU countries, 2010

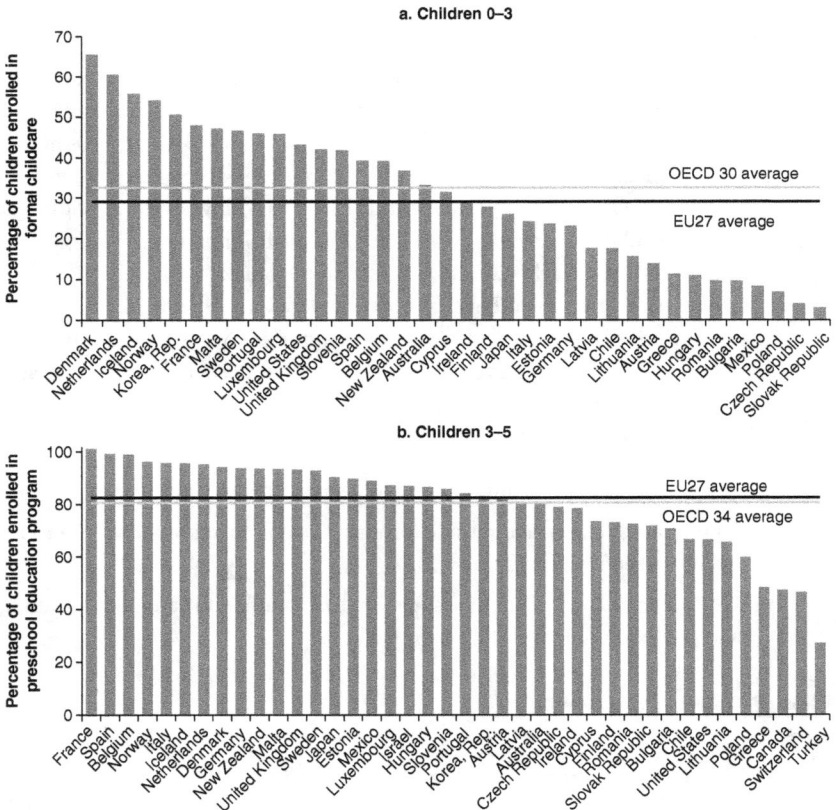

a. Children 0–3

b. Children 3–5

Source: OECD 2013a.
Note: EU = European Union; OECD = Organisation for Economic Co-operation and Development.

models for the provision of early care and education services. The unitary model offers a single organizational setting for children 0–6. The dual model, which is more prevalent in Europe, structures early education and care services separately for two age groups (0–3 and 3–6).

The unitary model has the same management structure for all age groups, with similar qualification requirements and salary scales for staff. One ministry is usually responsible for all services. All children are granted the right to a place from the very early years. Staff-child ratios tend to be higher than the dual model for all age groups.

The unitary model is used in the Nordic countries except Denmark. After World War II, the Nordic countries engaged in a process of progressive integration of childcare and early education and moved all child-related services into education. They no longer distinguish between early care and education, both of which are considered part of child well-being (Bennett 2008). Moving toward unitary models in LAC could help integrate childcare and educational functions through the various stages of childhood and facilitate policy consistency and smoother transitions from the very early years into preschool and then school.

Program and Service Features

Since the 1980s, it has become common practice in education to develop standards for achievement (Britto and Kagan 2010). These standards serve as a reference for "what teachers should teach, what students should learn, and what should be assessed to determine the degree to which schools have been effective in helping students learn the content articulated in the standards" (Scott-Little 2010, p. 132). Because of a lack of knowledge of how early child development occurs and the potential benefits of early stimulation and the need to increase public spending to fund these programs, it took almost two decades for the use of standards to be adopted (Scott-Little 2010).

The development of early learning and development standards (ELDS) is an important step toward improving the quality of early education and stimulation programs. The Going Global with Early Learning and Development Standards initiative brings together governments, international agencies, and relevant stakeholders to agree on the guiding principles, the domains of development and learning, and the way in which ELDS should be used (Britto and Kagan 2010). All states in the United States have adopted ELDS at the preschool level, and more than half use ELDS at the infant-toddler level (Scott-Little 2010). The standards concentrate on behaviors and performance related to physical and motor development, social and emotional development, cognition and general knowledge, and language and communication development (Britto and Kagan 2010; Scott-Little 2010). The United Kingdom has developed its own benchmarking tool for early education services (see https://www.gov.uk/government/publications/early-years -benchmarking-tool).

Based on evidence of the effects of programs on young children's development, Bowman, Donovan, and Burns (2000) identify a number of features to consider in designing early childhood education and care programs:

- Class size and adult-child ratios
- Educational materials and curricula integrated across development domains (cognitive, social, emotional, and physical) with well-specified aims
- Professional development of teachers (training and career progression)
- Active engagement and high-quality supervision of teachers
- Development of program standards and effective monitoring of them
- Development of relationships between the center or school and the home to create complementary environments
- Promotion of public understanding of early childhood education and care.

Most of the benchmarks presented in table 6.1 were created following consultation with countries, experts, practitioners, and a broad range of stakeholders in the field (Bennett 2008). Their views on the structural requirements and core

TABLE 6.1 Structural and program requirements for early childhood care and education programs

Benchmark	Indicator	Minimum level required
Social and family context		
B1. Effective public network of child and family health services	Infant mortality rate	Fewer than 4 per 1,000 live births
	Babies born with low birth weight (less than 2,500 grams)	Fewer than 6 per 100
	Immunization rate for 12- to 23-month-olds[a]	More than 95 per 100
B2. Effective national policies to reduce child poverty	Child poverty rate	Below 10 per 100
B3. Parental leave	Length of parental leave	About a year (maternity and parental leave combined)
	Wage replacement level	At least 50 percent
	Paternity leave	At least two weeks
Governance of early childhood systems		
B4. National or state responsibility for early childhood education and care assigned to one agency or ministry	Goal-setting, policy making, funding, and regulatory systems (including support/supervision) effectively integrated	Not specified

(continued on next page)

TABLE 6.1 Structural and program requirements for early childhood care and education programs *(continued)*

Benchmark	Indicator	Minimum level required
	National policy or plan for development of universal early childhood system published	Not specified
B5. Childhood policy is evidence based	Responsible agency commissioned and published independent national evaluation of early childhood services	At least 1 in 10 years
B6. Focus on well-being and holistic development of children	Regulatory framework enacted and applied equally to public and private settings[b]	Not specified
B7. Public expenditure on early childhood education for children 0–6[c]	Level of public expenditure in early childhood education	Equal or greater than 1 percent of GDP
	Costs per child in high-quality early education, with no more than 10 children per trained adult	$8,000–$14,000 a year per child 1–3; $6,000–$10,000 a year per child 3–6
	Cost per child based on number of hours in services with qualified educators	At least $5,000 a year per child for a half-day school-year program; About $9,000 a year per child for a full-day school-year program; About $13,000 a year per child for a full-day year-round integrated childcare program
Access to services		
B8. Access for all children, with opening hours and fees adjusted to meet the needs of parents	Priority to most vulnerable groups of young children	Not specified
B9. Level of childcare provision for children younger than 3	Access of children younger than 3 to places in publicly subsidized and regulated early childhood education services	At least 25 per 100
B10. Level of provision for 4-year-olds	Access of 4-year-olds to places in publicly subsidized and accredited early childhood education services	At least 80 per 100
	Hours per week of attendance	At least 15
Program quality		
B11. National/state guidelines or pedagogical framework developed for all early childhood services	Not specified	Not specified

(continued on next page)

TABLE 6.1 Structural and program requirements for early childhood care and education programs *(continued)*

Benchmark	Indicator	Minimum level required
B12. Governing agencies provide effective support structures to assist educators to achieve curriculum goals and values in cooperation with parents	Not specified	Not specified
B13. Level of training for all staff in regulated early childhood education services	Personnel with primary responsibility for care and education of young children have initial training	At least 80 percent
	Move toward a unified staffing system envisaged or in place, including qualifications, work conditions, and salaries aligned with the education or social services sector	Not specified
B14. Proportion of staff with higher level education and training in regulated early education centers (children 3–6)	Number of staff that are professionals (educators, pedagogues, or teachers)	At least 50 per 100
	Years of post–senior secondary training and certification in early childhood education and care required	At least 3 years
B15. Child-staff trained ratios and group sizes in publicly subsidized, center-based services	Child-staff trained ratio for children 4–5	Not greater than 15:1
	Group size	Does not exceed 24
	Low staff turnover	Not specified
B16. Space per child[d]	Childcare: Regulated indoor space Regulated outdoor space Preschool and kindergarten: Regulated indoor space Regulated outdoor space	 OECD average is 3.6 square meters OECD average is 8.9 square meters OECD average is 2.9 square meters OECD average is 7 square meters
B17. Monitoring and data collection mechanisms	Data collection mechanisms related to ECEC are in place Data are regularly updated Data are publicly shared and disseminated	Not specified
B18. Parental involvement	Not specified	Not specified

Sources: Bennett 2008; OECD 2012; Pascal and others 2013.
Note: ECEC = early childhood education and care; OECD = Organisation for Economic Co-operation and Development.
a. Averaged over measles, polio, and DPT3 vaccination.
b. A regulatory framework should define provider profiles, child eligibility for program, staff profiles, staff composition and career development, staff-child ratios, group sizes, program standards and curriculum, child assessments, and parent and community involvement (Bennett 2008).
c. Figures based on evidence from various sources, programs, and studies in OECD countries.
d. Not part of benchmarks proposed by Bennet (2008); OECD averages introduced as reference.

program elements necessary to ensure the quality of early childhood interventions were fairly consistent (OECD 2012; Pascal and others 2013). Among the critical components of center-based early childhood development and education programs, there appears to be broad consensus that high staff-child ratios, small group sizes, and low staff turnover have positive effects on outcomes (OECD 2012). Working conditions, staff qualifications, education, and training also affect child development (Taguma, Litjens, and Makowiecki 2012).

According to Heckman (2008), the largest returns are for disadvantaged children with low-quality parenting (which is not always correlated with income or education). He recommends that programs start as early as possible and not focus exclusively on cognition; that they include home visits, which can produce changes in the family environment when center-based interventions end; and that they be culturally diverse, to deal with tensions that may exist between the values of society transmitted to children through the programs and the children's family values. Universal programs avoid stigmatization, but financing them can create deadweight losses; a sliding fee schedule can be a solution.

Public Spending on Childcare

Does money make a difference? The evidence suggests, with some nuances, that it does. The Lien Foundation commissioned the Economist Intelligence Unit (EIU) to conduct a benchmarking exercise (EIU 2012). The EIU ranked preschool systems (for children 3–6) in 45 countries on what it called the Starting Well Index.[2] The results show that national income is highly correlated with the quality of early childhood care and education systems and that the affordability of preschool is strongly inversely correlated with income inequality (countries with high degrees of income inequality, such as Argentina, Brazil, China, Mexico, and South Africa, tend to show low levels of preschool affordability). Countries that are committed to early education are also more likely to ensure that these services are affordable for parents.

Data on the funding, spending, and costs of early childhood services are spotty (Atinc, Putcha, and Van der Gaag 2014). The data reported here capture public expenditure on preprimary education, the distribution of social expenditure by children's age (public investment strategy), and net childcare costs for families (affordability). Where data were available from different sources, priority was given to information that allowed for comparisons between LAC countries and countries outside the region.

Table 6.2 shows public expenditure on education and preprimary education expressed as a percentage of GDP. United Nations Educational, Scientific and Cultural Organization (UNESCO) data were used because they include European Union (EU27), OECD, and LAC countries.

Between 1998 and 2009, Iceland and the Netherlands increased public expenditure on early childhood education by almost 1 percent of GDP. During the same

TABLE 6.2 Public expenditure on preprimary education in selected countries, 2010 *(percentage of GDP)*

Region/economy	Expenditure on all education	Expenditure on preprimary education
Latin America and the Caribbean		
Argentina	5.78	0.43
Bahamas, The	—	—
Barbados	5.61[a]	0.02[b]
Belize	6.61	0.10
Bolivia	7.60	0.21
Brazil	5.82	0.44
Chile	4.18	0.56
Colombia	4.83	0.28
Costa Rica	6.28[c]	0.34[c]
Dominican Republic	2.22[a]	0.12[a]
Ecuador	4.20	0.12
El Salvador	3.49	0.28
Guatemala	2.80	0.31
Guyana	3.66	0.42
Haiti	—	—
Honduras	—	0.47
Jamaica	6.37	0.25
Mexico	5.21	0.53
Nicaragua	4.57	0.16
Panama	3.50[d]	0.11[d]
Paraguay	3.77	0.25
Peru	2.69	0.32
Suriname	—	—
Trinidad and Tobago	—	0.24[c]
Uruguay	4.50[d]	0.46[d]
Venezuela, RB	6.87[c]	0.80[c]
Average	4.79	0.31
OECD		
Australia	5.59	0.07
Austria	5.92	0.61

(continued on next page)

TABLE 6.2 Public expenditure on preprimary education in selected countries, 2010 *(continued)*

Region/economy	Expenditure on all education	Expenditure on preprimary education
Belgium	6.58	0.62
Bulgaria	4.10	0.92
Canada	5.50	—
Chile	4.18	0.56
Cyprus	7.27	0.40
Czech Republic	4.25	0.49
Denmark	8.74[a]	0.98[e]
Estonia	5.66	0.44
Finland	6.85	0.40
France	5.86	0.68
Germany	5.08	0.46
Greece	—	—
Hungary	4.90	0.71
Iceland	7.60	0.73
Ireland	6.41	0.10
Israel	5.59	0.62
Italy	4.50	0.45
Latvia	5.03	0.85
Lithuania	5.42	0.70
Japan	3.78	0.10
Luxembourg	—	0.76
Malta	6.91	0.51
Netherlands	5.98	0.41
New Zealand	7.17	0.48
Norway	6.87	0.33
Poland	5.17	0.52
Portugal	5.62	0.41
Korea, Rep.	5.25[b]	0.16[f]
Romania	3.53	0.35
Slovak Republic	4.23	0.40
Slovenia	5.69	0.59

(continued on next page)

TABLE 6.2 Public expenditure on preprimary education in selected countries, 2010 *(continued)*

Region/economy	Expenditure on all education	Expenditure on preprimary education
Spain	4.98	0.70
Sweden	6.98	0.71
Switzerland	5.24	0.19
United Kingdom	6.23	0.32
United States	5.42	0.35
Average EU27	5.65	0.57
Average OECD	5.76	0.47

Source: UIS 2014.
Note: Data are for 2010 except where indicated otherwise. — = Not available; EU = European Union; OECD = Organisation for Economic Co-operation and Development.
a. 2012.
b. 2008.
c. 2009.
d. 2011.
e. 2009.
f. 2011.

period, Chile, the Republic of Korea, and the United Kingdom increased their investments by 0.6 percent of GDP. Other countries already allocated more than 1 percent of their GDP to investments in childcare and preschool. They include Denmark (1.4 percent), Finland (1.1 percent), France (1.1 percent), Norway (1.2 percent), and Sweden (1.4 percent). Investments in the United States remained constant over the period, at about 0.4 percent of GDP (OECD 2013b).

Figure 6.2 shows wide variation in investment strategies. Some countries, such as Hungary and Iceland, spend more on early childhood than other age groups. Most countries, including Austria, Japan, the Republic of Korea, Mexico, Poland, Portugal, and the United States, spend more on middle and late childhood. Differences in spending are greater in early than in middle or late childhood.

Cash benefits, tax breaks, and childcare account for the majority of spending on children 0–5. In contrast, expenses on education represent the largest share of investments in children 6–17.

How affordable is childcare? Richardson (2012) considers net childcare costs of less than 10 percent of disposable income as affordable and costs of more than 30 percent as unaffordable. Figure 6.3 presents net childcare costs in selected countries, calculated based on the average wage of a dual-income family after accounting for childcare and other benefits and tax reductions (fee rebates, cash benefits, tax allowances, and tax credits). Gross childcare fees are unaffordable in

FIGURE 6.2 Public expenditure on child development and education in selected countries, by age of children, 2009

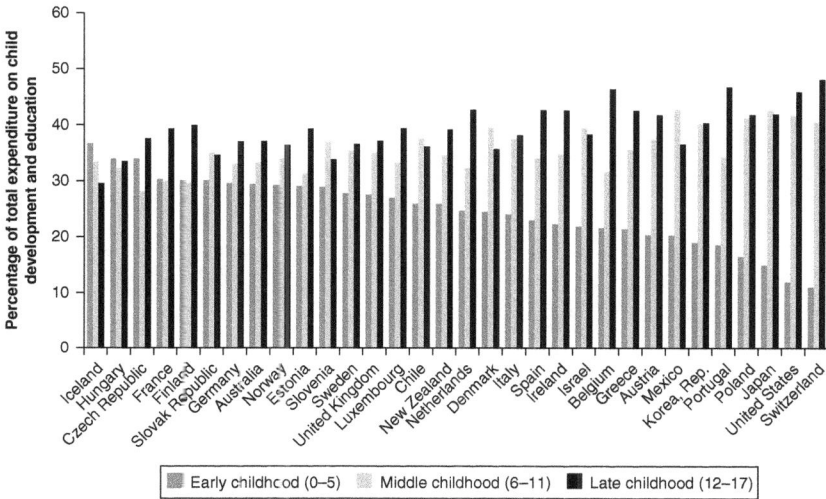

Sources: OECD 2013a, 2013b.
Note: Data for Canada and Turkey are missing. In Israel the population 0–5 represents 37 percent of the total population 0–17; in the Republic of Korea it represents 26 percent. In all other countries, children in each the three age groups represent about a third of the total number of children 0–17.

Australia, Belgium, Japan, Luxemburg, the Netherlands, Slovenia, and Switzerland. Once benefits are incorporated, however, costs are affordable in all seven countries. In contrast, even after assistance, costs to parents in Canada, Ireland, New Zealand, the United Kingdom, and the United States represent 30–50 percent of average wages.

These figures can be compared with the information presented in chapters 4 and 5 on childcare fees in LAC. Those data indicate that all publicly supported programs are either affordable (below 10 percent of average household per capita income) or moderately affordable (10–20 percent of average household per capita income). The household survey data present a less positive picture in the six countries for which they were available. They show that two-thirds of households report not paying fees for childcare. Among the third that do, the average out-of-pocket expenditure per child represents more than 10 percent of household income in all countries; it approaches the 30 percent threshold in Guatemala.

There is a debate about whether a supply-side (subsidies or transfers to service providers) or a demand-side (fee rebates or cash benefits to households) strategy

FIGURE 6.3 Net childcare costs for a dual-income family with full-time earnings of 150 percent of average wage, 2012

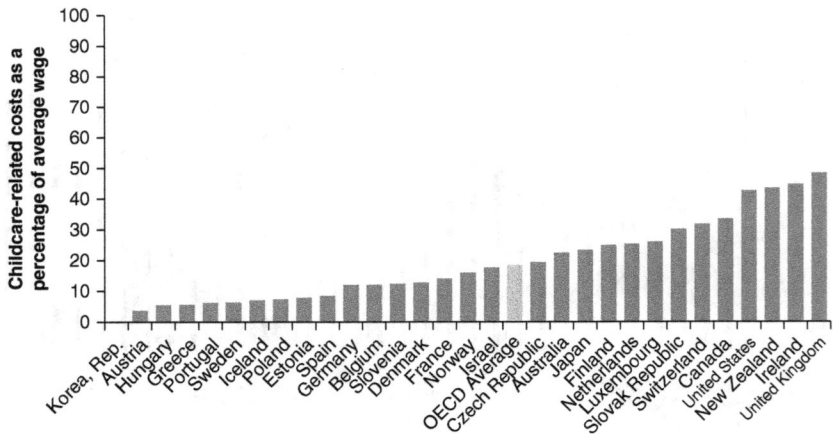

Source: OECD 2014.
Note: Figures show out-of-pocket childcare costs for full-time care at a typical childcare center. Childcare cost calculations for Austria are for Vienna; for Belgium, the French community; for Canada, the province of Ontario; for the Czech Republic, villages and towns with more than 2,000 inhabitants; for Germany, Hamburg; for Iceland, Reykjavík; for Switzerland, Zurich; for the United Kingdom, England; for the United States, Michigan. The government, at either the national or local level, determines childcare fees in Belgium, the Czech Republic, Finland, France, Hungary, Iceland, Israel, Japan, the Republic of Korea, Latvia, Lithuania, Poland, the Slovak Republic, and Slovenia. Childcare fees for Greece are calculated based on national guidelines. OECD = Organisation for Economic Co-operation and Development.

is better for funding childcare. Demand-side subsidies foster competition but do not ensure that quality objectives are met (EIU 2012; Leseman 2009). Many experts therefore suggest implementing a combination of the two.

Interactions and Transitions between Childcare and Complementary Policies

Countries in the OECD have adopted two models to handle the transitions into and out of childcare. Both begin when parental leave following the birth of a child ends. The parallel model offers a choice between childcare services or a home-care allowance.[3] The sequential model offers only childcare services.

Figure 6.4 shows the evolution of participation rates in childcare for children younger than 3 in the Nordic countries. Norway's policies are among the most gender-friendly in the world. It was the first country to introduce paid maternity leave, in 1956; the initial benefits were extended in 1993 to parental leave of 42 weeks at full pay or 52 weeks at 80 percent pay, 4 weeks of which are reserved for fathers. Norway also adopted important work and family conciliation policies,

FIGURE 6.4 Share of children younger than 3 enrolled in formal childcare or preschool in the Nordic countries, 1995–2010

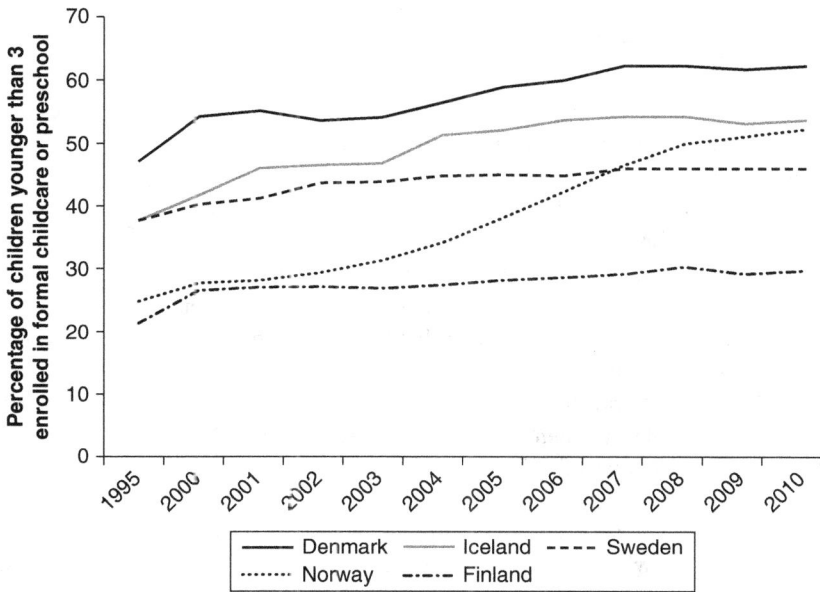

Source: OECD 2013a.

ranging from breastfeeding breaks to 20–30 days a year for parents to stay at home with sick children (Rindfuss and others 2010).

These policies were accompanied by an aggressive expansion of childcare, particularly during the 1980s and 1990s. Enrollment in childcare rose from about 20 percent in 1995 to about 50 percent in 2010. The increase was initially motivated by the desire to support child development. Policy makers later sought to accommodate working parents' needs (Bernhardt, Turid, and Torkild Hovde 2008; Rindfuss and others 2010; Sörensen and Bergqvist 2002) and increase the involvement of fathers in parenting and raise productivity and growth by facilitating FLFP (Brandth and Kvande 2009; Datta Gupta, Smith, and Verner 2006; Duvander, Lappegård, and Andersson 2010; Lappegård 2009; Rindfuss and others 2010; Rønsen 2004; Rønsen and Sundström 1996).

Childcare supply in Norway is provided both publicly and privately. The private supply is not-for-profit and emerged as a response to shortages in public supply. It is heavily subsidized by the national government: Both public and private centers receive about €500 per month per enrolled child, which covers a little more than half the total cost (Rindfuss and others 2010). Some public centers also receive municipal subsidies, and low-income families usually benefit from additional help. Childcare is very affordable for parents, representing about 6 percent of average household income. The national government regulates both public and private childcare provision, and there is a general sense that the quality is very high (Rindfuss and others 2010).

In Finland, in contrast, only 26 percent of children younger than 3 are enrolled in childcare services. All children younger than 3 are guaranteed a place in a municipal childcare, but this entitlement complements a home-care allowance system that enables parents to stay at home with their child with full job security until the child reaches the age of 3. Along with Norway and Sweden, Finland has implemented a cash-for-childcare scheme; it is the country with the highest proportion of parents taking up this benefit (Sweden has the lowest proportion) (Ellingsæter 2012). Platenga and Remery (2009) argue that the supply of public childcare has met demand for the last 20 years and that the 26 percent take-up rate reflects the popularity of the home-care alternative.

In Finland, Norway, and Sweden, the profile of beneficiaries of the home-care allowance is similar. Women with low incomes, low qualifications and education levels, a large number of children, and immigrant backgrounds are overrepresented (Eydal and Rostgaard 2011).

The consequences of a policy cannot be viewed in isolation. Publicly subsidized childcare will have greater effects if it is combined with other policies, such as extended parental leave. Households will behave differently if they have only one or several options to choose from; their choices may exacerbate rather than reduce segmentation. In Finland, for instance, the right to municipal childcare services and the right to a cash benefit were passed together, as the result of a compromise between the Left and Center parties. As in other countries, the Left opposed the cash benefit; conservatives presented the policy as a mechanism to support parents' choice to stay at home with their children. In fact, the cash benefit was introduced in a context of growing demand and insufficient supply (Ellingsæter 2012; Rantalaiho 2009). Parental leave in Finland is shorter and less generous than it is in Norway or Sweden: It lasts nine months and covers 70 percent of wages.[4] Confronted with both options, lower income households tended to choose the cash benefit instead of the center-based childcare services, whereas higher income households preferred that second option.

Home-care allowances appear to have a short-term positive redistributive effect but to promote longer-term inequality in at least three dimensions (Government of Norway 2009; Plantenga and Remery 2009). They promote socioeconomic inequality, because they deter low-income families from using daycare services (Ellingsæter 2012; Repo 2010). They promote geographic inequality, because the behavior of families differs greatly across regions and municipalities, depending on the demographic composition. They promote gender inequality, because home care tends to reinforce gender patterns of care and reduce mothers' labor supply (Kosonen 2011), keeping women away from the market for extended periods (Nelander 2007).

Implications for Policy

The experiences described in this chapter yield some lessons for policy makers interested in integrating lower income-women into the labor market and allowing their children to benefit from good-quality childcare:

- Unitary models provide a unique organizational setting that can help integrate childcare and educational functions through the various stages of childhood.
- Parallel models that start with a period of parental leave and then offer a choice between childcare services or a home care allowance provide more options for parents, but they can increase inequalities between families.
- Universal programs could reduce the segmentation in the provision and use of childcare that reinforces inequalities; a sliding fee schedule could be incorporated to prevent deadweight losses (Heckman 2008).
- If the system is well regulated, direct or private provision of publicly subsidized childcare should not necessarily affect the affordability or quality of services.
- In countries with wide heterogeneity and inequality, decentralization of services will reinforce segmentation.
- The best strategy for paying for childcare appears to be a combination of demand and supply subsidies, which foster competition while maintaining quality.
- Home care allowances can have short-term positive redistributive effects, but they tend to promote longer-term inequalities. Households that choose the home care allowance tend to have lower income, worse qualifications, less education, and more children than households that send their children to a daycare facility; they are also much more likely to have an immigrant background (Ellingsæter 2012; Eydal and Rostgaard 2011; Kosonen 2011; Government of Norway 2009; Nelander 2007).

Notes

1. In 2002 the European Council met in Barcelona for its second annual spring meeting on the economic, social, and environmental situation in the European Union. It prioritized active policies that support full employment to complete a common economic area and pursue the Union's long-term objectives.

2. Twenty-nine OECD countries and 16 other developed and emerging market economies are included: Argentina; Australia; Austria; Belgium; Brazil; Canada; Chile; China; the Czech Republic; Denmark; Finland; France; Germany; Ghana; Greece; Hong Kong SAR, China; Hungary; India; Indonesia; Ireland; Israel; Italy; Japan; the Republic of Korea; Malaysia; Mexico; the Netherlands; New Zealand; Norway; the Philippines; Poland; Portugal; Singapore; South Africa; Spain; Sweden; Switzerland; Taiwan, China; the Russian Federation; Turkey; Thailand; the United Arab Emirates; the United Kingdom; the United States; and Vietnam.

3. For more details about maternity, paternity, and parental leaves in advanced economies, see ILO (2014).

4. In Norway leave lasts 47 weeks with 100 percent wage replacement or 57 weeks with 80 percent wage replacement. In Sweden leave lasts 13 months with 80 percent wage replacement, plus three months at a flat rate (Ellingsæter 2012).

References

Atinc, T., V. Putcha, and J. Van der Gaag. 2014. "Costing Early Childhood Development Services: The Need to Do Better." Policy Paper 2014-04, Brookings Institution, Washington, DC.

Bennett, J. 2008. "Benchmarks for Early Childhood Services in OECD Countries." Working Paper 2008-02, UNICEF Innocenti Research Center, Florence.

Bernhardt E., N. Turid, and L. Torkild Hovde. "Shared Housework in Norway and Sweden: Advancing the Gender Revolution." *Journal of European Social Policy* 18 (3): 275–88.

Bowman, B. T., M. S. Donovan, and M. S. Burns, eds. 2000. *Eager to Learn: Educating Our Preschoolers*. Washington, DC: National Academies Press.

Brandth, B., and E. Kvande. "Gendered or Gender-neutral Care Politics for Fathers." *Annals of the American Academy of Political and Social Science* 624: 177–89.

Britto, P. R., and S. L. Kagan. 2010. "Global Status of Early Learning and Development Standards." In *International Encyclopedia of Education*, 3rd. ed., edited by P. Peterson, E. Baker, and B. McGaw. Oxford: Elsevier.

Datta Gupta, N., N. Smith, and M. Verner. 2006. "Child Care and Parental Leave in the Nordic Countries: A Model to Aspire To?" IZA Discussion Paper 2014, Institute for the Study of Labor, Bonn.

Duvander, A-Z., T. Lappegård, and G. Andersson. 2010. "Family Policy and Fertility: Father's and Mother's Use of Parental Leave and Continued Childbearing in Norway and Sweden." *Journal of European Social Policy* 20 (1): 45–57.

EACEA (Education, Audiovisual and Culture Executive Agency). 2009. *Tackling Social and Cultural Inequalities through Early Childhood Education and Care in Europe*. Brussels.

EIU (Economist Intelligence Unit). 2012. *Starting Well: Benchmarking Early Education across the World*. Report commissioned by the LIEN Foundation. Available at http://www.lienfoundation.org/pdf/publications/sw_report.pdf.

Ellingsæter, A. L. 2012. *Cash for Childcare: Experiences from Finland, Norway and Sweden*. Washington, DC: Friedrich-Ebert-Stiftung.

European Council. 2002. "Presidency Conclusions." Presentation at the Barcelona European Council, March 15–16. Available at http://ec.europa.eu/invest-in-research /pdf/download_en/barcelona_european_council.pdf.

Eydal, G., and T. Rostgaard. 2011. "Day-Care Schemes and Cash-for-Care at Home." In *Parental Leave, Childcare and Gender Equality in the Nordic Countries*, edited by I. V. Gìslason and G. B. Eydal. Copenhagen: Nordic Council of Ministers.

Government of Norway. 2009. *Fordelingsutvalget, NOU 2009: 10.* Ministry of Finance, Oslo.

Heckman, J. J. 2008. "Schools, Skills, and Synapses." IZA Discussion Paper 3515, Institute for the Study of Labor, Bonn.

ILO (International Labor Office). 2014. *Maternity and Paternity at Work: Law and Practice across the World.* Geneva: ILO.

Kosonen, T. 2011. "To Work or Not to Work? The Effect of Child-Care Subsidies on the Labour Supply of Parents." Working Paper 23, Government Institute for Economic Research, Helsinki.

Lappegård, T. 2009. "Family Policies and Fertility in Norway." *European Journal of Population* 26: 99–116.

Leseman, P. P. M. 2009. "The Impact of High Quality Education and Care on the Development of Young Children: Review of the Literature." In *Tackling Social and Cultural Inequalities through Early Childhood Education and Care in Europe.* Brussels: Education, Audiovisual and Culture Executive Agency (EACEA).

Nelander, Å. 2007. *Vårdnadsbidrag: En tillbakagång i svensk familjepolitik.* Rapport 5/2007, Arbetarrörelsens Tankesmedja, Stockholm.

OECD (Organisation for Economic Co-operation and Development). 2012. *Starting Strong III: A Quality Toolbox for Early Childhood Education and Care.* Paris: OECD Publishing.

———. 2013a. OECD Family Database. Paris.

———. 2013b. OECD Social Expenditure Database. Paris.

———. 2014. OECD Tax-Benefit Model. Paris

Pascal, C., T. Bertram, S. Delaney, and C. Nelson. 2013. *A Comparison of International Childcare Systems.* Center for Research in Early Childhood (CREC), Birmingham, United Kingdom.

Plantenga, J., and C. Remery. 2009. *The Provision of Childcare Services: A Comparative Review of 30 European Countries.* Luxembourg: Office for Official Publications of the European Communities.

Rantalaiho, M. 2009. *Kvoter, valgfrihet, fleksibilitet.* Nordic Gender Institute (NIKK), Oslo.

Repo, K. 2010. "Finnish Child Home Care Allowance: Users' Perspectives and Perceptions." In *Cash-for-Childcare: The Consequences for Caring Mothers*, edited by J. Sipilä, K. Repo, and T. Rissanen. Surrey, United Kingdom: Edward Elgar.

Richardson, L. 2012. *Costs of Childcare across OECD Countries.* Organisation for Economic Co-operation and Development (OECD), Paris.

Rindfuss, R. R., D. K. Guilkey, P. S. Morgan, and Ø. Kravdal. 2010. "Child-Care Availability and Fertility in Norway." *Population and Development Review* 36 (4): 725–48.

Rønsen, M. 2004. "Fertility and Public Policies: Evidence from Norway and Finland." *Demographic Research* 10 (6): 143–70. Available at http://demographic-research.org /volumes/vol10/6/10-6.pdf.

Rønsen, M., and M. Sundström. 1996. "Maternal Employment in Scandinavia: A Comparison of the After-Birth Employment Activity of Norwegian and Swedish Women." *Journal of Population Economics* 9 (3): 267–85.

Scott-Little, C. 2010. "Development and Implementation of Early Learning Standards in the United States." In *International Encyclopedia of Education*, 3rd. ed., edited by P. Peterson, E. Baker, and B. McGaw. Oxford: Elsevier.

Sörensen, K., and C. Bergqvist. 2002. *Gender and the Social Democratic Welfare Regime: A Comparison of Gender-Equality Friendly Policies in Sweden and Norway.* Stockholm: National Institute for Working Life.

Taguma, M., I. Litjens, and K. Makowiecki. 2012. *Quality Matters in Early Childhood Education and Care: Finland 2012.* Paris: Organisation for Economic Co-operation and Development (OECD).

UIS (UNESCO Institute for Statistics). 2014. Education Statistics: All Indicators. Montreal: UIS.

CHAPTER 7

Assessing Demand for Formal Childcare: A Case Study of Chile

To avoid investing resources in programs that fail to attract the intended beneficiaries, policy makers need to understand the behavior of households and assess potential demand for formal childcare.

In Chile enrollment in formal childcare programs has been consistently increasing since the 1990s, from an estimated 16 to 40 percent (Contreras, Puentes, and Bravo 2012; Medrano 2009). Large differences in participation hide behind these aggregated numbers in favor of older children. The current government is in the process of expanding childcare services, including opening 4,500 new centers to incorporate an additional 90,000 children 0–2 and 1,200 new spaces for 34,000 additional children 3–5. If these targets materialize, coverage for children 0–3 will approach OECD average levels (about 29 percent). However 2014 administrative data show that, on average, 9 percent of spaces went unused in the centers of the largest national program, Junta Nacional de Jardines Infantiles (JUNJI) (Mateo Díaz and Vasquez 2016). The new centers were not strategically located using mothers' potential work places as a reference, however, and opening hours did not necessarily match mothers' working hours. The main criterion used for this first expansion was availability of land to build the new centers. Existing evidence shows no effect of the policy on female labor supply (Encina and Martinez 2009; Medrano 2009), unless location and opening hours of centers are taken into account (Contreras, Puentes, and Bravo 2012).

The first section of this chapter briefly discusses the different factors influencing families' choices regarding the use of childcare, based on self-reported reasons. The second section proposes a model for assessing demand for childcare by clustering similar nonusers, quantifying them, identifying vulnerable households, and assessing how difficult it would be to induce each cluster to use formal childcare. Section three discusses the projected impact of increasing take-up by different groups of nonusers. The last section identifies policy actions that can prevent inefficiencies and ensure that new spaces created do not go unused.

What Determines Use (and Nonuse) of Formal Childcare?

Many factors shape individual and family choices about childcare, including employment opportunities and restrictions, preferences, and values. The evidence suggests that demand for childcare services is segmented (Mateo Díaz and Rodriguez-Chamussy 2013; Mateo Díaz, Rodriguez-Chamussy, and Grafe 2014). At the level of parents' daily decision making, social norms, economic opportunities, and access to (or the lack of) childcare determine the degree to which households rely on formal care arrangements (box 7.1). It is not easy to project how increases in the availability, affordability, or quality of childcare are likely to increase use.

BOX 7.1 Mothers' voices on family decision making on childcare

Interviewer: What alternative do you have but decide not to pursue because you prefer to send your children to childcare?

Monse: No alternative other than childcare.

Marisela: I have no other options; it's childcare whether I like it or not.

Liliana: If my mother-in-law could take care of my daughter, but she's big now and I'm afraid my mother-in-law might trip and fall while holding her.

Valeria: My mother-in-law took care of my children, but sometimes she would get nosy and fussy; she would tell me that she was tired of cleaning up after them and that the children would make a mess and that was when I told her that the children would be much better off [in childcare].

Interviewer: Why do you think other mothers with children the same age don't take them to childcare?

Lizet: Because they have the wrong idea about the programs or believe that childcare is only for working mothers.

Sandra: I didn't work, so my husband asked why I would use childcare when I had nothing to do; he changed his mind seeing that all of our nieces went to childcare, and then I pointed out to him that his sister doesn't work.

Itzel: My husband thought the same, and said to me, you are his mother and you have to take care of him.

Marisela: My sister didn't like it, and she said that her son would get sick in childcare.

Source: Focus group interviews with users of publicly subsidized childcare in Toluca, Mexico.

Surveys show that the main reasons children do not attend formal childcare include the following:

- Lack of affordability and availability
- Schedules and distance from home or work
- Lack of quality and trust in the service
- Children's age
- Social pressure and strong household beliefs that bringing children to centers is not good
- Lack of information about potential benefits in terms of a child's stimulation
- Preference for alternative care arrangements.[1]

Assessing Demand for Formal Childcare

To inform public policy, this study created a model for assessing demand for formal childcare. The model

- Clusters similar types of nonusers to provide some idea of magnitudes, in particular of vulnerable households
- Assesses the likelihood of inducing each cluster to use formal childcare
- Estimates the elasticity of demand for childcare in each cluster with respect to changes in different aspects of care services
- Identifies potential benefits if different profiles of nonusers are induced to use formal childcare.

This section describes the model and runs it using data from the 2012 early childhood survey in Chile (the Encuesta Longitudinal de la Primera Infancia [ELPI]), the only survey in Latin America and the Caribbean that includes information on the reasons for both use and nonuse of formal childcare. Results for other countries may be different. The purpose of the exercise is to show decision makers how to identify potential demand and to support policy design by increasing their understanding of the composition of the population not using childcare.

Step 1: Group Households by Self-Reported Reasons for Use and Nonuse of Formal Childcare

Households can be classified into three groups based on self-report: households that already outsource care but prefer informal over formal arrangements,[2] households that make decisions about childcare based on cultural reasons,[3] and households that make decisions based on supply and service characteristics, including availability, affordability, convenience, and quality.[4] (For a description

TABLE 7.1 Reasons why households in Chile do not use formal childcare

Reason	Percentage of households not using formal childcare
Strong preference for other arrangements	71
Cultural attitudes	68
Father does not want child to attend	76
Mother takes care of child	68
Sensitivity to various aspects of supply	43
Lack of availability or affordability	47
Perception that child doesn't benefit from formal childcare	46
Problems with service characteristics (hours, quality, and so forth)	35

Source: Centro MicroDatos (2012) Encuesta Longitudinal de la Primera Infancia (ELPI).

of the variables used in the model and the classification of reasons for childcare use/nonuse, see annex 7A). The two first groups have low levels of use (table 7.1). Households in the third group tend to use formal childcare much more.

Step 2: Determine Employability of Mothers

The mother's education, the labor trajectory of the mother, the cultural values of the parent and other relatives, and the level of local economic activity strongly affect how households respond to increases in the supply of formal childcare options. In the absence of a very strong conviction about the benefits of childcare for early childhood development (ECD), the decisions to use childcare and to work are often made at the same time. Households that currently do not use formal childcare but in which the mother has more education and work experience are more likely to respond positively to policy changes, because the mother is more likely to become economically active. Female labor force participation (FLFP) also depends on structural factors: Job opportunities are more likely to materialize in economically active areas. Cultural values also play a strong role in labor market decisions (see chapter 2). Cultural conservatism is measured using a question on opinions about the distribution of work and family roles between men and women (see annex 7A).

Households were classified into three groups. The first group comprises households in which women have low employability and little education, the household lives in a depressed economic area, and the household's values are strongly conservative regarding family roles. The third group comprises households in which women have high employability and education, the household lives in an economically active area, and the household has more progressive family values.

The second group lies in between. The incidence of use of formal childcare was 37 percent in the first group, 51 percent in the second group, and 59 percent in the third group.

Step 3: Classify Nonusers of Formal Childcare

Information from Steps 1 and 2 was used to classify households based on their reasons for not using formal childcare. Understanding which types of households belong to each group helps policy makers induce households to use formal childcare and project the benefits that are likely to ensue from targeting each group.

Nonusers can be divided into two groups. The first group ("structural nonusers") includes households that report a strong preference for other arrangements and households that report not using childcare because the husband or partner does not want to or the mother takes care of the child. Inducing these households to use formal childcare is difficult. Women in households with a strong preference for nonformal childcare arrangements that have already entrusted care to a third party tend to have more education and better labor market prospects and less conservative views about gender roles than women in other households. Many of these households will not be eligible for targeted childcare programs; for households that are eligible, center-based services will not be attractive. In households with more conservative values, mothers tend to have less education. Households with conservative attitudes toward formal childcare will also be very difficult to induce to use formal services, both because of strong cultural barriers and because mothers tend to be less employable than women in other groups. It is possible that these mothers tend to justify their absence from paid labor to some extent by what they believe will be their main responsibilities as caregivers.

The second group ("nonusers at the margin") includes households reporting sensitivity to certain characteristics of services. They are likely to be responsive to changes in supply, particularly in households in which the mother is highly employable. Tweaking specific service features—such as increasing coverage, changing schedules, staff-child ratios, and safety and security standards—is likely to induce some of these households to use formal childcare. This group tends to be at the lower end of the income distribution. Table 7.2 shows how difficult it will be to induce both types of nonusers to use childcare.

Figure 7.1 shows the size of both groups of nonusers. It shows that 42 percent of nonusers are structural nonusers, a relatively small share of whom are in the bottom two income quintiles. The proportion of low-income households is higher among nonusers at the margin. The largest group of nonusers comprises households that are concerned about the impact of formal centers on child development.

TABLE 7.2 Level of effort needed to induce nonusers to use formal childcare

Type of nonuser and reason for not using formal childcare	Employability of mother			Level of effort needed to induce nonusers to use
	Low	Medium	High	
Structural nonuser				High (> 51)
Strong preference for other arrangements	64	74	69	
Cultural attitudes	74	66	59	
Partner disagrees	81	73	68	
Mother should take care of child	74	65	59	
Nonuser at the margin				Low/moderate (< 51)
Sensitive to different aspects of supply	59	41	29	
Price/availability	63	43	31	
Benefits of early childhood development	55	44	38	
Service characteristics	73	35	16	

Source: Centro MicroDatos (2012) Encuesta Longitudinal de la Primera Infancia (ELPI).
Note: Figures in table are mean percentages per cluster. The average level of nonusers for all clusters was 51 percent; this number was used to distinguish between clusters that will require a high level of effort to induce nonusers to use and clusters that will require a low to moderate level of effort.

FIGURE 7.1 Size and income distribution of groups of nonusers of formal childcare in Chile

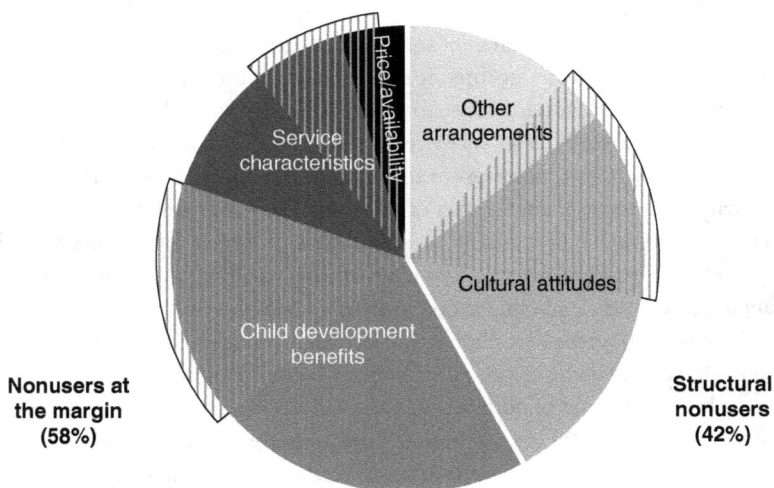

☐ Indicates the share of bottom two income quintiles.
For nonusers at the margin the share is 44%;
for structural nonusers the share is 39%.

Source: Centro MicroDatos (2012) Encuesta Longitudinal de la Primera Infancia (ELPI).

Projected Impact of Increasing Take-up of Formal Childcare

Table 7.3 presents the projected impact of inducing nonusers to use formal child-care. If the objective is to maximize benefits in terms of both ECD and FLFP and to expand take-up quickly, the focus should be on nonusers at the margin. If instead the goal is to reach larger numbers of vulnerable households, the focus should be on structural nonusers with conservative attitudes or nonusers at the margin who lack access to or cannot afford formal childcare. A strategy that focuses on structural nonusers will take time, because values and beliefs are difficult to change.

TABLE 7.3 Estimated benefits of increasing take-up of formal childcare in Chile

Type of nonuser/reason for not using childcare	Income and employability	Heterogeneity of group	Effect on early childhood development (ECD)	Effect on female labor force participation (FLFP)	Projected effect size
Structural nonuser					
Strong preference for other arrangements	Higher-income population (23 percent in bottom two quintiles); higher employability of mothers	Low	Yes	No (crowding-out effects)	Medium to large effects for ECD
Cultural attitudes	Lower-income population (47 percent in bottom two quintiles); lower employability of mothers	Low	Yes	No (in short term)	Large effects for ECD
Nonuser at the margin					
Price/ availability	Lower-income population (57 percent in bottom two quintiles); medium/ low employability of mothers	Low	Yes	Yes	Moderate effects on FLFP; large effects on ECD
Early childhood development benefits	Heterogeneous population (43 percent in bottom two quintiles; 34 percent in top two quintiles); medium/ low employability of mothers	High	Yes	Yes	Moderate effects on ECD and FLFP
Service characteristics	Heterogeneous population (41 percent in bottom two quintiles; 32 percent in top two quintiles); higher employability of mothers	High	Yes	Yes	Large effects on FLFP; moderate effects on ECD

Source: Author's elaboration.

The greatest returns to labor market outcomes should come from inducing women who do not use formal childcare because of service restrictions; inducing women who already use informal arrangements will probably not affect labor supply. More availability, lower prices, and higher quality would broaden their options but could crowd out informal arrangements. Notwithstanding any effect on the FLFP (extensive margin), there are potential effects on working hours and the job quality of women already in the labor force (intensive margin).[5] The evidence for children 3 and older also suggests better development outcomes for children attending childcare centers than for children cared for by family members (grandmothers and others) (Bernal and Fernandez 2013).

The outcomes presented in table 7.4 assume that FLFP is held constant. Taking a dynamic perspective yields a richer picture of the interactions that take place as behavior changes. For instance, an increase in FLFP among nonusers at the margin could influence structural nonusers who avoid formal childcare for cultural reasons, through its effect on norms and values (Fernandez 2013; Fogli and Veldkamp 2011). Demand can change quickly: The profile of women on the margin of participating in the labor market has changed significantly over time (Fitzpatrick 2010). Assessments of demand should therefore be conducted frequently.

Recommended Policy Actions and Interventions

Table 7.4 suggests policy actions and interventions that could be used to increase demand. It is divided into two categories: interventions specific to childcare programs and other policies that could be used in combination with childcare. The types of policies recommended depend on the type of nonusers targeted. The policies believed to have the greatest effects on inducing nonusers to use formal childcare are prioritized.

Three sets of policies are common to all: expanding access, increasing quality, and improving incentives (Lun Wong and others 2013). Policies that expand access should be a priority, especially in areas without childcare centers. A certain level of quality should be ensured, not only to increase ECD benefits but also to convince households to enroll their children. Incentives should be used to reduce inequalities in participation by different socioeconomic groups and to speed the process of changing norms and values that prevent households from using formal childcare.

Influencing Attitudes

Policies aimed at increasing the use of childcare must do more than just increase the number of spaces. They should include incentives and sensitization programs emphasizing the potential benefits of formal childcare for working families and their children. Fogli and Veldkamp (2011) claim that when women learn about the effects of maternal employment on children by observing other employed women in their surroundings, they are more likely to join the labor force. These policies are particularly effective with nonusers with strong beliefs about gender roles or apprehensions

TABLE 7.4 Interventions and policies for inducing nonusers to use formal childcare

Type of nonuser/ reason for not using childcare	Interventions specific to childcare program						Other policies to use in combination with childcare				
	Expand access (coverage and age of children)	Reduce price	Modify hours/days/ months of operation	Increase quality	Launch information campaigns (on service features)	Launch sensitization campaigns (on benefits of early childhood development)	Incentive-based policies (for example, conditional cash transfers)	Education policies	Changes in labor market composition	Productivity policies	Work and family conciliation policies
Structural nonuser											
Strong preference for other arrangements	✓			✓		✓	✓				
Cultural attitudes	✓	✓		✓		✓	✓	✓	✓	✓	
Nonuser at the margin											
Price/availability	✓	✓		✓	✓		✓		✓	✓	
Early childhood development benefits	✓			✓		✓	✓	✓	✓	✓	
Service characteristics	✓		✓	✓	✓		✓	✓	✓	✓	✓

Source: Author's elaboration.

183

about the impact of centers on ECD. Increasing awareness can come as part of existing parenting interventions or through sessions with experts as early as the first checkup for babies. Sensitization campaigns on the benefits of early stimulation should target households (including grandmothers), particularly among structural nonusers.

Interventions to modify behavior based purely on sensitization campaigns often increase awareness but do not modify attitudes or lead to the desired behavior change (Croker, Lucas, and Wardle 2012; Flay and Sobel 1983; Horsfall, Bromfield, and McDonald 2010; Rogers and Storey 1987; Walls and others 2011). Certain approaches can be very powerful in changing behaviors (Backer 1990; Palmgreen and Donohew 2006; Perloff 1993). The collaboration of important local stakeholders (Melkote, Moore, and Velu 2014); the use of segmentation strategies (Backer, Rogers, and Sopory 1992; Slater 1996); an emphasis on the benefits of modified behaviors rather than undesirable features and consequences (Walls and others 2011); and personalized feedback have been found to be effective.

Learning from Success

Renca, a low-income municipality near Santiago, has been extremely successful in increasing take-up (for detailed information about the program, see Mateo Díaz and Vasquez, 2016). In 2007 it started a childcare program with blended financing from municipal funds and transfers from the Junta Nacional de Jardines Infantiles (JUNJI) (the largest national program for early care and education run by the Ministry of Education). Today the municipality operates 10 centers with the capacity to serve 1,328 children. The program targets beneficiaries using vulnerability criteria. It gives priority to working mothers (about 60 percent of mothers using the centers are employed), children suffering from abuse or violence, and households that benefit from other social programs. On average, centers run by the municipality have half the excess capacity (5 percent) of centers run by JUNJI and Fundación Integra (a national network of childcare providers run by the President's Office) (20 percent). Table 7.5 describe the most important features of the program.

TABLE 7.5 Features of the municipal childcare program in Renca, Chile

Feature	Description
Affordability	• Parents pay no fees.
Location	• Centers are located in neighborhoods where target population lives.
Schedules	• Opening hours match mothers' working hours. Normal opening hours are from 8 a.m.–5 p.m., Monday through Friday. Mothers who provide proof of work or study can use centers' extended hours (7:30 a.m. –7 p.m.).

(continued on next page)

TABLE 7.5 Features of the municipal childcare program in Renca, Chile *(continued)*

Feature	Description
Quality	• All centers use one of the following teaching methods: High Scope, Montessori, Waldorf, Reggio Emilia, or Curriculo Integral (Curriculo Integral was created by a group of preschool teachers at the University of Chile during the 1970s; it considers children as active agents and teachers as facilitators of learning). • Staff-child ratios are low: 0.20 for children 0–2, 0.13 for children 3–4, and 0.09 for children 4–5. • A trained preschool teacher is required in every classroom, a standard that goes beyond the legal requirement. • Educational programs include pedagogical workshops with an emphasis on psychomotricity, language, math, science, and English. • Centers have developed their own identities, specializing and developing content around issues, such as the environment, sports, and arts. • All centers have libraries. • Staff take children to museums, farms, and other places. • Nutrition follows the guidelines of the Programa de Alimentación Preescholar for a well-balanced diet. • Staff and management teams work with families to ensure continuity and consistency between school and home.
Incentives for staff	• Staff members are offered regular training to improve their qualifications. • Staff salaries are slightly below the average of Junta Nacional de Jardines Infantiles (JUNJI) staff, but staff receive monetary and nonmonetary incentives linked to performance. • Performance is measured based on staff attendance and punctuality, registered complaints (if any) from parents, and child attendance. • Staff members receive vacation bonuses, annual trip to the beach, and free passes to municipal swimming pool for them and their families. • Staff members with school-age children receive gift cards and school packages at beginning of every school year.
Incentives for families	• Childcare is integrated with other social programs (such as vaccination, dental hygiene, and nutrition programs) and the social protection network of the municipality. Users who fail to comply with rules of any program risk losing rights to other programs.
Transitions with school	• Programs are well articulated with primary education programs, providing continuity when children transition to school.

Source: Author's elaboration based on administrative data.

Annex 7A: Methodological Issues in Assessing Demand

In its childcare module, the Chilean Longitudinal Survey of Early Childhood (Encuesta Longitudinal de Primera Infancia [ELPI]) asks the primary caregiver retrospectively if the child attended a nursery or educational institution during a given age range.[6] The survey also collects information about current attendance at an educational institution by each household member (including children).

Using these two variables, we constructed a categorical variable (*status*) that classifies children according to their current (t) and immediate past ($t-1$)

attendance at formal childcare institutions. The categories are newcomers, stayers, dissidents, and always-out. *Newcomers* are children who were not attending a childcare institution in t-1 but were currently. *Dissidents* are children who used formal childcare services in t-1 but did not use them currently. *Stayers* are children that attended a childcare institution in t-1 and still attended. *Always-out* children did not attend a childcare institution in either t-1 or t.

Reasons for Using or Not Using Formal Childcare

The reasons for using or not using formal childcare services are captured in a variable that has five categories: culture, price/availability, service characteristics, beliefs about early childhood development, and other arrangements. The construction of this variable involved the recoding of three other variables available in the ELPI database: reasons for using a formal childcare service (15 categories) and the two main reasons for not using a formal childcare service (10 categories) in the immediate past (t-1).[7] The two main reasons were coded to construct two variables, each with six categories: my spouse does not want, price/availability, service characteristics, beliefs about early childhood development, other arrangements, and mother takes care of the child. These category variables were summarized in one five-category variable (*reasons2*): culture, price/availability, service characteristics, beliefs about early childhood development, and other arrangements. This transformation was made based on the following criteria:

- For children with information on only one of the two reasons, *reasons2* takes the value of the nonmissing reason.

- If one of the reasons is "mother takes care of the child" and the other reason had a missing value, *reasons2* takes the correspondent value "culture."

- For children with nonmissing values for both reasons and for whom the first reason is the same as the second reason, *reasons2* takes that value.

- If the first reason is "mother takes care of the child" and the second reason has a nonmissing value, *reasons2* takes the value of the second reason.

- For children with nonmissing values for both reasons and all other possible combinations, *reasons2* takes the value of the first reason.

Information about reasons for attending was available only for children who attended a childcare institution. Reasons for not attending were available only for children who did not attend a childcare institution. Therefore, after the recoding process, we constructed a unified variable for reasons of use and nonuse that takes the value of *e20* if the child attended an educational institution in the immediate past and the value of *reasons2* if the child did not.

Mothers' Employability

The likelihood that the mother works is captured in a categorical variable dividing mothers into three groups: low, medium, and high. To construct this variable, we first took the average of four categorical variables: level of education, maternal labor trajectory, cultural attitudes about work and family, and economic activity (participation rate) of the commune (Chile's most basic administrative division). Each of these variables has five categories except for attitude toward gender roles, which has only four; in each case the lowest value represents the most vulnerable profile. After taking the mean, we established two cut points—2.25 and 3.37—which correspond to the 25th and 75th percentile. A woman with an average below or equal to 2.25 has a low probability of working, and a woman whose average is above 3.375 has a high probability of working.

We measured the cultural attitudes about work and family (1 = most conservative, 4 = most liberal) using the average of two variables available in the "Meaning of Job and Family Responsibilities" module of the ELPI 2012. For the two corresponding questions, the respondent had to indicate the level of agreement on a scale of 1–4 (with 1 meaning "strongly agree" and 4 meaning "strongly disagree") with the following statements: (a) It is better for everyone if the man is the one who works and the woman takes care of home and family, and (b) If my partner earned enough, I would not work for pay. If the average of these variables is close to 1, we conclude that the respondent is conservative.

The maternal labor trajectory is represented by a categorical variable that can take five values: inactive and never worked, inactive and worked, looking for job for the first time, unemployed, and working. We constructed this variable using the raw employment situation variable ($d2$), taking advantage of the design of the "employment history of primary caregiver" module of the survey, in which the current employment situation determines whether the respondent continues with the module questions and which question is answered next. We classified a respondent as "inactive but has worked" if he or she answered the first question of the module part designed only for people with this characteristic. We applied the same logic to identify "inactive people who never worked." To identify unemployed and employed people, we used $d2$ for the current period.[8]

We capture the mother's level of education by a categorical variable with five possible values: no or basic education, intermediate education, incomplete tertiary education, complete tertiary education, and graduate education. We constructed this variable from a raw variable that comes from a question in the ELPI 2012 education module ($j2n$). It identifies the level of education for people older than 5 through 15 categories (distinguishing between the old and new system for basic and intermediate education and between technical/tertiary education with and without a diploma).

Economic activity in the commune is measured by a five-category variable (1 = low, 5 = high), the construction of which was based on information from the 2011 National Socioeconomic Characterization Survey (Encuesta de Caracterización Socioeconómica Nacional [CASEN]). From this survey, we calculated the participation rate by commune, defined as the proportion of economically active people older than 15 in the district. We then projected the participation rate on a scale of 1–5 by dividing by five the difference between the maximum and minimum value of the participation rates. In this way, we established six cut points that allowed us to classify the sample into five groups: 32–42.55 (first category, low economic activity), 42.55–48.98, 48.98–55.41, 55.41–61.84, and 61.84–68.27 (fifth category, high economic activity).

Income Quintiles

In its household income module, the ELPI 2012 collects information about average monthly household income in the past 12 months from all sources of income. Dividing this information by the number of household members, we obtained the average per capita income of each individual in a household (*ingpc*). Using the corresponding expansion factor, we constructed a new variable that categorized *ingpc* by quintiles. A 1 in this category variable means that the individual is in the bottom 20 percent of the distribution.

Notes

1. Results are based on seven surveys. Two gathered data on older children only: age 4 and older in the 2012 Encuesta de Hogares de Propósitos Múltiples (EHMP) (El Salvador) and age 5 and older in the 2006 Encuesta de Condiciones de Vida (ECV) (Ecuador). The other five collected data on children from birth to the mandatory school age. They are the 2012 Encuesta Longitudinal de la Primera Infancia (ELPI) (Chile), the 2011 Encuesta Nacional de Calidad de Vida (ENCV) (Colombia), the 2004 Encuesta Nacional de Condiciones de Vida (ENCOVI) (Honduras), the 2009 Encuesta Nacional de Empleo y Seguridad Social (ENESS) (Mexico), and the 2009 Encuesta Nacional de Hogares sobre Medición del Nivel de Vida (EMNV) (Nicaragua).

2. This group includes households that did not use formal care and cited, "I do not need the service; I prefer paying a nonrelative to take care of my child" or "I do not need the service; a relative takes care of my child" as the reason why and households that reported using formal care because, "I had to work and I had no relative to help out."

3. This group includes households that reported, "My spouse prefers the child does not attend a center" or "I do not need the service; I take care of my child".

4. This group includes households that did not use formal daycare for the following reasons: "There were no free centers available"; "There were no centers back then"; "I need to send my child to a center, but the enrollment and monthly tuition fees are too expensive"; "I need the service, but it is too far"; "I need the service, but

the schedule is incompatible with my working hours"; "I needed a center but none had good quality"; "I do not trust or I do not like the centers"; "My child is too young"; "Children get sick at childcare centers"; "My child has health issues"; and "I preferred a nursery school or a kindergarten." It also included households that used formal daycare for the following reasons: "I had to work and I could not afford someone to take care of my child at home"; "Although I did not work, I trusted that the center would offer better conditions than what my child would have at home"; "To look for a job/go to school"; "By recommendation of the pediatrician"; "For my child to socialize with other children"; "To stimulate learning"; and "The school year already started."

5. See Mateo Díaz and Rodriguez-Chamussy (2013) for a summary of the evidence of the effect of childcare on these dimensions.

6. The age ranges are 0–3 months, 3–6 months, 6–12 months, 12–18 months, 2–3 years, 3–4 years, 4–5 years, 5–6 years, and 6–7 years.

7. All questions in the childcare module are asked for all age ranges before the current age of the child.

8. This module asks each question for every period since January 2004.

References

Backer, T. E. 1990. "Comparative Synthesis of Mass Media Health Behavior Campaigns." *Science Communication* 11: 315–29.

Backer, T. E., E. M. Rogers, and R. Sopory. 1992. *Designing Health Communication Campaigns: What Works?* Newbury Park, CA: Sage.

Bernal, R., and C. Fernandez. 2013. "Subsidized Child Care and Child Development in Colombia: Effects of Hogares Comunitarios de Bienestar as a Function of Timing and Length of Exposure." *Social Science & Medicine* 97: 241–9.

Centro MicroDatos. 2012. Encuesta Longitudinal de la Primera Infancia (ELPI). Departamento de Economía, Universidad de Chile.

Contreras, D., E. Puentes, and D. Bravo. 2012. "Female Labor Supply and Child Care Supply in Chile." Working Paper SDT 370, Department of Economics, University of Chile, Santiago.

Croker, H., R. Lucas, and J. Wardle. 2012. "Cluster-Randomized Trial to Evaluate the 'Change for Life' Mass Media/Social Marketing Campaign in the UK." *BMC Public Health* 6 (12): 404.

Encina, J., and C. Martinez. 2009. "Efecto de una mayor cobertura de salas cuna en la participación laboral femenina: Evidencia de Chile." Working Paper SDT 303, Department of Economics University of Chile, Santiago.

Fernandez, R. 2013. "Cultural Change as Learning: The Evolution of Female Labor Force Participation over a Century." *American Economic Review* 103 (1): 472–500.

Fitzpatrick, M. D. 2010. "Preschoolers Enrolled and Mothers at Work? The Effects of Universal Pre-Kindergarten." *Journal of Labor Economics* 28 (1): 51–85.

Flay, B. R., and J. L. Sobel. 1983. "The Role of Mass Media in Preventing Adolescent Substance Abuse." In *Preventing Adolescent Drug Abuse: Intervention Strategies,* edited by T. J. Glynn, C. G. Leukefeld, and J. P. Ludford. Rockville, MD: National Institute on Drug Abuse.

Fogli, A., and L. Veldkamp. 2011. "Nature or Nurture? Learning and the Geography of Female Labor Force Participation." *Econometrica* 79 (4): 1103–38.

Horsfall, B., L. Bromfield, and M. McDonald. 2010. "Are Social Marketing Campaigns Effective in Preventing Child Abuse and Neglect?" *National Child Protection Clearinghouse Issues* 32: 28.

Lun Wong, H., R. Luo, L. Zhang, and S. Rozelle. 2013. "The Impact of Vouchers on Preschool Attendance and Elementary School Readiness: A Randomized Controlled Trial in Rural China." *Economics of Education Review* 35: 53–65.

Mateo Díaz, M. and L. Rodriguez-Chamussy. 2013. "Childcare and Women's Labor Participation: Evidence for Latin America and the Caribbean." Technical Note 586, Inter-American Development Bank, Washington, DC. Available at https://publications.iadb.org/handle/11319/6493.

Mateo Díaz, M., L. Rodriguez-Chamussy, and F. Grafe. 2014. "Ley de Guarderías in México y los desafíos institucionales de conectar familia y trabajo." Policy Brief 219, Inter-American Development Bank, Washington, DC. Available at http://publications.iadb.org/handle/11319/6650.

Mateo Díaz, M., and J. Vasquez. 2016. "¿Demanda insuficiente o insatisfecha? El caso de un programa municipal de provisión de guarderías en Chile?" Nota Técnica, Inter-American Development Bank, Washington, DC.

Medrano, P. 2009. "Public Day Care and Female Labor Force Participation: Evidence from Chile." Working Paper SDT 306, Department of Economics, University of Chile, Santiago.

Melkote, S. R., D. Moore, and S. Velu. 2014. "What Makes an Effective HIV/AIDS Prevention Communication Campaign? Insights from Theory and Practice." *Journal of Creative Communications* 9 (1): 85–92.

Palmgreen, P., and L. Donohew. 2006. "Effective Mass Media Strategies for Drug Abuse Prevention Campaigns." In *Handbook of Drug Abuse Prevention,* edited by Z. Sloboda and W. J. Bukoski. New York: Springer.

Perloff, R. M. 1993. *The Dynamics of Persuasion.* Hillsdale, NJ: Lawrence Erlbaum.

Rogers, E. M., and J. D. Storey. 1987. "Communication Campaigns." *Handbook of Communication Science,* edited by C. R. Berger and S. H. Chaffee. Newbury Park, CA: Sage.

Slater, M. D. 1996. "Theory and Method in Health Audience Segmentation." *Journal of Health Communication* 1: 267–83.

Walls, H. L., A. Peeters, J. Proietto, and J. J. McNeil. 2011. "Public Health Campaigns and Obesity: A Critique." *BMC Public Health* 11: 136.

CHAPTER 8

Formulating a Basic Package for Childcare Programs

In a context of limited resources, there is a tradeoff between reaching as many children as possible and providing good-quality care at a reasonable cost. Policy makers need to consider these tradeoffs as they try to make programs reach the desired scale.

This chapter examines the costs, scale, and features of programs. It provides a set of possible combinations to be included in a basic package of services that ensures a minimum level of well-being for children and mothers. Because it is difficult to meet all objectives at once, policy makers need to make choices about expanding access, making access compatible with working families' schedules, and improving quality. These three aspects are key to program design because no child should be left behind, children should not be worse off attending a program than not attending it, and programs should provide certain convenience features to ensure that families use them.

The chapter is organized as follows: The first section documents the costs of existing programs. The second section proposes a list of features that should be considered as a minimum in any childcare program.

Costs, Staff Qualifications, and Compensation at Existing Programs

Costs of Programs

Table 8.1 shows the costs per child of 28 of the 40 programs analyzed (information was not available on the other programs).

Two sets of figures are reported for the costs per child. The first is based on the information reported by program directors and specialists; the second is the total budget divided by the number of children enrolled. The fact that the figures differ suggests the need for better data.

TABLE 8.1 Per child costs of selected childcare programs in Latin America and the Caribbean

Program/country	Total annual budget (millions of local currency units)	Number of children enrolled	Estimated average monthly cost per child (total budget/number of children enrolled/12)	Estimated monthly average cost per child (international purchasing power parity dollars)	Reported monthly average cost per child	
					Local currency unit	International purchasing power parity dollars
Programa Nacional Abrazo, Centros Comunitarios (Paraguay)	31,000	2,246	1,150,193	485	1,291,666	544
Jardines de Administración Directa, Junta Nacional de Jardines Infantiles (JUNJI) (Chile)	223,463	168,883	110,265	279	182,191	461
Estancias Infantiles, Instituto de Seguridad y Servicios Sociales de los Trabajadores del Estado (ISSSTE) (Mexico)	1,456	34,318	3,535	377	4,283	457
Jardines Vía Transferencia de Fondos (VTF) (JUNJI) (Chile)	—	—	—	279	156,297	395
Jardines Infantiles, Buenos Aires (Argentina)	600	46,818	1,069	386	975	352
Centros Infantiles del Buen Vivir, Ministerio de Inclusión Económica y Social (MIES) (Ecuador)	160	93,226	143	250	199	348
Guarderías, Instituto Mexicano del Seguro Social (IMSS) (Mexico)	8,698	209,056	3,467	370	3,151	336
Fundación Integra (Chile)	161,175	73,185	183,524	467	120,574	307
Centros Educativo, Culturales de Infancia (JUNJI) (Chile)	1,013	1,697	49,724	126	116,880	296
Programa de Mejoramiento a la Infancia (PMI) (JUNJI) (Chile)	1,450	2,352	51,387	130	85,830	217

(continued on next page)

TABLE 8.1 Per child costs of selected childcare programs in Latin America and the Caribbean *(continued)*

Program/country	Total annual budget (millions of local currency units)	Number of children enrolled	Estimated average monthly cost per child (total budget/number of children enrolled/12)	Estimated monthly average cost per child (international purchasing power parity dollars)	Reported monthly average cost per child	
					Local currency unit	International purchasing power parity dollars
Jardín Infantil Familiar/Laboral/Étnico (JUNJI) (Chile)	—	—	—	279	81,220	205
Modalidad Institucional, Instituto Colombiano de Bienestar Familiar (ICBF) (Colombia)	1,350,000	701,961	160,265	132	243,000	200
Espacios de Desarrollo Infantil, Rio de Janeiro (Brazil)	268	130,006	172	107	251	157
Plan Centros de Atención a la Infancia y a la Familia (CAIF) (Uruguay)	1,549	45,549	2,834	152	2,834	152
Centros de Primera Infancia (CPI) (Argentina)	14	6,400	183	66	392	142
Programa de Atención Integral a la Primera Infancia, Consejo Nacional para la Niñez y la Adolescencia (CONANI) (Dominican Republic)	166	7,910	1,750	83	2,962	141
Estancias Infantiles, Secretaría de Desarrollo Social (SEDESOL) (Mexico)	3,532	268,577	1,096	117	1,263	135
Centros de Desarrollo Integral, Instituto Salvadoreño para el Desarrollo Integral de la Niñez y la Adolescencia (CDI ISNA) (El Salvador)	1	1,428	68	129	69	130
Cuna Más (Peru)	241	56,766	354	220	208	129
Centros de Desarrollo Infantil (CDI) (Nicaragua)	121	7,800	1,297	135	1,235	128

(continued on next page)

TABLE 8.1 Per child costs of selected childcare programs in Latin America and the Caribbean *(continued)*

Program/country	Total annual budget (millions of local currency units)	Number of children enrolled	Estimated average monthly cost per child (total budget/number of children enrolled/12)	Estimated monthly average cost per child (international purchasing power parity dollars)	Reported monthly average cost per child	
					Local currency unit	International purchasing power parity dollars
Centros de Desarrollo Infantil (CENDI DF), Secretaría de Educación Pública Distrito Federal (SEP-DF) (Mexico)	73	5,311	1,138	121	1,126	120
Atención en Educación Infantil, Fortaleza (Brazil)	72	32,232	186	116	186	116
Hogares Comunitarios, Secretaría de Obras Sociales de la Esposa del Presidente (SOSEP) (Guatemala)	84	16,024	435	107	405	100
Centros de Atención Integral, Instituto Hondureño de la Niñez y la Familia (IHNFA) (Honduras)	17	1,997	717	67	584	54
Hogares Comunitarios (ICBF) (Colombia)	844,300	1,058,593	66,464	55	64,800	53
Programa de Atención Integral al Niño Menor de Seis Años (PAIN) (Guatemala)	33	22,011	126	31	—	—
Centros de Bienestar Infantil, Instituto Salvadoreño para el Desarrollo Integral de la Niñez y la Adolescencia (CBI ISNA) (El Salvador)	1	5,854	15	29	—	—
Centros de Educación y Nutrición y Centros Infantiles de Atención Integral (CEN-CINAI) (Costa Rica)	41,526	19,100	181,178	496	—	—

Source: Authors' elaboration based on administrative data.
Note: Only one budget was available for the three modalities of JUNJI in Chile. The data reported by program staff have different unit costs for each modality. — = Not available.

The numbers reveal wide variation in costs per child, ranging from about $50 to more than $500 a month. These figures are close to the international benchmarks or actual investment in some countries in the Organisation for Economic Co-operation and Development (OECD) (see chapter 6).

Figure 8.1 shows the average cost per child (x-axis), the number of services in the program (y-axis), and the number of children served (the size of each circle).[1] The service index represents the sum of 14 dichotomous variables indicating the presence (1) or absence (0) of certain characteristics plus an indicator of the average staff-child ratio. These variables include whether the program provides at least eight hours of service; offers extended service beyond eight hours; is open Monday–Friday; is open on weekends; is open year round; provides at least three meals; receives nutritional advice from experts; has a curriculum; accepts children younger than 1; accepts children 1–2; accepts children 2–3; has a cap on the number of children younger than 1; has a cap on the number of children 1–2;

FIGURE 8.1 Number of services provided by, number of children served by, and average per child cost of selected childcare programs in Latin America and the Caribbean

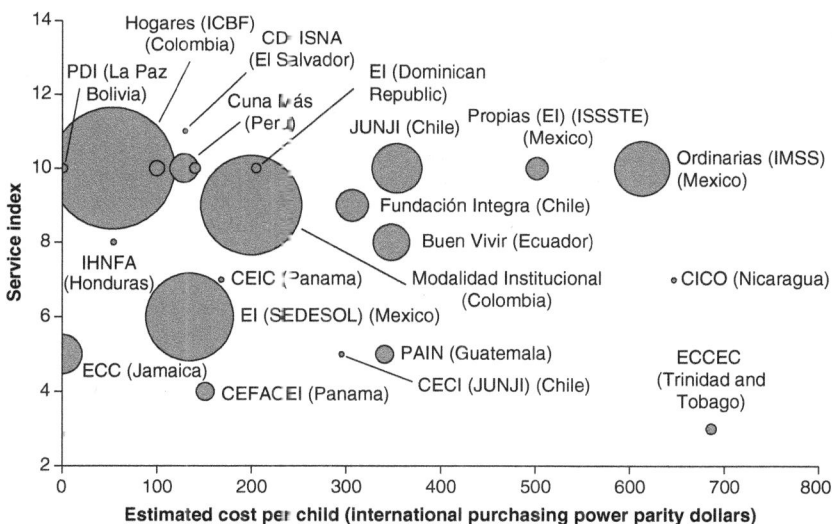

Source: Authors' elaboration based on administrative data.
Note: Size of circles indicates number of children enrolled. Buen Vivir = Centros Infantiles del Buen Vivir; I; CDI ISNA = Centros de Desarrollo Integral; CECI = Centro Educativo Cultural de Infancia; CEFACEI = Centros Familiares y Comunitarios de Educación Inicial; CEIC = Centros de Educación Inicial Comunitario; CICO = Centros Infantiles Comunitarios; ECC = Early Childhood Commission; ECCEC = Early Childhood Care and Education Centers; EI = Estancias Infantiles; ICBF = Instituto Colombiano de Bienestar Familiar; IHNFA = Instituto Hondureño de la Niñez y la Familia; IMSS = Instituto Mexicano del Seguro Social; ISSSTE = Instituto de Seguridad y Servicios Sociales de los Trabajadores del Estado; JUNJI = Junta Nacional de Jardines Infantiles; PAIN = Programa de Atención Integral al Niño Menor de Seis Añosl; PDI = Programa de Desarrollo Inicial; SEDESOL = Secretaría de Desarrollo Social.

FIGURE 8.2 Relation between child-staff ratio and average cost per child at selected childcare programs in Latin America and the Caribbean

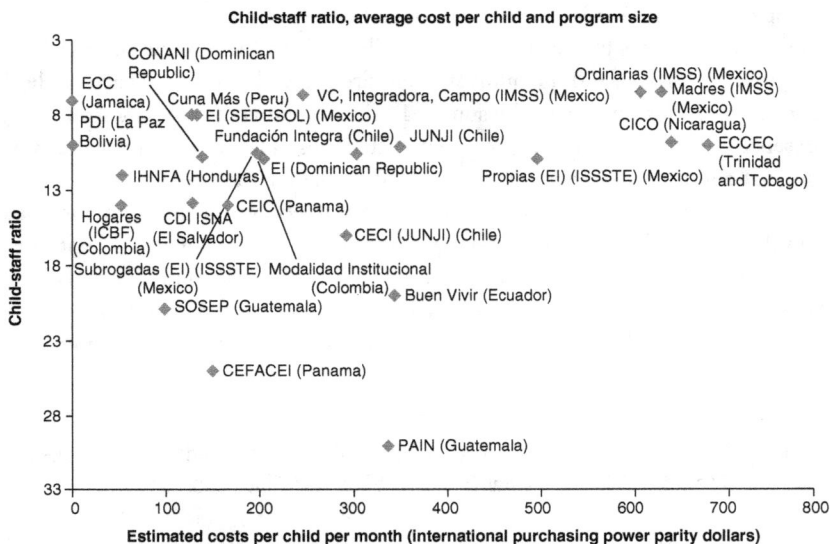

Child-staff ratio, average cost per child and program size

Source: Authors' elaboration based on administrative data.
Note: Buen Vivir = Centros Infantiles del Buen Vivir; CDI ISNA = Centros de Desarrollo Integral; CECI = Centro Educativo Cultural de Infancia; CEFACEI = Centros Familiares y Comunitarios de Educación Inicial; CEIC = Centros de Educación Inicial Comunitario; CICO = Centros Infantiles Comunitarios; CONANI = Consejo Nacional para la Niñez y la Adolescencia; ECC = Early Childhood Commission; ECCEC = Early Childhood Care and Education Centers; EI = Estancias Infantiles; ICBF = Instituto Colombiano de Bienestar Familiar; IHNFA = Instituto Hondureño de la Niñez y la Familia; IMSS = Instituto Mexicano del Seguro Social; ISSSTE = Instituto de Seguridad y Servicios Sociales de los Trabajadores del Estado; JUNJI = Junta Nacional de Jardines Infantiles; PAIN = Programa de Atención Integral al Niño Menor de Seis Años!; PDI = Programa de Desarrollo Inicial; SEDESOL = Secretaría de Desarrollo Social; SOSEP = Secretaría de Obras Sociales de la Esposa del Presidente; VC = Vecino Comunal.

and has an age-differentiated staff-child ratio. The higher the service index, the more complete the childcare program.

Factors other than just services explain variations in per child costs: Staff costs vary across countries, for example, and economies of scale may reduce costs at larger programs. Overall, staff-child ratios drive a large part of program costs (figure 8.2). Services for younger children are more expensive than services for older children because of significant differences in staff-child ratios.

Staff Qualifications and Compensation

Staff-related expenses represent a large share of costs across all programs, although the differences are large. The share of the annual budget that went to wages was 43 percent at Hogares Comunitarios in Colombia, 45 percent at Centros del Buen

Vivir in Ecuador, 52 percent at Centros de Educação Infantil in Brazil, 77 percent at Jardines Infantiles in Argentina, 92 percent at the Early Childhood Commission in Jamaica, and 95 percent at the Programa de Atención Integral al Niño Menor de Seis Años (PAIN) in Guatemala.[2]

To ensure that quality does not suffer, policy makers need to ensure that staff-child ratios can be maintained and that a sufficient number of trained professionals is available—or that a strategy can be developed in the short run to overcome the shortage of professionals.[3] Professionals can be trained to meet expanded demand only if expansion can be staggered.

Table 8.2 presents the staff qualification requirements for 36 of the 40 programs studied (information was not available on two programs in Brazil and two in Mexico). Seventeen programs (47 percent) require a university degree for teachers, with 10 of them requiring that the degree be in early education or a technical equivalent. Thirteen programs (37 percent) require some secondary education. One program in Chile and one in El Salvador have no particular requirements; one program in Peru has only a literacy requirement; one program in Mexico

TABLE 8.2 Educational requirements for staff at selected childcare programs in Latin America and the Caribbean

Level of education	Program
Bachelor's degree in early education or technical equivalent	Centros de Desarrollo Infantil (CDI) (Nicaragua)
	Centro Educativo Cultural de Infancia (CECI), Junta Nacional de Jardines Infantiles (JUNJI)
	Centros de Desarrollo Infantil, Secretaría de Educación Pública Distrito Federal (CENDI DF) (Mexico)
	Centros Infantiles de Buen Vivir (Ecuador)
	Centro de Orientación Infantil y Familiar (COIF) (Panama)[a]
	Consejo Nacional para la Niñez y la Adolescencia (CONANI) (Dominican Republic)
	Centros de Primera Infancia (CPI) (Argentina)[b]
	Early Childhood Commission (ECC) (Jamaica)[c]
	Early Childhood Care and Education Centers (ECCEC) (Trinidad and Tobago)[a]
	Estancias Infantiles (EI) (Dominican Republic)
	Estancias Infantiles, Instituto de Seguridad y Servicios Sociales de los Trabajadores del Estado (ISSSTE) (Mexico)[a]
	Guarderias, Instituto Mexicano del Seguro Social (IMSS) (Mexico)[d]

(continued on next page)

TABLE 8.2 Educational requirements for staff at selected childcare programs in Latin America and the Caribbean *(continued)*

Level of education	Program
	Instituto Hondureño de la Niñez y la Familia (IHNFA) (Honduras)[e]
	Fundación Integra (Chile)[e]
	Jardines Infantiles (Argentina)[a]
	Jardines Infantiles (SEP-DF) (Mexico)
	JUNJI (Chile)
Upper secondary	Programa Nacional Abrazo, Centros Comunitarios (Paraguay)
	Centros de Educación y Nutrición y Centros Infantiles de Atención Integral (CEN-CINAI) (Costa Rica)
	Centros de Proteccion Programa Abrazo (Paraguay)
	Day Care Services (The Bahamas)
	Programa de Desarrollo Inicial (PDI) (Bolivia)
Lower secondary	Plan Centros de Atención a la Infancia y a la Familia (CAIF) (Uruguay)
	Centros de Bienestar Infantil (CBI ISNA) (El Salvador)
	Centros Infantiles Comunitarios (CICO) (Nicaragua)
	Estancias Infantiles, Secretaría de Desarrollo Social (SEDESOL) (Mexico)
	Hogares Comunitarios, Instituto Colombiano de Bienestar Familiar (ICBF) (Colombia)
	Hogares Comunitarios, Secretaría de Obras Sociales de la Esposa del Presidente (SOSEP) (Guatemala)
	Modalidad Institucional (ICBF) (Colombia)
	Programa de Atención Integral al Niño Menor de Seis Años (PAIN) (Guatemala)
Primary	Centros Familiar y Comunitarios de Educación Inicial (CEFACEI) and Centros de Educación Inicial Comunitario (CEIC) (Panama)
	Centros de Educación Inicial (CEI) (SEP-DF) (Mexico)
Training on early childhood education, basic childcare	Daycare Centre, Child Care Board (CCB) (Barbados)
Ability to read and write	Cuna Más (Peru)
No requirements	Programa de Mejoramiento a la Infancia (PMI) (JUNJI) (Chile)
	Centros de Desarrollo Integral (El Salvador)

a. Assistants must have upper-secondary education.
b. Assistants must be studying for a bachelor's degree in early education.
c. Assistants must have upper-secondary education with a specialization in early education.
d. Assistants must have lower-secondary education.
e. Assistants must have primary education.

and one in Panama require completed primary education; and one program in Barbados requires training in early childhood education/basic childcare.

Table 8.3 shows the average compensation of childcare workers and managers, based on information from program directors and staff (table 8.3). On average managers receive more than twice the salary of a childcare worker (about $1,380 a month versus $640). Average salaries of childcare workers are slightly lower than average salaries in the health and education sectors; salaries for managers are slightly higher. However, wide variation lies behind those numbers. A childcare worker at the Instituto Mexicano del Seguro Social (IMSS) earns only a fifth as much as the average public sector employee, whereas a similar worker in Uruguay makes about a third as much. In all countries except Bolivia and Uruguay, childcare workers earn

TABLE 8.3 Average monthly wage of childcare workers and managers at selected programs in Latin America and the Caribbean

Country	Program	Childcare Center Workers			Childcare Center Managers		
		In US dollars	As percentage of average monthly wage in public sector	As percentage of average monthly wage in health and education sector	In US dollars	As percentage of average monthly wage in public sector	As percentage of average monthly wage in health and education sector
Argentina	Centros de Primera Infancia (CPI)	755	51	59	—	—	—
Argentina	Jardines Infantiles	1,068	72	84	—	—	—
Bolivia	Programa de Desarrollo Inicial (PDI) (Servicio Departamental de Gestión Social [SEDEGES]) La Paz	710	144	174	710	144	174
Chile	Fundación Integra	1,005	87	89	1,694	146	150
Chile	Junta Nacional de Jardines Infantiles (JUNJI)	700	60	62	3,122	270	276
Chile	Programa de Mejoramiento a la Infancia (JUNJI)	700	60	62	3,122	270	276
Chile	Centros Educativo-Culturales de Infancia (CECI) (JUNJI)	700	60	62	3,122	270	276

(continued on next page)

TABLE 8.3 Average monthly wage of childcare workers and managers at selected programs in Latin America and the Caribbean *(continued)*

Country	Program	Childcare center workers			Childcare center managers		
		In US dollars	As percentage of average monthly wage in public sector	As percentage of average monthly wage in health and education sector	In US dollars	As percentage of average monthly wage in public sector	As percentage of average monthly wage in health and education sector
Colombia	Hogares Comunitarios (Instituto Colombiano de Bienestar Familiar [ICBF])	342	28	51	—	—	—
Colombia	Modalidad Institucional (ICBF)	419	34	63	723	59	109
Costa Rica	Centros de Educación y Nutrición y Centros Infantiles de Atención Integral (CEN-CINAI)	617	43	57	1,016	70	94
Dominican Republic	Estancias Infantiles (Instituto Dominicano de Seguros Sociales [IDSS])	321	79	93	407	100	118
Dominican Republic	Programa de Atención Integral a la Primera Infancia (Consejo Nacional para la Niñez y la Adolescencia [CONANI])	281	69	82	—	—	—
Ecuador	Centros Infantiles del Buen Vivir (Ministerio de Inclusión Económica y Social [MIES])	648	87	117	1,128	152	204
El Salvador	Centros de Desarrollo Integral, Instituto Salvadoreño para el Desarrollo Integral de la Niñez y la Adolescencia (CDI ISNA)	402	72	103	798	143	205

(continued on next page)

TABLE 8.3 Average monthly wage of childcare workers and managers at selected programs in Latin America and the Caribbean *(continued)*

Country	Program	Childcare center workers			Childcare center managers		
		In US dollars	As percentage of average monthly wage in public sector	As percentage of average monthly wage in health and education sector	In US dollars	As percentage of average monthly wage in public sector	As percentage of average monthly wage in health and education sector
El Salvador	Centros de Bienestar Infantil (CBI ISNA)	39	12	18	649	116	166
Guatemala	Hogares Comunitarios (Secretaría de Obras Sociales de la Esposa del Presidente [SOSEP])	358	64	85	—	—	—
Honduras	Centros de Atención Integral (Instituto Hondureño de la Niñez y a Familia [IHNFA])	439	67	101	659	101	151
Mexico	Estancias Infantiles (EI) (Instituto de Seguridad y Servicos Sociales de los Trabajadores del Estado [ISSSTE])	367	43	56	1,957	232	297
Mexico	Guarderías (Instituto Mexicano del Seguro Social [IMSS])	157	19	24	309	37	47
Paraguay	Programa Nacional Abrazo, Centros Comunitarios	420	73	82	—	—	—
Paraguay	Programa Nacional Abrazo, Centros de Protección	420	73	82	—	—	—

(continued on next page)

TABLE 8.3 Average monthly wage of childcare workers and managers at selected programs in Latin America and the Caribbean *(continued)*

Country	Program	Childcare center workers			Childcare center managers		
		In US dollars	As percentage of average monthly wage in public sector	As percentage of average monthly wage in health and education sector	In US dollars	As percentage of average monthly wage in public sector	As percentage of average monthly wage in health and education sector
Trinidad and Tobago	Early Childhood Care and Education Centers (ECCEC)	773	—	—	1,846	—	—
Uruguay	Plan Centros de Atención a la Infancia y a la Familia (CAIF)	3,077	312	378	886	90	109

Source: Authors' elaboration based on administrative data.
Note: — = Not available. Childcare workers include caregivers and other personnel directly in charge of children. Managers include directors of centers and administrators. Average wages for part-time staff in charge of cleaning, cooking, security, and maintenance are not included. No information was available for programs in The Bahamas, Barbados, Brazil, Jamaica, Nicaragua, Panama, or Peru; on PAIN in Guatemala; or on five programs in Mexico, including the Secretaría de Desarrollo Social (SEDESOL). Some programs did not report information on managers' wages because they are home-based and therefore run by mothers or because the information was not available.

less than their counterparts in either the public sector or the health and education sectors. Except in Costa Rica and Mexico (IMSS), the opposite is true of center directors and administrators, who earn significantly more than their counterparts in the health and education sectors. Salaries of center directors and administrators are also lower than the average for the public sector in Colombia and Uruguay.

Features That Should Be Included in a Basic Package

"Suppose I am a minister of finance and I tell you I want to expand a childcare service to reach as many as possible. What would the basic package include?" This section tries to answer this question. The basic package it describes represents the minimum standards for which there is significant agreement among experts from different countries.

Formal childcare facilitates female labor force participation (FLFP) and supports early childhood development (ECD). Sometimes trade-offs have to be made between investing in features that support one of these goals over the other. In many cases, however, fostering ECD and FLFP potentiate each other. Strengthening staff qualifications or reducing the number of children assigned to trained staff, for example, probably increases the use of childcare services, which facilitates FLFP. Having highly vulnerable children spend more hours at a center will likely improve their developmental outcomes.

The basic package (table 8.4) is a minimum standard, not an optimum package. Benchmarks for it come from a UNICEF consultation with a broad range of

TABLE 8.4 Basic package of features for childcare programs

Basic package feature	Early childhood development ⟵ Basic package ⟶ Female labor force participation
Coverage	
Access by children younger than 3	At least 25%
Access by 4-year-olds	At least 80%
Service features	
Safety	✓
Hours per week of attendance	At least 15 hours
Full-time (5–8 hours)	
Extended hours (more than 8 hours)	
Full-year calendar	
Distance (fewer big centers versus more small centers)	
Nutrition	✓
Curricula (national/state guideline or pedagogical framework for all early childhood services)	✓
Human resources	
Move toward a unified staffing system, including qualifications, work conditions, and salaries aligned on the education or social care sector	✓
Child-staff trained ratio for 4- to 5-year-olds	Not greater than 15:1
Group size	≤ 24 children per group

(continued on next page)

TABLE 8.4 Basic package of features for childcare programs *(continued)*

Basic package feature	Early childhood development	Basic package	Female labor force participation
Personnel with primary responsibility for care and education of young children have initial training		At least 80%	
Number of staff that are professionals (educators, pedagogues and/or teachers)		At least 50%	
Years of postsenior secondary training and certification in early childhood education and care required for this staff		At least 3 years	
Governance, management, and monitoring			
Registry of public providers		✓	
Registry of private providers		✓	
Regulatory framework enacted and applied equally to public and private providers		✓	
Goal setting, policy making, funding, and regulatory systems (including support/ supervision) effectively integrated		✓	
National policy or plan for development of universal early childhood system		✓	
Periodic independent national evaluations of early childhood services ensure that childhood policy is evidence based		At least 1 in 10 years	
Monitoring and data-collection mechanisms		✓	
Data regularly updated and publicly shared and disseminated		✓	
Level of public expenditure in early childcare and development		At least 1% of GDP	

Source: Authors' elaboration.
Note: Checks indicate item should be included in a basic package.

stakeholders in the field (Bennett 2008) complemented with information from OECD (2012) and Pascal and others (2013). Apart from safety considerations, infrastructure requirements are not included. In some cases, regulations about indoor and outdoor space are very specific (see chapter 5). No clear benchmark was found for staff-child ratios for children younger than 4 or for group sizes by age group (also not included in the table). Various organizations, including the American Academy of Pediatrics, the American Public Health Association, and the National Resource Center for Health and Safety in Child Care and Early Education (2011) in the United States, have established standards for these measures (see also Araujo, López Bóo, and Puyana 2013). Countries may prefer to use OECD averages as benchmarks (one staff member per 7 children for children 0–3 and one staff member per 18 children in preschool [OECD 2012]).

Everything below the cost line in table 8.4 is considered a mandatory component or "fixed cost." All programs should have an integrated ECD system and good registries, monitoring and evaluation mechanisms, and regulatory frameworks. A regulatory framework should define provider profiles, child eligibility, staff profiles, staff composition and career development, staff-child ratios, group sizes, program standards and curriculum, child assessments, and parent and community involvement (Bennett 2008).

The most expensive programs are not always the best. Some provision models may be more efficient at delivering similar packages of services than others. Factors such as staff remuneration and reach (geographic spread of smaller centers versus larger centers concentrated about high density/urban areas for example) affect program costs. Decisions related to models of provision (with or without private involvement in the delivery of the service) also matter.

Because the market for childcare is segmented, different program features will attract different types of users. The type of user has equity implications in terms of the allocation of public resources and program benefits. Policy makers should avoid choosing options that may inadvertently make programs unattractive to the intended population.

Notes

1. Some programs use more than one service modality. Guarderias, Instituto Mexicano del Seguro Social (IMSS) (in Mexico) has three: Madres IMSS, IMSS Ordinario, and IMSS in Campo/Vecino Comunal/Integradora. Estancias Infantiles, Instituto de Seguridad y Servicios Sociales de los Trabajadores del Estado (ISSSTE) (also in Mexico) has two: ISSSTE de Administración Directa and ISSSTE Subrogadas. Junta Nacional de Jardines Infantiles (JUNJI) (in Chile) has three: Jardines de Administración Directa, Jardines Via Transferencia de Fondos, and Jardín Infantil Familiar/Laboral/Etnico. Cuna Más (in Peru) has two modalities of service

provision—direct public provision and subsidies to private providers; program directors report no differences in costs or service features.

2. Araujo, López-Bóo, and Puyana (2013) find that wages account for the largest share of costs in most of the centers in their analysis.

3. Teachers in Mexico expressed concern about their ability to provide individualized attention and teaching in the face of expansion (Yosikawa and others 2007).

References

American Academy of Pediatrics, American Public Health Association, and National Resource Center for Health and Safety in Child Care and Early Education. 2011. *Caring for Our Children: National Health and Safety Performance Standards: Guidelines for Early Care and Education Programs*, 3rd ed. Elk Grove Village, IL. Available at http://cfoc.nrckids.org/StandardView/2.2.0.1.

Araujo, M. C., F. López-Bóo, and J. M. Puyana. 2013. "Panorama sobre los servicios de desarrollo infantil en América Latina y el Caribe." [Overview of Child Development Services in Latin America and the Caribbean.] IDB Monograph IDB-MG-149, Inter-American Development Bank, Washington, DC. Available at https://publications.iadb .org/handle/11319/3617?locale-attribute=es.

Bennett, J. 2008. "Benchmarks for Early Childhood Services in OECD Countries." Innocenti Working Paper 2008-02, UNICEF Innocenti Research Center, Florence.

OECD (Organisation for Economic Co-operation and Development). 2012. *Starting Strong III: A Quality Toolbox for Early Childhood Education and Care*. Paris: OECD Publishing.

Pascal, C., T. Bertram, S. Delaney, and C. Nelson. 2013. *A Comparison of International Childcare Systems*. Center for Research in Early Childhood (CREC), Birmingham, United Kingdom.

Yosikawa H., K. McCartney, R. Myers, K. L. Bub, J. Lugo-Gil, M. A. Ramos, and F. Knaul. 2007. "Early Childhood Education in Mexico: Expansion, Quality Improvement, and Curricular Reform." UNICEF Innocenti Research Center, Florence.

CHAPTER 9

Challenges Ahead

To strengthen its position in the world's economy, Latin America and the Caribbean (LAC) has to make the best possible use of its present and future human capital assets. The central argument in this book is that childcare policies are crucial to doing so. Significantly increasing the labor supply over the coming years requires the incorporation of women 25–45 into the labor market. The majority of mothers of children younger than 6 are concentrated in this age group. Access to good-quality and convenient childcare services can modify female labor force participation (FLFP) decisions, increasing a household's income and opportunities, especially among the most vulnerable segments of the population.

Time is of the essence, because other countries have already taken this path. In Norway 83 percent of mothers with young children are employed, and almost 90 percent of children 1–5 are in childcare (Johnsen 2012). The country's minister of finance described the contribution of FLFP to net national wealth as equivalent to the country's total petroleum wealth (Johnsen 2012). Japan has placed "womenomics" at the center of the country's growth strategy, shifting priorities from a social strategy to a strategy in which women actively participate and contribute to the economy.

This chapter elaborates on six messages:

- Countries should take a long-term perspective on human capital and social policy.
- Policy makers need to work on childcare policies together with complementary policies that affect female labor force participation.
- More and better data need to be gathered in order to assess the public and private stock of, use of, and potential demand for childcare services.
- Governance, management, and monitoring systems need to be improved to

increase policy coherence, help policy makers make better decisions based on evidence, enhance the efficiency and effectiveness of programs, and disseminate information that allows parents to make better choices.

- Increasing access without accounting for children's and mother's well-being may not be the right policy decision.
- Policy makers should always consider what the alternatives are for the mothers and children programs target.

Taking a Long-Term Perspective on Human Capital Assets and Social Policy

Taking a long-term perspective on human capital implies adopting a sustainable and coherent management strategy for both the stock and flow of policies and a life cycle perspective when designing social policy. It requires mapping all programs by age group to identify where programs overlap, to determine the reasons they do so, and to identify where programs are missing, in order to prevent people from falling through the cracks of social protection nets. Overlaps may exist because of the need to meet different objectives or target different populations based on demographic criteria, such as income, gender, and race. This exercise helps identify areas where there may be too many or too few social policies and programs.

The politics of reforms often provide strong incentives for policy makers to invest in policies with shorter-term payoffs. But childcare policies are at the heart of key social and economic development outcomes. They have to be understood as powerful instruments that play a role at the crossroads of child development, labor, demography, fiscal sustainability, productivity, growth, and equity. Behind these policies are real opportunities to capitalize on past and current investments in better education for girls, improve the human capital of tomorrow, make the best of the demographic dividend that many countries in the region are enjoying, strengthen public finances, and raise productivity and promote sustainable growth.

Adopting Complementary Policies to Improve Female Labor Force Participation

The conventional role of women as caregivers is partly responsible for low FLFP and the low earnings of women. These outcomes create a vicious cycle of more time allocated to unpaid informal childcare and less opportunity to engage in paid employment. Childcare policies can help break this cycle, but they are not sufficient.

Barriers to FLFP include skills mismatches, labor market constraints, lack of work and family conciliation policies, and cultural factors. Tackling the multiplicity of obstacles women face accessing jobs requires multiple policy actions.

LAC countries face the challenge of boosting labor demand in sustainable ways. Given the simultaneous nature of women's decisions to work and use childcare, childcare interventions should accompany all other policies intended to improve female labor market outcomes.

Education

Labor outcomes are related to education and skills acquisition. Ensuring that girls stay in school and receive good-quality education are important inputs for FLFP. LAC countries have been successful in increasing school attendance, but the time spent in school does not guarantee the acquisition of relevant skills. Girls and boys enter school with similar abilities, but the gender gap develops and widens over time. Results of the 2012 Programme for International Student Assessment (PISA), for example, show that in Chile the average girl performs as if she has half a year less education than the average boy. These gaps are not universal: In Norway and Sweden, for example, there are no gender gaps in PISA math scores, and girls in Iceland outperform boys. Math results are important because they are a good predictor of future earnings, and school test scores and results on university access exams determine career decisions that contribute to occupational segregation in the labor market (Bassi, Busso, and Muñoz 2013; Bos, Ganimian, and Vegas 2014; Heckman 2011; Mizala 2014; Ñopo 2012). Policy options to improve inputs in the school system and reduce gender inequalities include early childhood interventions, review of textbooks to correct for stereotypes and gender biases, teacher training, and mentoring programs.

Labor Market Rigidities

The evidence suggests that two interventions could significantly improve the functioning of the labor market for women: solving information problems through active labor market policies and adapting institutional arrangements to allow more flexibility at work (Autor 2008; Goldin 2014; Todd 2012; World Bank 2012). Active labor market policies are government programs (including public employment services, training programs, and employment subsidies) that affect the interaction between labor demand and supply. They are responses to costly, incomplete, and asymmetric information that makes it difficult for individual actors to solve coordination problems. These policies are often implemented during economic downturns. There is evidence that skills training and wage subsidies in particular have positive impacts on FLFP.[1]

Flexible arrangements and work-time policies help women enter and remain in the labor market.[2] They include telecommuting, flexible hours, flexible use of paid annual and family paid leave, and compressed work schedules.

Work and Family Conciliation Policies

Two main policies reduce the impact of parenthood on labor market outcomes: parental leave and childcare policies. Leave provisions vary widely across the world (see chapter 5 for a description of parental, maternity, and paternity leave policies in LAC). The impact of these policies on FLFP depends on who pays for them. Evidence from advanced economies suggests that mothers entitled to maternity leave benefits are more likely to return to work than mothers without such benefits (Berger and Waldfogel 2004; Espinola-Arredondo and Mondal 2009; Han and others 2009; OECD 2011). Extended paid maternity leave can also have negative effects on female employment, however (OECD 2011).

Cultural Factors

Economic factors and formal institutions alone cannot explain FLFP and fertility decisions.[3] Differences in social norms and beliefs have to be factored in when crafting policies that affect these outcomes (Fernández 2013; Fernández and Fogli 2009; Fogli and Veldkamp 2011).[4] Fernández and Fogli (2009) provide robust evidence that cultural proxies are significant (statistically and in magnitude) in explaining how much women work.[5]

Cross-country comparisons illustrate the relationship between beliefs and women's participation in the labor market (figure 9.1). When designing specific interventions, countries need to account for these preferences and beliefs.

Gathering More and Better Data

One of the striking challenges encountered during the preparation of this book is the lack of data on both demand for and supply of childcare in the region. More information is needed about care arrangements in general and the use of formal childcare for younger children in particular; households' reasons for using or not using certain types of services; and the services themselves (costs, financing, and operating models for both public and private supply). Many countries are missing the fundamental data they need to make cost-effective decisions about formal services for children and their families.

Costs of Programs

Packages of services can be produced at different unit costs; country-specific factors and decisions such as the model of provision or the geographic spread of services (having smaller centers instead of larger centers concentrated around high density/urban areas, for example) significantly affect these costs. When comparing costs of programs, it is important to think in terms of the costs' functions rather than average unit costs (Glassman 2015).

FIGURE 9.1 Female labor force participation rates and beliefs about gender roles in selected countries in Latin America and the Caribbean

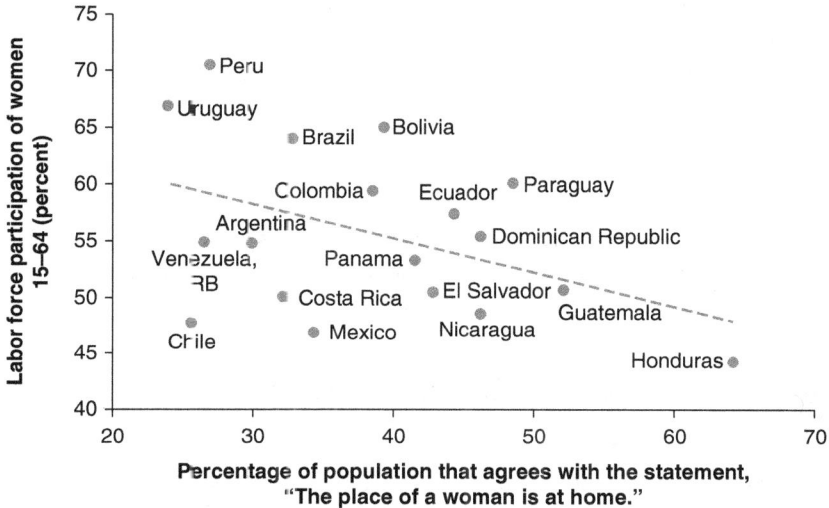

Sources: Latinobarómetro 2009; World Bank 2012.

Registries

Good registries of both public and private providers, combined with good regulation and accreditation mechanisms to ensure quality, are critical. Most providers of private childcare services are required to register and obtain operating permits. But simply registering does not mean that information is consolidated in a single state or national registry, which would allow for a better understanding of how supply is distributed, who is using specific services, the dynamics between public and private provision, and the most pressing needs in terms of coverage or service requirements for more vulnerable populations. At least 60 percent of children 0–5 enrolled in all countries studied use public childcare programs. Many of these programs are either outsourced by the public sector or run directly by private providers.

Survey Data

Less than half of the countries in the region collect survey data on childcare programs (Mateo Diaz and Rodriguez-Chamussy, 2015). Even if incomplete, household surveys are the main source of information. Household surveys collect socioeconomic and demographic data that are used by national statistic offices as inputs to calculate indicators and measures related to household and individual income, labor status, poverty, and life conditions of the population.

These data provide a credible source of information for the development and evaluation of public policies in each country. Some surveys include only one question about attendance and one about the type of program attended. Some surveys do not include information on the mother in the household, making it difficult to understand the relationship between her working status, education, and other characteristics and the childcare arrangement she uses. A few surveys collect information for children younger than 3 years old. Very few surveys collect information on informal childcare arrangements and costs.

Coordination among governments, researchers, international institutions, and donor agencies is crucial to set standard practices for gathering data across countries. Annex 9A proposes a module that national surveys could use to gather information on the use of childcare and education services by families of very young children that could be added to countries' household surveys.

Improving the Governance, Management, and Monitoring of Childcare Programs

Experts and practitioners stress the importance of governance requirements and institutional features for childcare programs (Bennett 2008) based on four principles:

- A unified early childhood development (ECD) system to ensure the coherence of and integration between different levels of policy-making processes

- A shared and integrated vision of child development across units

- An evidence-based approach to policy design and implementation

- Accountability and transparency mechanisms.

These principles have several implications. First, institutions should promote multisectoral integration and develop coordination mechanisms to ensure efficiency and effectiveness in the delivery of ECD services. To increase the coherence and integration of goal-setting, policy making, funding, and regulation (including support and supervision mechanisms), national or state responsibility for ECD should be assigned to a single agency or ministry where possible. A national policy or plan is also recommended as a roadmap for developing a unified ECD system that covers education, health, social protection, and labor. Policy choices should also be streamlined. Offering too many different programs increases costs and makes it difficult to create a coherent support system and to coordinate and manage parallel systems. Spreading resources too thin, governments lose the overall perspective and end up managing a huge number of daily transactions rather than managing public services.

Second, an integrated or holistic approach to child development is needed. Multiple risk factors in child development need to be addressed simultaneously.

Interventions to reduce stunting and increase cognitive stimulation are more effective if combined, for example, although it is unclear which combinations work best (Engle and others 2011). For certain core aspects related to quality of care and education, public and private provision are currently not governed by the same regulatory framework.

Third, decision makers need to take an evidence-based approach to policy design and implementation. An independent agency should monitor and evaluate the ECD system, and the information gathered should be a key input in to decisions to scale up programs. Good program-specific data are critical (Wolfensohn Center for Development 2009). Registries of providers need to be created. Most private providers are required to register to obtain permits to start operating. This information is not always consolidated into a single state or national registry. Creation of such registries would improve the understanding of where public and private childcare centers are located, who is using specific services, and what the most pressing needs are for vulnerable populations.

Fourth, accountability and transparency mechanisms are vital. Once good data collection and evaluation instruments have been put in place, data should be published, made easily accessible, regularly updated, and disseminated for use by all stakeholders, particularly parents. Making information available reduces information asymmetries and potential market failures in private service provision, allowing parents to make better-informed choices.

Mexico's experience illustrates the challenges of improving the governance of childcare (box 9.1).

BOX 9.1 Integrating policies and programs in Mexico through a childcare law

Mexico has increased childcare coverage, but it faces quality and efficiency challenges. Fragmentation of interventions and programs makes it difficult to improve equity in access to good-quality services.

The Childcare Law (*Ley de Guarderias*), passed in 2011, represents an opportunity to integrate policies and programs and improve their compatibility and coherence in the medium and long term. Several issues need to be resolved before it can do so, however:

- A board was created to coordinate policy decisions, but there is much institutional asymmetry between its members, and no clear mandates and coordination rules were established.
- A unified registry of providers was created, but it was not implemented. The registry should be the main tool for planning, monitoring, and evaluation. The Federal District was entrusted with responsibility for the state registries, but it does not have the institutional capacity or resources to handle them effectively.
- Policies for early childcare and initial education were not successfully integrated.

(continued on next page)

Fostering Early Childhood Development and Making It Easier for Mothers to Work

"Care and education cannot be thought of as separate entities in dealing with young children" (Bowman, Donovan, and Burns 2000, p. 2). Likewise, the well-being of parents and children should not be considered separate entities when designing early childhood care and education policies.

Raising staff qualifications and reducing the number of children per trained staff member would likely result in greater use of childcare services. Having highly vulnerable children attend more hours at a good-quality center is likely to improve their developmental outcomes.

Focusing on both parents and children is more expensive than investing in either early childhood development or FLFP, but the cost of designing a program that affects both simultaneously should be lower than the cost of investing in each separately. A package that focuses on early childhood development would reduce staff-child ratios, strengthen staff training, and develop better curricula; a few hours a day of service could suffice. In contrast, a package that seeks to increase FLFP would provide expanded opening hours, convenient locations, and transportation. If countries rank both early childhood development and FLFP among their top priorities, they must avoid developing policy solutions in isolation. The most cost-effective formula will incorporate features that respond to both goals.

Considering the Counterfactual

Countries should be concerned not only about the provision of good-quality and convenient childcare in sufficient numbers but also about getting children, in particular the most vulnerable children, to centers. Demand for childcare services is segmented. Because there is an unequal distribution of opportunities, the costs (including opportunity costs) and benefits of childcare are different across income levels.

Some children in the region are subject to extremely precarious care arrangements, such as staying with another minor, being left alone, or being taken to the mother's workplace.[6] Such arrangements affect as many as 5 percent of young children in some countries, according to survey data—which may underestimate the reality, given the shame associated with accurate reporting (social desirability effects). These children would be better off in a suboptimal formal service. Policy makers should consider these counterfactuals when designing policies.

In some households the idea of a mother not working to stay at home with her children is not an option. Some countries in the world can afford one, two, or three year parental leave policies, but this is not foreseeable in the near future for most LAC countries. Keeping one parent at home, for instance, by using vouchers, solves the problem of current income by simply replacing it but does not provide a solution for future income, generating a structural dependency on social assistance programs in many cases for those individuals.

Having a large share of the active population outside the labor market poses fiscal sustainability issues, and it reduces labor supply in the economy both in the short and long run, as in two, three, or four years the possibilities for those workers to return to the labor force will be very limited (Blank 1989; Del Boca and Sauer 2009; Eckstein and Wolpin 1989; Francesconi 2002; Heckman and Willis 1977; Jaumotte 2003; Nakamura and Nakamura 1985; OECD 2007; Plantenga and Remery 2009; Shapiro and Mott 1994; Soldani 2015).

Given the level of vulnerability, would these children be better off with or without the program? Even if childcare programs are a second-best choice, families could still be better off with them than without them.

Annex 9A: Proposed Module on Childcare for Household Surveys

This annex presents a set of questions that is compatible with the logic and objectives of existing household surveys in Latin America and the Caribbean.[*] It is based on a review of household surveys as well as the specialized questionnaires of the Early Childhood Survey in Chile (Encuesta Longitudinal de la Primera Infancia [ELPI]); the Longitudinal Survey of Wealth, Income, Labor, and Land in Colombia (Encuesta Longitudinal Colombiana [ELCA]); the National Survey of Employment and Social Security in Mexico (Encuesta Nacional de Empleo y Seguridad Social [ENESS]); and the European Statistics on Income and Living Conditions (EU–SILC). Items were selected, redesigned, and adapted to come up with the

---

[*] The authors developed this questionnaire with Paul J. Lavrakas, Ph.D, a survey research expert and former president of the American Association for Public Opinion Research.

most complete set of questions on childcare use. The module, which is designed for respondents with children younger than 6 years old or younger than the mandatory schooling age, is based largely on Chile's ELPI, the most complete and extensive survey on early childhood in the region. It proposes alternative questions and, in some cases, more detailed response options to questions in existing surveys.

Questions are formatted for administration by an interviewer. **BOLD UPPERCASE** instructions are for both interviewers and users of computer-assisted programming. The interviewer should read the question and response choices in lower-case letters to the respondent. The interviewer should not read the response choices that appear in all UPPERCASE letters; the associated questions are open-ended (respondents should answer in their own words). The interviewer should emphasize wording that is underlined. If the questionnaire is administered using paper and pencil, the interviewer should circle the number associated with the response and record verbatim the respondent's answers to open-ended questions.

MODULE A. *Questions to be added to household members' identification section of the household survey. They should be administered only to respondents with children younger than 6 or the mandatory schooling age. The survey should be completed separately for each child.*

1. Where does the child's mother live?

    1. In the same household as the child (INCLUDE MOTHER'S ID IF DIFFERENT FROM RESPONDENT)
    2. In the same dwelling unit as the child but in a different household
    3. Somewhere else in the same country as the child
    4. In a different country
    5. MOTHER IS DECEASED
    9. UNKNOWN

2. On what day, month, and year was the child born?

    FULL DATE: DD/MM/YYYY

    99/99/9999. UNKNOWN

MODULE B. *Question to be added to the Labor and Occupation module of the household survey. It should be administered only to individuals who responded "not working."*

1. What is the <u>one main reason</u> you are not working or looking for work? **(READ ALL RESPONSE CHOICES; CODE ONLY ONE ANSWER; PROBE AS NEEDED TO CLARIFY)**

    1. You are a student.
    2. You are retired.

3. You are a homemaker.

4. You are temporarily disabled.

5. You are permanently disabled.

6. You are waiting for an employer's decision on a future job.

7. There are no jobs in your profession or craft.

8. You do not have the schooling or experience necessary for a job.

9. You are waiting for the working season.

10. You are recovering from an illness/accident.

11. (ASK WOMEN ONLY) You are pregnant.

12. You need to take care of your children.

13. You need to take care of elders or disabled family members.

14. Another family member won't let you work.

15. Another reason (SPECIFY):_____

MODULE C. *Questions to be included in a separate Childcare module of the survey.*

1. Does the child attend any formal childcare service, kindergarten, or nursery school?

   1. Yes **(SKIP TO QUESTION 7)**

   2. No **(CONTINUE WITH QUESTION 2)**

   9. UNKNOWN **(CONTINUE TO QUESTION 2)**

[QUESTIONS 2–6 ARE TO BE ASKED ONLY IF RESPONDENT RESPONDS "NO" TO QUESTION 1]

2. Is this child on a waiting list to get into a formal childcare service, kindergarten, or nursery school?

   1. Yes

   2. No

   9. UNKNOWN

3. Who is the child's <u>main caregiver</u> during the week? **(ACCEPT ONLY ONE ANSWER; PROBE TO CLARIFY AS NEEDED)**

   1. The mother

   2. The father

   3. A grandparent

   4. Another relative

5. A nanny or maid

6. A friend or neighbor

7. The child is mostly left alone

8. Other (SPECIFY): _____

9. UNKNOWN

4. Where does this caregiving take place?

   1. At the child's home

   2. Mother takes child to work

   3. Somewhere else (SPECIFY): _____

   9. UNKNOWN

5. Does the household use any childcare arrangement other than what is provided by the main caregiver?

   1. Yes (**ASK QUESTION 5b**)

   2. No (**SKIP TO QUESTION 6**)

   9. UNKNOWN

5b. Who provides the other childcare? (**READ AND RECORD AN ANSWER FOR ALL OF THE FOLLOWING CHOICES**)

5b1.	The mother	1. yes	2. no	9. UNKNOWN
5b2.	The father	1. yes	2. no	9. UNKNOWN
5b3.	A grandparent	1. yes	2. no	9. UNKNOWN
5b4.	Some other relative	1. yes	2. no	9. UNKNOWN
5b5.	A nanny or maid	1. yes	2. no	9. UNKNOWN
5b6.	A friend or neighbor	1. yes	2. no	9. UNKNOWN
5b7.	Someone else	1. yes	2. no	9. UNKNOWN

6. What is the <u>one main reason</u> the child <u>does not</u> attend a formal childcare center, kindergarten, or nursery school? (**READ ALL STATEMENTS; CODE ONLY ONE "YES" ANSWER, MARK ALL THE OTHER ONES "NO" or "UNKNOWN"; PROBE TO GET ONE "YES" ANSWER AS NEEDED TO CLARIFY**)

6a. It is too expensive.

   1. yes   2. no   9. UNKNOWN

6b. There are no openings in the preferred childcare facility.

   1. yes   2. no   9. UNKNOWN

6c. The child is below the minimum age for attendance.

    1. yes   2. no   9. UNKNOWN

6d. Mother or father thinks child is too young to go.

    1. yes   2. no   9. UNKNOWN

6e. The closest childcare facility is too far away.

    1. yes   2. no   9. UNKNOWN

6f. There is no transportation available.

    1. yes   2. no   9. UNKNOWN

6g. Transportation is too expensive.

    1. yes   2. no   9. UNKNOWN

6h. Mother or father does not trust the childcare facility.

    1. yes   2. no   9. UNKNOWN

6i. The child is sick or otherwise needs special attention.

    1. yes   2. no   9. UNKNOWN

6j. The facility's schedule is not compatible with the mother's job.

    1. yes   2. no   9. UNKNOWN

6k. The mother takes care of the child.

    1. yes   2. no   9. UNKNOWN

6l. Someone else takes care of the child.

    1. yes   2. no   9. UNKNOWN

6m. The pediatrician didn't recommend childcare attendance.

    1. yes   2. no   9. UNKNOWN

6n. Child´s development and learning will be better stimulated in an environment different from the childcare facility.

    1. yes   2. no   9. UNKNOWN

6o. Other (SPECIFY):_____

    1. yes   2. no   9. UNKNOWN

[QUESTIONS 7–25 ARE ASKED ONLY IF RESPONDENT ANWERS "YES" TO QUESTION 1. IF RESPONDENT ANSWERS "NO," SKIP TO QUESTION 26.]

7. What is the <u>one main reason</u> the child does attend a formal childcare center, kindergarten, or nursery school? (**READ ALL STATEMENTS; CODE ONLY ONE "YES" ANSWER, MARK ALL OTHERS "NO" or**

"UNKNOWN"; PROBE TO GET ONE "YES" ANSWER AS NEEDED TO CLARIFY)

7a. It is affordable.

    1. yes   2. no   9. UNKNOWN

7b. There were openings in the preferred childcare facility.

    1. yes   2. no   9. UNKNOWN

7c. The child reached the minimum age for attendance.

    1. yes   2. no   9. UNKNOWN

7d. Mother or father thinks child is the right age to go.

    1. yes   2. no   9. UNKNOWN

7e. The childcare facility is close.

    1. yes   2. no   9. UNKNOWN

7f. Transportation is available.

    1. yes   2. no   9. UNKNOWN

7g. Transportation is affordable.

    1. yes   2. no   9. UNKNOWN

7h. Mother or father trust that the childcare facility will offer better conditions than those at home.

    1. yes   2. no   9. UNKNOWN

7i. Childcare facility is adapted to the special needs of my child.

    1. yes   2. no   9. UNKNOWN

7j. Facility's schedule is compatible with mother's job.

    1. yes   2. no   9. UNKNOWN

7k. Mother couldn't take care of child/she had to work or study.

    1. yes   2. no   9. UNKNOWN

7l. No one else could take care of child.

    1. yes   2. no   9. UNKNOWN

7m. Pediatrician recommended that child start attendance.

    1. yes   2. no   9. UNKNOWN

7n. To stimulate the child´s development and learning.

    1. yes   2. no   9. UNKNOWN

7o. Other (SPECIFY) _____

    1. yes   2. no   9. UNKNOWN

8. About how much—if anything—does the household have to pay out of pocket each month for the child to attend childcare, kindergarten, or nursery school?

    _____ [ADD LOCAL DENOMINATION] **(DO NOT ENTER A RANGE)**

    999999. UNKNOWN

9. Does the household use another care arrangement in addition to sending the child to the childcare facility, kindergarten, or nursery school?

    1. yes **(ASK QUESTION 9b)**

    2. no **(SKIP TO QUESTION 10)**

    9. UNKNOWN

9b. Who provides this additional childcare?

    1. The mother

    2. The father

    3. A grandparent

    4. Another relative

    5. A nanny or maid

    6. A friend or neighbor

    7. Someone else (SPECIFY): _____

    9. UNKNOWN

10. What kind of childcare facility, kindergarten, or nursery school does the child attend?

    1. Public [CAN PROVIDE LIST OF AVAILABLE SERVICES]

    2. Private

    3. Church

    4. Other nongovernment facility (SPECIFY): _____

    9. UNKNOWN

11. Who regularly drops off and picks up up the child from the childcare facility, kindergarten, or nursery school?

    1. The mother

    2. The father

    3. Another relative

4. A nonrelative who is the child's legal guardian

5. Another nonrelative

9. UNKNOWN

12. What is the main form of transportation the child uses to go to and from this place?

   1. Walking

   2. Public transportation

   3. School bus

   4. Private car

   5. Animal cart

   6. Boat

   7. Some other form of transportation (SPECIFY): _____

   9. UNKNOWN

13. About how much does the household spend a month on transportation to childcare?

   _____ [ADD LOCAL DENOMINATION] (**DO NOT ENTER A RANGE**)

   9999999. UNKNOWN

14. About how many minutes does it usually take to travel from the child's home to the childcare location?

   _____ NUMBER OF MINUTES (**DO NOT ENTER A RANGE**)

   999. UNKNOWN

15. About how many minutes does it take to travel from the childcare facility to the mother's place of employment?

   _____ NUMBER OF MINUTES (**DO NOT ENTER A RANGE**)

   888. MOTHER IS NOT EMPLOYED

   999. UNKNOWN

16. Which days of the week does the child go to the childcare facility, kindergarten, or nursery school? (**READ AND RECORD ANSWER FOR EACH DAY**)

16a.	Monday	1. yes	2. no	9. UNKNOWN
16b.	Tuesday	1. yes	2. no	9. UNKNOWN
16c.	Wednesday	1. yes	2. no	9. UNKNOWN

16d.	Thursday	1. yes	2. no	9. UNKNOWN
16e.	Friday	1. yes	2. no	9. UNKNOWN
16f.	Saturday	1. yes	2. no	9. UNKNOWN
16g.	Sunday	1. yes	2. no	9. UNKNOWN

17. What time of day does the child normally attend the childcare facility, kindergarten, or nursery school? (**ENTER TIME AND CIRCLE AM OR PM**)

STARTING TIME: _____ AM PM

FINISHING TIME: _____ AM PM

9999. UNKNOWN

18. For how many hours a day does the child normally attend childcare facility, kindergarten, or nursery school?

_____ (**DO NOT ENTER RANGE**)

99. UNKNOWN

19. For how many months of the year does the child go to the childcare facility, kindergarten, or nursery school?

_____ (**DO NOT ENTER RANGE**)

99. UNKNOWN

20. Does the household pay (any other) monthly childcare fee?

1. yes (**ASK QUESTION 20b**)

2. no (**SKIP TO QUESTION 21**)

9. UNKNOWN

20b. About how much is that fee?

_____ AMOUNT OF FEE [ADD LOCAL DENOMINATION] (**DO NOT ENTER RANGE**)

999999. UNKNOWN

21. Did the household have to pay a one-time enrollment/registration/inscription fee during this school year?

1. yes (**ASK QUESTION 21b**)

2. no (**SKIP TO QUESTION 22**)

9. UNKNOWN

21b. About how much was that fee?

_____ AMOUNT OF FEE [ADD LOCAL DENOMINATION] (**DO NOT ENTER RANGE**)

999999. UNKNOWN

22. Did your household have to pay for childcare uniforms this school year?

1. yes (**ASK QUESTION 22b**)

2. no (**SKIP TO QUESTION 23**)

9. UNKNOWN

22b. About how much did it pay?

_____ AMOUNT OF UNIFORM FEE [ADD LOCAL DENOMINATION]

999999. UNKNOWN

23. Did your household have to pay for books, school supplies, or grooming items during this school year?

1. yes (**ASK QUESTION 23b**)

2. no (**SKIP TO QUESTION 24**)

9. UNKNOWN

23b. About how much did it pay?

_____ AMOUNT OF FEE [ADD LOCAL DENOMINATION]

999999. UNKNOWN

24. Does your household pay a monthly meal fee for childcare?

1. yes (**ASK QUESTION 24b**)

2. no (**SKIP TO QUESTION 25**)

9. UNKNOWN

24b. About how much does it pay?

_____ AMOUNT OF FEE [ADD LOCAL DENOMINATION]

999999. UNKNOWN

25. Did the household pay any other monthly fees to the childcare facility, kindergarten, or nursery school?

1. yes (**ASK QUESTION 25b**)

2. no (**SKIP TO NEXT QUESTIONNAIRE MODULE**)

9. UNKNOWN

25b. About how much was that?

_____ AMOUNT OF FEE [ADD LOCAL DENOMINATION]

999999. UNKNOWN

TO BE ASKED TO ALL RESPONDENTS

26. What is the quality of the care your child currently receives?

1. Very good

2. Good

3. Fair

4. Poor

5. Very poor

9. UNKNOWN

27. How important is each of the following in choosing your child's caregiver/childcare facility? (**INCLUDE UNKNOWN AS CHOICE**)

SCALE: 1. not at all important 10. Extremely important   99. UNKNOWN

27a. Number of children per adult

27b. Warm and loving environment

27c. Flexible or convenient hours

27d. Training and credentials of staff

27e. Rate of provider turnover or changes in staff

27f. Physical facilities and equipment for play and learning

27h. Convenient location

27i. Cost

27j. Child health and safety

27k. Provider is someone you know and trust

27l. Educational and stimulating activities or programs

27m. Provider enrolls children with special needs

27n. Provider accepts infants

27o. Communication with parents

Notes

1. Job boards, referrals agencies, and temporary subsidies help communicate workers' true ability to employers and overcome challenges women entering the labor force face. Because few women work in certain types of jobs, employers lack good information about their ability and productivity. This lack of familiarity may reinforce beliefs that women are not as productive as men, perpetuating low FLFP in these jobs. Training

programs provide employers with an opportunity to see participants' true abilities. Wage subsidies reduce the cost to employers of hiring women and give them an opportunity to assess their performance.

2. Golden (2011) analyzes the impact of reductions in working hours and flexible working arrangements on productivity and firm performance.

3. External shocks can generate rapid changes that will have long-term impacts on values and labor market behavior. During World War II, FLFP in the United States and Europe rose from about 14 million women in 1940 to about 21 million in 1944 (Goldin and Olivetti 2013), as working became acceptable for women whose husbands were in the armed services or wanted to contribute to the war effort. Once the war ended, many women with low levels of education lost their jobs. In contrast, many women with higher levels of educations remained in their jobs (Goldin and Olivetti 2013).

4. The literature identifies uncertainty about the consequences of working as one of the reasons behind female labor market decisions. The nature of this uncertainty evolved remarkably over the last century. Half a century ago, working by a married women was often considered an indication that her husband could not provide for the family. Later it was thought that a working woman could reduce family stability or that women were not suited for certain occupations. More recently, fears have been expressed that women working may adversely affect child development (Fernández 2013). Changes in values can alter human behavior (Harrison and Huntington 2000; Inglehart and Norris 2003).

5. Fogli and Veldkamp (2011) describe the process in which countries transition from lower to higher FLFP rates as similar to a process of local information transmission. Cultural transmission occurs through family and the neighborhood. Women learn about the effects of maternal employment on children by observing other employed women in their surroundings, which would explain why FLFP tends to concentrate in certain areas.

6. Grandmothers are frequently the main caregiver when the mother works. Even with less precarious arrangements like this, there is evidence, at least for children 3 and older, of better development outcomes for children attending childcare centers compared to children cared for by family members (Bernal and Fernandez 2013).

References

Autor, D. 2008. "The Economics of Labor Market Intermediation: An Analytic Framework." NBER Working Paper 14348, National Bureau of Economic Research, Cambridge, MA.

Bassi, M., M. Busso, and J. S. Muñoz. 2013. "Is the Glass Half Empty or Half Full? School Enrollment, Graduation, and Dropout Rates in Latin America." Working Paper 462, Inter-American Development Bank, Washington, DC.

Bennett, J. 2008. "Benchmarks for Early Childhood Services in OECD Countries." Innocenti Working Paper 2008-02, UNICEF Innocenti Research Center, Florence.

Berger, L. M., and J. Waldfogel. 2004. "Maternity Leave and the Employment of New Mothers in the United States." *Journal of Population Economics* 17 (2): 331–49.

Bernal, R., and C. Fernandez. 2013. "Subsidized Child Care and Child Development in Colombia: Effects of Hogares Comunitarios de Bienestar as a Function of Timing and Length of Exposure." *Social Science & Medicine* 97: 241–49.

Blank, R. M. 1989. "The Role of Part-Time Work in Women's Labor Market Choices over Time." *American Economic Review Papers and Proceedings* 79 (2): 295–99.

Bos, M. S., A. Ganimian, and E. Vegas. 2014. "América Latina en PISA 2012: Cómo se desempeñan los varones y las mujeres?" Inter-American Development Bank, Washington, DC.

Bowman, B. T., M. S. Donovan, and M. S. Burns, eds. 2000. *Eager to Learn: Educating Our Preschoolers.* Washington, DC: National Academies Press.

Del Boca, D., and R. M. Sauer. 2009. "Life Cycle Employment and Fertility across Institutional Environments." *European Economic Review* 53 (3): 274–92.

Eckstein, Z., and K. Wolpin. 1989. "Dynamic Labour Force Participation of Married Women and Endogenous Work Experience." *Review of Economic Studies* 56 (3): 375–90.

Engle, L., L. Patrice, C. H. Fernald, H. Alderman, J. Behrman, C. O'Gara, A. Yousafzai, M. Cabral de Mello, M.Hidrobo, N. Ulkuer, I. Ertem, S. Iltus, and the Global Child Development Steering Group. 2011. "Strategies for Reducing Inequalities and Improving Developmental Outcomes for Young Children in Low-income and Middle-income Countries." *Lancet* 378 (9799): 1339–53.

Espinola-Arredondo, A., and S. Mondal. 2009. "The Effect of Parental Leave on Female Employment: Evidence from State Policies." Working Paper 2008-15, School of Economic Sciences, Washington State University, Pullman, WA.

Fernández, R. 2013. "Cultural Change as Learning: The Evolution of Female Labor Force Participation over a Century." *American Economic Review* 103 (1): 472–500.

Fernández, R., and A. Fogli. 2009. "Culture: An Empirical Investigation of Beliefs, Work, and Fertility." *American Economic Journal: Macroeconomics, American Economic Association* 1 (1): 146–77.

Fogli, A., and L. Veldkamp. 2011. "Nature or Nurture? Learning and the Geography of Female Labor Force Participation." *Econometrica* 79 (4): 1103–38.

Francesconi, M. 2002. "A Joint Dynamic Model of Fertility and Work of Married Women." *Journal of Labor Economics* 20 (2): 336–80.

Glassman, A. 2015. *Early Childhood Development: Four Lessons from Health for Costing ECD Programs.* Brookings Series on Early Childhood Development. Washington, DC: Brookings Institute.

Golden, L. 2011. "The Effects of Working Time on Productivity and Firm Performance: A Research Synthesis Paper." Conditions of Work and Employment Series 33, International Labour Organization, Geneva.

Goldin, C. 2014. "A Grand Gender Convergence: Its Last Chapter." *American Economic Review* 104 (4): 1091–19.

Goldin, C., and C. Olivetti. 2013. "Shocking Labor Supply: A Reassessment of the Role of World War II on Women's Labor Supply." *American Economic Review: Papers and Proceedings* 103 (3): 257–62.

Han, W., C. Ruhm, J. Waldfogel, and E. Washbrook. 2009. "Public Policies and Women's Employment after Childbearing." NBER Working Paper 14660, National Bureau of Economic Research, Cambridge, MA.

Harrison, L. E., and S. P. Huntington. 2000. Culture Matters: *How Values Shape Human Progress*. New York: Basic Books.

Heckman, J. J. 2011. "The Economics of Inequality: The Value of Early Childhood Education." *American Educator* (Spring): 31–47.

Heckman, J. J., and R. J. Willis. 1977. "A Beta-Logistic Model for the Analysis of Sequential Labor Force Participation by Married Women." *Journal of Political Economy* 85 (1): 27–58.

Inglehart, R. F., and P. Norris. 2003. *Rising Tide: Gender Equality and Cultural Change Around the World*. New York: Cambridge University Press.

Jaumotte, F. 2003. *Female Labour Force Participation: Past Trends and Main Determinants in OECD Countries*. Paris: Organisation for Economic Co-operation and Development (OECD).

Johnsen, S. 2012. "Women in Work: The Norwegian Experience." *OECD Observer* 293 (Q4).

Latinobarómetro. 2009. Latinobarómetro Opinión Pública Latinoamericana 2009. http://www.latinobarometro.org/latContents.jsp.

Mateo Díaz, M. and L. Rodriguez-Chamussy. 2015. "Who Cares about Childcare? Estimations of Childcare Use in Latin America and the Caribbean." Technical Note 815, Inter-American Development Bank, Washington, DC.

Mateo Díaz, M., L. Rodriguez-Chamussy, and F. Grafe. 2014. "Ley de Guarderías in México y los desafíos institucionales de conectar familia y trabajo." [Childcare Law in Mexico and the Institutional Challenges of Connecting Family and Work.] IDB Policy Brief IDB-PB-219, Inter-American Development Bank, Washington, DC. Available at http://publications.iadb.org/handle/11319/6650.

Mizala, A. 2014. "Brecha de género, desempeño en matemáticas y elección de carreras." Proyecto FONDECYT, Fondo Nacional de Desarrollo Científico y Tecnológico, Santiago, Chile.

Nakamura, A. O., and M. Nakamura. 1985. "Dynamic Models of the Labor Force Behavior of Married Women Which Can Be Estimated Using Limited Amounts of Information." *Journal of Econometrics* 27 (3): 273–298.

Ñopo, H. 2012. *New Century, Old Disparities: Gender and Ethnic Earnings Gaps in Latin America and the Caribbean*. Washington, DC: Inter-American Development Bank.

OECD (Organisation for Economic Co-Operation and Development). 2007. *Babies and Bosses. Reconciling Work and Family Life. A Synthesis of Findings for OECD Countries*. Paris: OECD.

———. 2011. "Reducing Barriers to Parental Employment." In *Doing Better for Families*. Paris: OECD Publishing.

Plantenga, J., and C. Remery. 2009. *The Provision of Childcare Services: A Comparative Review of 30 European Countries*. European Commission's Expert Group on Gender and Employment Issues (EGGE), Brussels.

Shapiro, D., and F. L. Mott. 1994. "Long-Term Employment and Earnings of Women in Relation to Employment Behavior Surrounding the First Birth." *Journal of Human Resources* 29: 248–75.

Soldani, E. 2015. "What Took You So Long? The Short and Longer-Run Effects of Public Kindergarten on Maternal Labor Supply and Earnings." Working Paper, Department of Economics, New York University, New York.

Todd, P. E. 2012. "Effectiveness of Interventions Aimed at Improving Women's Employability and Quality of Work: A Critical Review." Policy Research Working Paper 6189, World Bank, Washington, DC.

Wolfensohn Center for Development. 2009. *Scaling Up Early Child Development in the Developing World*. Washington, DC: Brookings Institute.

World Bank. 2012. *World Development Report 2012: Gender Equality and Development*. Washington, DC: World Bank.

National Experts Consulted for This Report

Some of the information presented in this book is based on data in 2013 from directors and specialists of 40 publicly supported childcare programs in 21 countries in Latin America and the Caribbean. We distributed a questionnaire and followed up with telephone calls and emails to obtain and validate information. This appendix lists the experts consulted.

Argentina

Marcela Goenaga, Directora Nivel Inicial, Ciudad de Buenos Aires

The Bahamas

Agatha Archer, Assistant Director of Education Preschool, Ministry of Social Services and Community Development
Ellerie Seymour, Director, Early Childhood Development Centers, Ministry of Social Services and Community Development

Barbados

Joan Crawford, Director, Childcare Board, Ministry of Social Transformation

Bolivia

Luz Eliana Chambicari, Coordinadora, Programa de Desarrollo Inicial SEDEGES, La Paz
   Olga Alarcón, Directora, Educación Inicial en Familia Comunitaria, Ministerio de Educación

Brazil

Simone de Jesus Souza, Gerência de Educação Infantil/Primera Infancia Completa, Prefeitura Cidade Rio de Janeiro-Rio Educa

Chile

Maria De La Luz Cano Reveco, Directora, Jardines Infantiles, Junta Nacional de Jardines Infantiles (JUNJI)
   Antonia Feuereisen, Asesora de Dirección, Fundación Integra
   Maria de la Luz Morales Branif, Secretaria Ejecutiva de Primera Infancia, Ministerio de Educación

Colombia

Carlos del Castillo Cabrales, Subdirector de Gestión Técnica para la Atención de la Primera Infancia, Instituto Colombiano de Bienestar Familiar (ICBF)
   Ana Beatriz Cárdenas Restrepo, Directora de Primera Infancia, Ministerio de Educación

Costa Rica

Gabriela Castro, Directora Nacional, Centros de Educación y Nutrición y Centros Infantiles de Atención Integral (CEN-CINAI)
   Mainer Villalobos, Jefe, Centros Docencia Privada, Ministerio de Educación Pública
   Amalia Porta Nunez, Asesora, Centros Docencia Privada

Dominican Republic

Penélope Melo Ballesteros, Gerente, Programa de Atención Integral a la Primera Infancia, Consejo Nacional para la Niñez y la Adolescencia (CONANI)

Liliam Rodriguez, Directora Ejecutiva, Estancias Infantiles Salud Segura, Instituto Dominicano de Seguros Sociales (IDSS)

Ecuador

Marcelo Ordoñez, Subsecretario, Desarrollo Infantil Integral, Ministerio de Inclusión Económica y Social (MIES)

Zoila Ramos, Directora Nacional, Educación Inicial y Básica, Ministerio de Educación

El Salvador

Maria de la Paz Yanes de Garcia, Directora, Educación Inicial, Centros de Bienestar Infantil (CBI)/Centros de Desarrollo Integral - Instituto Salvadoreño para el Desarrollo Integral de la Niñez y la Adolescencia (CDI ISNA)

Janet Lopez, Gerente de Gestión Pedagógica, Ministerio de Educación

Guatemala

Flor de Maria Madrid, Directora, Programa Hogares Comunitarios, Secretaría de Obras Sociales de la Esposa del Presidente (SOSEP)

Evelyn Ortiz de Rodríguez, Directora, Programa de Atención Integral al Niño Menor de Seis Años (PAIN), Ministerio de Educación

Vivian Arcelí Palencia Peralta, Jefa, Departamento de los Niveles Inicial y Preprimario, Ministerio de Educación

Diana Romero, Subdirectora, Programa Hogares Comunitarios

Honduras

Felipe Morales, Director Ejecutivo, Centros de Atención Integral, Instituto Hondureño de la Niñez y la Familia (IHNFA)

Mayra Ibelis Valdez, Coordinadora, Nacional Educación Prebásica, Secretaría de Educación

Jamaica

Michelle Campbell, Director, Sector Support Services, Early Childhood Commission (ECC)

Karlene Deslandes, Director, Regulations and Monitoring, Early Childhood Commission (ECC)

Mexico

Gonzalo Cordero González, Jefe, División de Asuntos Multilaterales, Programa de Guarderías, Instituto Mexicano del Seguro Social (IMSS)

José Mena y Alvaro Carrillo, Subdirector de Operación, Programa de Estancias Infantiles, Secretaría de Desarrollo Social (SEDESOL)

Salua Quintero Soda, Subdirectora de Relaciones Internacionales, Programa de Estancias Infantiles, Instituto de Seguridad y Servicios Sociales de los Trabajadores del Estado (ISSSTE)

Gloria Xolot, Subdirectora de Apoyo Técnico, Complementario Coordinación Sectorial, SEP-DF

María del Rocío Juárez González, Encargada de la Dirección del Área de Educación Inicial, Secretaría de Educación Pública (SEP) Nacional

Nicaragua

Sobeyda Bárcenas, Coordinadora, Programa Amor por los más Chiquitos y Chiquitas, Ministerio de la Familia Adolescencia y Niñez

Deisy Cordero, Directora de Educación Inicial, Ministerio de Educación

Panama

Teresa Sanchez, Directora Nacional, Servicios de Protección Social, Centro de Orientación Infantil y Familiar (COIF), Ministerio de Desarrollo Social

Victoria Tello, Directora Educación Inicial, Centro Familiar y Comunitario de Educación Inicial (CEFACEI) y Centros de Educación Inicial Comunitario (CEIC), Ministerio de Educación

Paraguay

Bernarda Casco, Coordinadora Programa Nacional Abrazo, Secretaría Nacional de la Niñez y la Adolescencia

Maria del Carmen Gimenez de Sivulec, Directora General, Educación Inicial y Escolar Básica, Ministerio de Educación

Peru

Andrea Portugal Desmarchelier, Directora Ejecutiva, Programa Nacional Cuna Más

Neky Vanetty Molinero Nano, Directora de Educación Inicial, Ministerio de Educación

Sandra Vega, Presidenta, Asociación de Promotores de Educación Inicial

Trinidad and Tobago

Deborah Khan, Lead, Early Childhood Care and Education Centers (ECCEC)

Uruguay

Yolanda Echeverría, Coordinadora del Área de Educación en la Primera Infancia, Ministerio de Educación

Susana Mara, Directora Políticas Primera Infancia, Plan Centros de Atención a la Infancia y a la Familia (CAIF)